Paddling Colorado

Help Us Keep This Guide Up to Date

Every effort has been made by the author and editors to make this guide as accurate and useful as possible. However, many things can change after a guide is published— trails are rerouted, regulations change, techniques evolve, facilities come under new management, etc.

We appreciate hearing from you concerning your experiences with this guide and how you feel it could be improved and kept up to date. While we may not be able to respond to all comments and suggestions, we'll take them to heart and we'll also make certain to share them with the author. Please send your comments and suggestions to the following address:

Globe Pequot
Reader Response/Editorial Department
246 Goose Lane, Suite 200
Guilford, CT 06437

Thanks for your input!

Paddling Colorado

Kayak, Canoe, Paddleboard, and Raft
the Greatest Fresh Waters in the State

Second Edition

Dunbar Hardy
Revised by Kate Stepan

ESSEX, CONNECTICUT

FALCONGUIDES®

An imprint of Globe Pequot, the trade division of The Rowman & Littlefield
Publishing Group, Inc.
4501 Forbes Blvd., Ste. 200
Lanham, MD 20706
www.rowman.com

Falcon and FalconGuides are registered trademarks and Make Adventure Your Story is a trade-
mark of The Rowman & Littlefield Publishing Group, Inc.

Distributed by NATIONAL BOOK NETWORK

Photos by Kate Stepan unless otherwise noted
Maps by Melissa Baker and The Rowman & Littlefield Publishing Group, Inc.

British Library Cataloguing in Publication Information available

Library of Congress Cataloging-in-Publication Data available
Names: Hardy, Dunbar, author. | Stepan, Kate, author.
Title: Paddling Colorado : kayak, canoe, paddleboard, and raft the greatest fresh waters in the state
    / Dunbar Hardy, revised by Kate Stepan.
Description: Second edition. | Essex, Connecticut : Falcon [2023] | Summary: "Paddling Colo-
    rado describes 30–40 trips in a remarkable variety of settings-from downtown Denver to the
    remote canyons of the Dolores River. Offering useful guidance on river access, hazards, and
    regulations, this guide shows the way to the best paddling opportunities in the state"—Provided
    by publisher.
Identifiers: LCCN 2022056212 (print) | LCCN 2022056213 (ebook) | ISBN 9781493069347
    (trade paperback) | ISBN 9781493069354 (epub)
Subjects: LCSH: Canoes and canoeing—Colorado—Guidebooks. | Kayaking—Colorado—
    Guidebooks. | Colorado--Guidebooks.
Classification: LCC GV776.C6 H37 2023   (print) | LCC GV776.C6   (ebook) | DDC
    797.12209788—dc23/eng/20221209
LC record available at https://lccn.loc.gov/2022056212
LC ebook record available at https://lccn.loc.gov/2022056213

♾️™ The paper used in this publication meets the minimum requirements of American National
Standard for Information Sciences—Permanence of Paper for Printed Library Materials, ANSI/
NISO Z39.48-1992.

To Grandma Betty, who sparked my love for journalism before I could even drive myself to cover local events for the town paper. She couldn't see very well but could be an adult in the passenger seat while I piloted us to countless school board meetings, county fairs, and 24-hour photo counters on my learner's permit. And Mom and Dad, Dee and Dave, for always welcoming me back into the fold after a crazy adventure.

Also, Terry Breslin and the crew at Pocono Whitewater, who entrusted me with their borrowed gear and first rafts full of paying passengers. And Jerry McAward, who lent me his WaveSport Ace in my first summer kayaking even though I didn't know how to use a cam strap to tie it to the roof of my Subaru.

Finally, to Brandon Slate, Ryan Coulter, and my team at the Rocky Mountain Outdoor Center. For being there through rough waters and calm, supporting me, and believing in me against all odds. And through the times I probably should have been fired.

A spring paddling road trip in the Rockies.

Contents

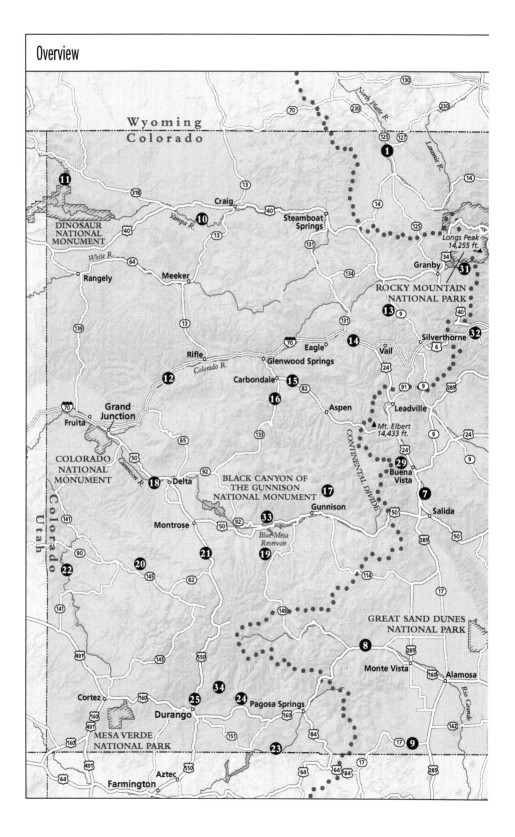

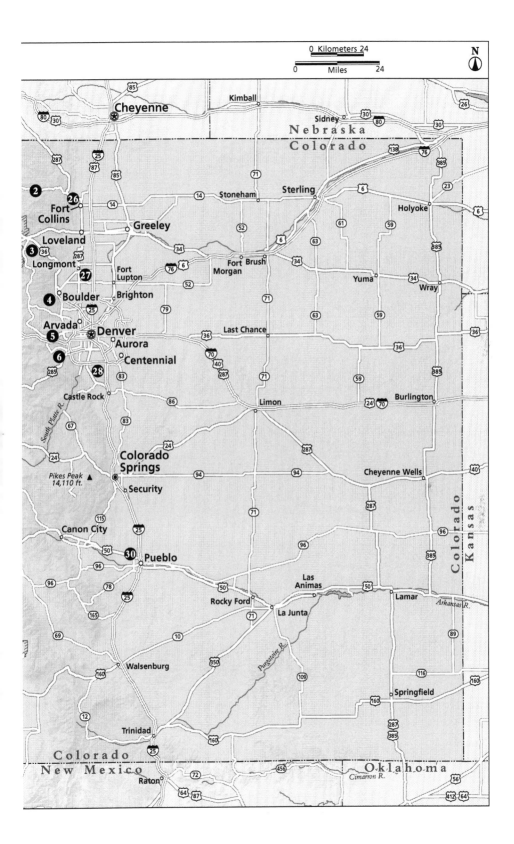

0 Kilometers 24

0 Miles 24

N

Cheyenne
Kimball
Sidney
Nebraska
Colorado

2
26
Fort
Collins
Stoneham
Sterling
Holyoke
Greeley
Loveland
3
Longmont
27
Fort
Lupton
Fort
Morgan
Brush
Yuma
Wray
4 Boulder
Brighton
Arvada
5
Denver
Aurora
Last Chance
6
Centennial
28
Castle Rock
Limon
Burlington
South Platte R.
Colorado
Springs
Cheyenne Wells
Colorado
Kansas
Pikes Peak
14,110 ft.
Security
Canon City
Pueblo
30
Las
Animas
Lamar
Arkansas R.
Rocky Ford
La Junta
Purgatoire R.
Walsenburg
Springfield
Trinidad
Colorado
New Mexico
Raton
Oklahoma
Cimarron R.

Flatwater Tours—Lakes and Reservoirs (North-South)

Acknowledgments

It would be remiss to write about paddling anywhere in the United States without mention of American Whitewater, and their steadfast advocacy for river access and runnable flows. Their work is immeasurable in making the paddling, writing, and photographing of the runs in this book possible.

We also must recognize those who have come before and pioneered our beloved river sport, but especially those who work and teach continually to educate paddlers in the realm of safety and rescue. I'd especially like to thank Mike Mather, swiftwater rescue guru and mentor, as I got my start as a rookie raft guide on the New and Gauley Rivers through Wildwater Expeditions.

Upon moving to Colorado, paddling various rivers around the state would not have been possible without those I met through mountainbuzz.com, before the era of Facebook groups. Special thanks to Rob Hurst and Kevin Hoffman for rallying

around the mountains during our early days of raft guiding in Colorado. I'd also like to thank Erik Rist for influencing me to move the Arkansas Valley, and the raft guides at disco night at the Rope in BV circa 2009 for giving me a reason to stay. And I acknowledge Kent Ford for his early and continued mentorship of my kayak instruction career, as well as the countless students I've encountered through teaching and guiding at the Rocky Mountain Outdoor Center. You are the inspiration for all we do.

Finally, I'd like to thank Logan Meyer for always being down to paddle some obscure Class II in the snow. And Dave Bumgarner for his wealth of information and drive to paddle every run in the state. Kit Davidson, hope to see you on a Colorado river sometime soon!

Foreword

"Epic Class II Adventures"

On April 22, 2022 (Earth Day), Mama Nature cloaked the southwest corner of Colorado in a montrous windstorm. Dust clouded the air, creating a dusk-like aura at 4 p.m. Scott Link and I were walking back to his truck after scouting the East Fork San Juan River, a swift-moving Class III creek with a propensity to collect new wood on the west side of Wolf Creek Pass. As we bent our heads against the gale force gusts, dirt particles gritted in our teeth, eyeballs, and clothing. Conditions were decidedly epic for such a tame section of paddling.

The impetus for this recon mission to the Rio Grande River drainage was the revision of this guidebook. While I was able to recall many of the included rivers and paddling runs from memory, having lived and boated in Colorado for the last 13 years, there were some places I had not been and could not decipher the directions in the existing book. In reality, some of the listed access points did not exist at all. The timeline for publication was lining up with the busy summer season at the outfitter I help manage on the Arkansas River (Rocky Mountain Outdoor Center), so it was now or never to get booties on the ground for the project this spring.

So I called my neighbor and fellow kayaker Logan Meyers. Logan is just the kind of paddling friend I like, confident in his advanced skill set but more apt to chase rivers for their novelty and beauty than potential for steep, gnarly whitewater action. While I've put down some Class V descents, mostly as a 25-year-old raft guide traveling the world to kayak, this kind of boating mission is now more my speed. Logan has also been all over southwest Colorado, particularly to the Rio Grande, taking photos, making note of satellite images, and dialing in river gauges and tributaries to determine the best paddling options.

Over that blustery April weekend, the Rio Grande drainage delivered. The dust clouds gave way to rain, which gave way to snow. Scott eased his F-250 pickup back up and over Wolf Creek Pass and past its namesake ski area, closed for the season but getting a dusting of fresh powder, before we posted up along the banks of the South Fork Rio Grande for the night. The wind finally stopped howling and gentle flakes blanketed our camp in snow.

The next day dawned cool, calm, and clear. Today's goal was to canvas the Rio Grande proper, from the headwaters to the confluence with the South Fork and on down to the newly engineered play wave in Del Norte. We checked off put-ins and takeouts, me furiously scribbling directions, shooting photos, and taking down GPS waypoints in the passenger seat. Late in the afternoon, with an increasing tailwind, we finally pumped up the 9.5-foot Tributary raft we'd brought and got ready to shove off into the Class II waters, and bridge abutments, of the Wagon Wheel Gap section (see description on pages 70–71). But not before I managed to put the nose of my kayak through the front window of Scott's truck topper while slamming the tailgate shut. After profuse apologies, and a few tears, we finally hit the water at about 3:30 p.m.

The winds brought increasing clouds as the cold front bearing down on us finally settled in. With icy fingers and toes, we paddled furiously through the last few miles of meandering current. Logan met us at the takeout with warm burgers from a local diner and a heated shuttle ride. Life was good.

Driving upriver to camp near the once booming mining town of Creede landed us just above 9,000 feet for the night. We stopped in Creede to buy a case of beer, the cardboard from which would serve as repair materials for the truck window. As the sun set, Scott duct-taped the patch job in place while Logan and I got a fire going. Stars dotted a clear sky, indicating cold temps overnight.

We awoke to frozen river shoes and a quick check of iPhone river gauges, which revealed our planned excursion to the Headwaters Box Canyon section, about 1,000 feet higher in elevation, was going to be bony. Last night's lows in the teens had shut off the spring melt that we had enjoyed the previous day. Logan and I would have to kayak the run while Scott ran shuttle and took photos; the raft remained rolled in the pickup bed.

As we set off for the headwaters, just below Rio Grande Reservoir, I remarked, "Now this is a put-in road!" Anything this far away from the highway that paralleled much of the river's lower reaches must be worth doing. Logan's truck fishtailed a few times on the washboards along FSR 520 before we arrived at the gated campground that would serve as our river access point. We were surrounded by the freshly burned Weminuche Wilderness, with most of the spring's whitewater goods locked up in the snowfields above. A few tiny flakes drifted down from the gathering clouds as we paddled in, scraping the river bottom in more than a few places. As the river gathered its braids and poured into a few mini gorges, the whitewater was fun and nonthreatening (see description on page 65). And the scenery was stunning. I had found what I was looking for in a wicked Colorado weekend kept warm with Tasty Bites, a campfire, and a sense of Class II adventure.

While I commend those that want to chase the biggest, hardest whitewater around, with age I've come to appreciate the beauty of simply spending time somewhere wild and new—particularly on a river. This book project is dedicated to my like-minded boating kin, with a few harder runs thrown in for those with the skill to enjoy the spice. Consider it a compilation of Colorado's "greatest hits" for paddlers of any craft, and fellow lovers of epic tales told around the campfire or local brewery.

—Kate Stepan

Introduction

Welcome to Colorado—home of the Rocky Mountains. Where people come for the winter, but paddlers stay for the summer. Come warmer weather and melting snow, the same snow-covered peaks enjoyed by throngs of skiing tourists become a stunning backdrop to spring and summertime river runs. With water projects contributing to consistent flows and the advent of drysuits and warmer paddling gear, many locals are now able to extend their boating season into the fall or even year-round. American Whitewater lists 268 runnable rivers with 2,515 readable gauges in a land where state tourism bureaus boast 300-plus days of sunshine a year and fresh clean air. Colorado is a prime paddling destination for those who relish the outdoors and welcome the beauty of clean rivers, pristine lakes, a dry temperate climate, and beautiful scenery.

While most whitewater kayaking flicks portray Colorado's remote waterfalls and Class V creeks, options do exist for paddlers of all skill levels around the state. Mountain lakes and reservoirs offer flatwater enthusiasts still-water paddling with 360-degree views. Beginning paddlers will find there are many sections appropriate for learning—albeit in Colorado's notoriously fast-moving, cold, shallow waters. Intermediate paddlers have numerous quality sections available to them, and should not shy away from jumping on a Rocky Mountain paddling road trip. Advanced/expert paddlers can tackle some of the most difficult whitewater found anywhere, with unique geology and hair-raising remote creeking adventures to be had; if you have those skills, check out *Whitewater of the Southern Rockies* by Evan Stafford and Kyle McCutchen, a modern whitewater tome that goes way beyond the scope of expert paddling than this book.

Lay of the Land

"That John Denver was full of sh★★!"—Lloyd Christmas, *Dumb and Dumber*. Not all Colorado is full of mountains. The eastern side of the state is a sloping high plain of open expanse that extends toward the flatlands of Nebraska, Kansas, and Oklahoma. This part of the state is better known for its agriculture than its paddling. Bumping up against the mountains is an area known as the Front Range, which is home to most of the state's population and the cities of Pueblo, Colorado Springs, Denver, Boulder, and Fort Collins. There are paddling opportunities along the Front Range, as well as crowds. Heading farther west, up and over the Continental Divide, is the central part of the state and its highest mountains. This is home to the majority of ski areas, as well as abundant snowmelt paddling options. And the Rocky Mountains here certainly live up to their name, with young geology and crumbling glacial outflow. Heading even farther west is the part of the state known as the Western Slope. The mountain scenery eventually transitions to a dry high desert–like environment as Colorado gives way to the sandstone cliffs of Utah.

With such a variety of ecosystems and scenery throughout the geography of the state, the different paddling options are equally varied among Colorado's 105,344 miles of river. Included in this guidebook are runs set in the incredibly urban setting of downtown Denver to runs on the remote lower canyons of the Dolores River tucked away down in the southwest corner of the state. Offering whatever style of paddling you most enjoy coupled with a variety of settings and beautiful scenery, Colorado affords a lifetime of diverse paddling options.

Safety on the Water

Do your homework before setting out for a paddle: Check the weather forecast, check the water levels, have the proper gear and equipment, have at least one paddling partner, and have a clear plan with an estimated takeout time and location. These simple rules are very important in preventing potential accidents and being prepared for any accidents that do happen.

Check the weather: Know what is forecast for the day of your paddle, as well as the days ahead if launching on a multi-day trip. Colorado weather is apt to change at a moment's notice, especially at high elevation. Never underestimate the potential for summer afternoon thunderstorms!

Water levels: Check the water level of your intended run before putting in, and be sure the current level is within the recommended flow range. (See the appendix for specific contact information.)

Bring proper clothing and equipment: Always wear a properly fitted personal flotation device (PFD), and wear appropriate clothing layers to stay warm in wet and cold. A drytop or drysuit is highly recommended for Colorado's snowmelt-fed rivers. At least one first-aid kit is recommended within each group.

Paddle with partners: There is safety, and enjoyment, in numbers; do your best to never paddle alone.

Let others know your plan: Relay the day's paddling plan to others outside the paddling group who will know when and where to look for you if you don't arrive when expected.

Be prepared: Prepare for the worst by taking extra clothing, bringing a first-aid kit, and having first-aid/river-rescue training.

Know your capabilities: Be honest about your skill level, and always paddle within your abilities.

Understand difficulty ratings: Many rivers increase in difficulty with an increase in flow, so know what you are getting into before you actually enter the water. Following are the general classifications of river difficulty:

- **Class I: Easy.** Flatwater or moving water with easy, small waves, if any; little to no maneuvering; no obstructions.

- **Class II: Medium.** Easy rapids with a few small obstructions that are easily avoidable with low consequences for missed moves; increased water speed; clear routes downstream.

- **Class III: Difficult.** Numerous rapids with larger irregular waves requiring more precise maneuvering between obstacles; increased water speed. More-obstructed routes may require scouting. Consequences could include a long swim in cold whitewater, or encountering boulders or other obstacles in the water.

- **Class IV: Very Difficult.** Longer, more powerful rapids with large waves between large rocks and other obstacles; very obstructed route. High skill level with scouting is highly recommended. Hazardous obstacles like strainers, sieves, or pin spots may be present.

- **Class V: Extremely Difficult.** Long, violent rapids that drop steeply with extremely fast current; complex route-finding required between hazardous features. Extensive experience and skill recommended; scouting is mandatory.

- **Class VI: Unrunnable.**

Flows

Each river run outlined in this guide has a recommended flow range coupled with the river difficulty rating. Of course, sections of rivers can be paddled outside the recommended flow range, but you risk a paddle of less quality if the waters are too low or one that's more difficult—and dangerous—if the waters are higher than the recommended flow.

In order to stay within a section of river that matches your difficulty level, check the flow of the section as close as possible to the time and day you are planning to paddle. Use the water level resources provided in the appendix of this guide to check the most current flows. Then reference the current flow with the recommended flow range for the section you are planning to paddle. This will give you an informed idea as to what to expect regarding the character and difficulty of that section prior to putting in.

With a few exceptions, there is a distinct season to most of the paddling within Colorado. Generally speaking, Colorado's rivers tend to run off and swell with melting snows in late spring (April and May), peak in early summer (May and June), and drop to low flows by late summer and fall (July through September).

Some of the rivers outlined in this guide are dam controlled and thus no longer follow this natural seasonal flow. Gather local knowledge about a dam's intended purpose—power generation, flood control, or irrigation—to help predict releases. Verify the actual dam releases and flows of these rivers either visually or by checking the corresponding gauge. The operations of these dams will ultimately determine the true length, or season, of the river's run, as well as the true flow range from low to high water.

How to Use This Guide

Each paddle description begins with a section that provides nuts-and-bolts information on that specific paddling destination. Each of these at-a-glance items is described below:

Section map: A general map is included with each river description to help paddlers get oriented in finding the access points for the put-in and takeout. This map also shows a few of the larger characteristics of the section to be paddled.

River summary: This briefly outlines the waterway's geographic location, outlines its general characteristics and paddling quality, and highlights the overall route.

Section description: More specific information on the characteristics and qualities of the section to be paddled.

Start: A recommended launching access point to begin the described section for paddling.

End: A recommended exit access point to conclude the described section for paddling.

Length: A fairly accurate measurement of the section to be paddled, measured in miles.

Approximate paddling time: A range of time, measured in hours, required to paddle the section at the fastest speed as well as at a slower, more leisurely pace.

Difficulty rating: The ideal skill level recommended for the section to be paddled.

Rapids: Class rating (See "Safety on the Water," page 2) of the most difficult rapids on the run, and quantity of those rapids to expect.

River gradient: Average elevation loss of the river section, expressed as feet per mile (fpm).

River gauge: The recommended flow range, measured in cubic feet per second (cfs), that will maintain the highest quality paddling while keeping this section within its previously mentioned difficulty rating. When applicable, dam-controlled sections are noted, providing paddlers with a heads-up that dam operations will ultimately determine the flows.

Elevation drop: Difference from highest to lowest elevation on the river section.

Hazards: Known dangerous obstacles and character of those obstacles on the river section.

Season: A recommended time frame for the best paddling flows on the section to be paddled. When applicable, dam-controlled sections are noted, providing paddlers with a heads-up that dam operations will ultimately determine the season.

Boats used: The recommended type of watercraft for the section to be paddled. (*Note:* Inflatable kayaks and packrafts are indicated if a run is deemed suitable for both kayaks and rafts. Decked canoes, or C-2s, are indicated if a run is deemed suitable for kayaks; "canoe" refers to open whitewater canoes.)

Special considerations: Additional paddling options related to the described paddle. This may include a higher or lower access point to lengthen or shorten the run or a brief description of a more advanced nearby paddling route that's beyond the scope of this guide.

Getting there: Detailed route descriptions for driving and completing the shuttle to access both the put-in and takeout for the described paddle.

The routes in the Flatwater Tours chapter include information on launch sites and access points rather than put-in, takeout, and shuttle descriptions. These write-ups also include sources of information on the specific reservoirs and lakes and related parklands plus "honorable mentions" for additional paddling options in the area.

Giving Back

What makes Colorado so special is its natural resources, including rivers and lakes. The numerous free-flowing rivers and creeks that gush out of the mountains are gifts to be respected and cherished. Ever-expanding population growth and unprecedented development threaten access to water paddlers once took for granted. The dedicated care and commitment of people and organizations have kept the majority of these paddling resources available for future generations to enjoy. If not for these groups and other people who love Colorado, we might not have the many options for paddling that exist today for all of us.

Whether you're visiting and paddling in Colorado for the first time or putting in for another day on the local run, please consider becoming involved in river and wilderness conservation within the state. The future protection of our resources depends on community involvement. For additional information on statewide and national organizations that are actively participating in protecting Colorado's natural resources, see this guide's appendix.

Thank you for your consideration and care for the future of paddling in Colorado.

Map Legend

Transportation

≡(70)≡   Freeway/Interstate Highway

≡(50)≡   U.S. Highway

≡(13)≡   State Highway

[344]   Other Road

▬▬▬   Railroad

Symbols

Boat Launch

Bridge

■   Building/Point of Interest

▲   Campground

➤   Put-In/Takeout

Water Features

Body of Water

Major River

Minor River or Creek

Intermittent River or Creek

Land Management

National Park/Forest

State Park, Wilderness Area

N   True North (Magnetic North is approximately 11.0° East)

Front Range Paddles (North-South)

Surf's up in the Salida Whitewater Park. Credit: Kevin Hoffman

Waterton hike.

1 North Platte River

Tucked up in the northern portion of the state, the North Platte River is formed by the confluence of various streams that drain the Rabbit Ears Wilderness Area to the west and the Medicine Bow Mountains to the east. Coming together in a broad, wide-open valley, the North Platte runs northward and slides into the Platte River Wilderness Area once it crosses into Wyoming. It then makes a hard turn to the east and flows out of the state and into Nebraska, where it runs the length of the state before eventually joining the Missouri River.

Free flowing up here along the border, the North Platte surges with spring snow-melt and runoff. It offers remote beginner/intermediate sections that can be linked together for a raft overnighter or first self-support kayak trip. Day paddling is also possible with multiple access points in Colorado and Wyoming. Pair a paddling trip in this area with a trip to the hot springs in the nearby town of Saratoga.

Northgate Canyon

Intermediate wilderness paddling set in a remote canyon that flows through the heart of the Platte River Wilderness Area straddling the Colorado–Wyoming border.

Nearest city/town: Walden
Start: Routt launch site (N40 57.112' / W106 20.626')
End: Six-Mile Gap, Wyoming (N41 02.666' / W106 23.939')
Length: 10.0 miles (longer runs possible)
Approximate paddling time: 3 to 4 hours
Difficulty: Intermediate
Rapids: Technical routes formed around large boulders
River type: Class III (2), Class III+ (2)
Current: Swift
Environment: Remote low-angle canyon with abundant wildlife
River gradient: 20 fpm
River gauge: 500 to 1,500 cfs, North Platte River near Northgate
Elevation drop: 36 feet
Hazards: Barbed wire fence

Season: May through August
Land status: USFS, BLM, private along Upper Valley section above Northgate Canyon
Boats used: Canoes, rafts, kayaks, stand-up paddleboards (SUPs)
Fees or permits: Not required for private trips; maximum group size is 25.
Maps: *Upper North Platte River Float Map* (Wyoming Fish and Game Department)
Other users: Commercial rafters, anglers
Contacts: USFS Brush Creek/Hayden Ranger District (307-326-5258), Parks Ranger District (970-723-8204)
Special considerations: Add 6 miles of meandering Class I by putting in at the County Road 6 bridge, or use this Upper Valley section as a mellow beginner day float down to the Routt launch site.

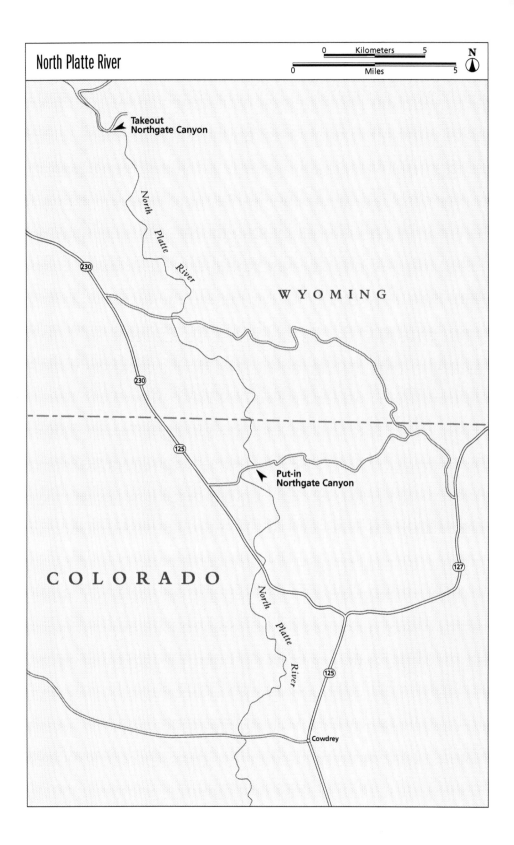

North Platte River

0   Kilometers   5

0   Miles   5

N

Takeout
Northgate Canyon

North Platte River

230

WYOMING

230

125

Put-in
Northgate Canyon

127

COLORADO

North Platte River

125

Cowdrey

Put-in/takeout information: To reach the takeout from Walden, head north on Highway 125. Cross into Wyoming, where Colorado Highway 125 becomes Wyoming Highway 230. Four miles north of the border, turn right (east) onto County Road 492 and follow it for 2 miles to a campground and trailhead; this is the takeout.

To get back to the put-in, head south on Highway 125 until it crosses the river. Shortly after this bridge, look for signs for Routt launch site. Turn left (east) and follow the signs to the boat launch area.

The Paddle

Rugged slopes, lush forests of firs, and frequent wildlife sightings all lend an "out there" feeling to this run—floaters report moose and wolf sightings, along with a host of birdlife. After a bit of a warm-up, most of the whitewater comes in a 4-mile section that starts about 7 miles in, after Elkhorn Creek enters on the right. Here, the gradient steepens and the North Platte funnels into its main canyon, where paddlers will face Cowpie (Class III+), Tootsie Roll (Class III), and Stovepipe Rapids (Class III). At flows above 1,200 cfs, the crux rapid (Narrow Falls) approaches Class IV in difficulty. Scout this blind horizon line from the talus slope on river left. Just below Stovepipe, a steep 200-yard-long trail challenges tourists on commercial rafting trips as it climbs up to the takeout. Consider scouting the takeout while running shuttle; it's a good trail but hard to see from the river. Pro tip: roll rafts for the carry; bonus points for rolling around oars like the commercial guides do.

2 Poudre River

The Cache la Poudre River tumbles out of the east side of the Medicine Bow Mountains and drains the northern side of Rocky Mountain National Park. As the Poudre gathers its tributaries during late-spring runoff, it runs strong and continuous through a dramatic river canyon. A designated wild and scenic River corridor, Poudre River Canyon offers beautiful driving along Highway 14, which closely parallels the river. The 50-plus miles of runnable river here also offer a range of beginner to expert paddling options, with many easy access points. As the Poudre exits its canyon just west of Fort Collins, various irrigation diversions take water out of its channel. The river flattens out as it heads east onto the Front Range plains toward Greeley, where it eventually becomes another tributary to the South Platte River. The Poudre drainage also plays host to many surrounding Class V creek descents, for those willing to explore.

Rustic Sections

A respite from the Class V gnar upstream and the harder Narrows section below.

Nearest city/town: Fort Collins
Start: Sleeping Elephant Campground (N40 40.998' / W105 46.281')
End: Narrows Campground (N40 41.454' / W105 25.959')
Length: 19.0 miles (shorter runs possible)
Approximate paddling time: 3 to 5 hours
Difficulty rating: Intermediate/advanced
Rapids: Class IV (1), Class III (multiple)
River type: Continuous
Current: Swift
Environment: Wide river canyon
River gradient: 60 fpm (feet per minute)
River gauge: 300 to 3,000 cfs, Cache la Poudre at Canyon Mouth near Fort Collins
Elevation drop: 1,140 feet
Hazards: Low bridges and pushy whitewater features at high water
Season: May through July

Land status: US Forest Service, National Park Service
Boats used: Kayaks, rafts, canoes
Fees or permits: None
Maps: *Cache La Poudre National Heritage Area*
Other users: Commercial rafters
Contacts: Arapaho and Roosevelt National Forests, Estes-Poudre Ranger District (303) 482-3822
Special considerations: Put in 2 miles farther up Highway 14 for the Class V Spencer Heights section. Scout and/or portage your way through the Upper, Middle, and Lower Narrows (Class V, Class IV, Class V–) in the 3.5 miles beyond the Rustic takeout at Narrows Picnic Ground.
Put-in/takeout information: Use Highway 14, which closely parallels the river, as the primary route for access along this section. Both the put-in and takeout are well marked and easy to find.

The Paddle

Various access points along the middles section of the Poudre allow intermediate paddlers to choose their own adventure in a wide river valley best enjoyed at peak runoff flows. On the Upper Rustic, the Miracle Mile (Class IV), near mile marker 86, is the

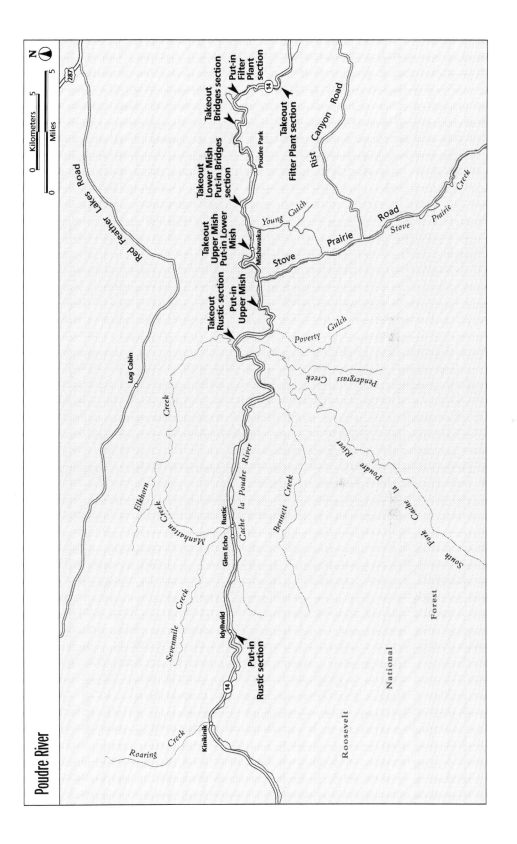

rapid of note, though it's perhaps more accurately described as a "busy quarter mile" of advanced paddling. The rest of the rapids fall into the straightforward Class II–III realm—long, choppy wave trains, with little technical maneuvering to worry about.

Shortly below the takeout for what is considered the Upper Rustic section, at Indian Meadows Picnic Area (N40 41.975' / W105 32.462'), the Poudre drops into a section known as Grandpa's Gorge (Class III+). When the river crosses to the south side of Highway 14, buckle up and charge through the fun waves. At high water, be prepared to dodge a few sticky holes—or just hit them straight and hard. There are a few other drops hiding above and below the bridge to Mountain Park campground. Look for some worthy surf waves around the campground, as well as below the island above Century Park. Highway 14 provides easy access and the potential for multiple laps at higher flows—locals look for 3.5 on the Pineview gauge. At 4 feet and above, there is little flatwater. Since it is higher up in the drainage, this section can be colder, requires more water, and will have a shorter season than the Narrows or other sections below.

Stevens Down

Twelve miles of the Poudre's most popular whitewater sections, broken down.

Upper Mishawaka

The most difficult section of the reach. Catch a show at the takeout, a historic riverside music venue!

Nearest city/town: Fort Collins
Start: Steven's Gulch Campground (40 41.010 / W105 32.549)
End: Mishawaka Amphitheatre (N40 41.251' / W105 21.975')
Length: 3.3 miles
Approximate paddling time: 1 to 3 hours
Difficulty rating: Advanced
Rapids: Class IV (3)
River type: Continuous read-and-run with a few walled-in rapids
Current: Swift
Environment: Wild and scenic roadside canyon
River gradient: 64 fpm
River gauge: 200 to 1,000 cfs, Cache la Poudre at Canyon Mouth
Elevation drop: 210 feet
Hazards: Cold water, sharp granite
Season: May through August

Land status: US Forest Service, National Park Service
Boats used: Kayaks, canoes, rafts
Fees or permits: None
Maps: *Cache La Poudre National Heritage Area*
Other users: Commercial rafters
Contacts: Arapaho and Roosevelt National Forests, Estes-Poudre Ranger District (303-482-3822)
Special considerations: Sometimes you watch the show, sometimes you are the show.
Put-in/takeout information: Use Highway 14, which closely parallels the river, as the primary access route along this section. The takeout is at the iconic Mishawaka Inn near mile marker 108. Use one of the pullouts downstream of the music venue unless you are planning to stop in for a beer or food. Find Stevens Gulch Campground near mile marker 104.7; this is the put-in.

The Paddle

Upper Mish is another Class IV read-and-run that's considered a Colorado classic with a cool bonus—riverside jams at one of the state's most historic venues at the takeout. At high flows (above 900 cfs, or 2.5 feet on the Pineview Rock gauge), this section is known for flushy, catch-on-the-fly play with the chance for long, cold swims. Mellow to medium flows make it more of a Class III+ affair with the exception of three prominent rapids considered Class IV at most water levels.

The first is Split Rock (also known as Twin Pin, Triple Rock, and a host of other names), generally run in the middle until the hole becomes retentive. The next is Tunnel, upstream of the Baldwin Highway Tunnel near mile marker 107.2. Here the river becomes a series of powerful waves and hydraulics, constricted by the canyon walls and slamming into an undercut ledge at the bottom left. Shortly downstream is a notorious place for eddyline play, known as Ultimate Squirt Spot (U.S.S.). Just upstream of the Mish amphitheatre lies its eponymous drop, Mishawaka Falls. It's the final and most consequential rapid of the section, and a place where paddlers are highly likely to be included in a tourist photo album. Scout from the right and try to ignore the drunken bikers and boaters lounging on the Mishawaka deck.

Lower Mishawaka

The next step down from the Narrows and Upper Mish, in difficulty and on the river.

Nearest city/town: Fort Collins
Start: Mishawaka Amphitheatre (N40 41.251' / W105 21.975')
End: Poudre Park Day Use Area (N40 41.383' / W105 19.463')
Length: 3.0 miles
Approximate paddling time: 1 to 2 hours
Difficulty rating: Intermediate
Rapids: Class III (multiple)
River type: Continuous, cold mountain stream
Current: Swift
Environment: Wild and scenic roadside canyon
River gradient: 62 fpm
River gauge: 200 to 1,000 cfs, Cache la Poudre at Canyon Mouth
Elevation drop: 185 feet
Hazards: Cold water, sharp granite
Season: June, July
Land status: US Forest Service, National Park Service
Boats used: Kayaks, rafts, canoes
Fees or permits: None

Maps: *Cache La Poudre National Heritage Area*
Other users: Commercial rafters
Contacts: Arapaho and Roosevelt National Forests, Estes-Poudre Ranger District (303) 482-3822
Special considerations: This takeout access point is about a mile of flat and uninteresting whitewater above Hewlett's Gulch, the put-in for the next river section (Poudre Park); it is often skipped unless running the entire section from Stevens Gulch down to Bridges Take Out.
Put-in/takeout information: Use Highway 14, which closely parallels the river, as the primary access route along this section. Find Poudre Park Day Use Area near mile marker 110.7; this is the takeout. The put-in is at the iconic Mishawaka Inn near mile marker 108. Use one of the pullouts downstream of the music venue unless you are planning to stop in for a beer or food.

The Paddle

Lower Mish is a short Class III romp sandwiched between sections of harder white-water. It's perfect for those stepping up from Filter Plant or wanting a notch easier than the sections around Lower Mish. It's still cold, shallow, and continuous—and will test a shaky combat roll. Other than a few sticky holes, medium to high flows will bring solid intermediate maneuvering and splashy wave hits.

Poudre Park

A fun splat-and-play run, or Class IV test piece.

Nearest city/town: Fort Collins
Start: Hewlett's Gulch bridge (N40 41.291' / W105 18.695')
End: Below Pineview Falls (N40 41.478' / W105 17.220')
Length: 2.0 miles
Approximate paddling time: 1 hour
Difficulty rating: Advanced
Rapids: Class IV (3)
River type: Cold, continuous mountain stream
Current: Swift
Environment: Wild and scenic roadside canyon
River gradient: 67 fpm
River gauge: 250 to 2,500 cfs, Cache la Poudre at Canyon Mouth
Elevation drop: 140 feet
Hazards: Bridge pilings and man-made debris
Season: June, July
Land status: US Forest Service, National Park Service
Boats used: Kayaks, canoes, rafts
Fees or permits: None

Maps: *Cache La Poudre National Heritage Area*
Other users: Fewer commercial rafters than on the easier sections
Contacts: Poudre Rock Report, poudrerockreport.com
Special considerations: Pineview Falls rapid is also the site of the Pineview Rock gauge, a river-left boulder spray-painted with lines indicating the "foot" levels most locals use in lieu of cfs measurements.
Put-in/takeout information: Use Highway 14, which closely parallels the river, as the primary access route along this section. The takeout is just below Pineview Falls near mile marker 112.7. To get to the put-in, head west on Highway 14, turn right (north) on Hewlett's Gulch Road just upstream of the small borough of Poudre Park, and cross the river; this is the put-in. Or go upstream about a mile to Poudre Park Day Use Area (see Upper Mishawaka takeout on page 14).

The Paddle

Five small road bridges to various private properties form the first rapids on the Poudre Park section. After the last bridge, prepare for Cardiac Corner (Class IV), an acute right-hand turn that slams current into some small cliffs on the left. This area is littered with large boulders and hard to see from the road, but the few intrepid commercial raft guides that run here may have the most elevated heart rates of any boaters.

The run finishes off with Pineview Falls (Class IV), with its picturesque nature and legendary splat rock known as Disneyland Slide. Here the canyon walls constrict the riverbed and tip it into a few decent-sized holes. Go right of the largest one at 4 feet and above on the Pineview Rock Gauge, located at the start of the rapid.

Bridges

More bridges.

Nearest city/town: Fort Collins
Start: Below Pineview Falls (N40 41.478' / W105 17.220')
End: Bridges Takeout (N40 41.419' / W105 17.237')
Length: 2.0 miles
Approximate paddling time: 1 hour or less
Difficulty rating: Intermediate
Rapids: Class III (2)
River type: Continuous, cold mountain stream
Current: Swift
Environment: Wild and scenic, increasingly crowded in the lower Poudre sections
River gradient: 33 fpm
River gauge: 250 to 3,000 cfs, Cache la Poudre at Canyon Mouth
Elevation drop: 65 feet
Hazards: Bridge pilings plus whitewater

Season: May through August
Land status: US Forest Service, National Park Service
Boats used: Kayaks, rafts, canoes, SUPs (?)
Fees or permits: None
Maps: *Cache La Poudre National Heritage Area*
Other users: Commercial rafters
Contacts: Poudre Paddlers Canoe and Kayak Club, poudrepaddlers.org
Special considerations: A late season special that runs at extremely low flows (.3 on the Pineview Rock Gauge)
Put-in/takeout information: Use Highway 14, which closely parallels the river, as the primary access route along this section. The takeout is a pullout near mile marker 114.7. The put-in is just below Pineview Falls near mile marker 112.7.

The Paddle

With mellow gradient and gentle whitewater, Bridges would be a great beginner run if weren't for the . . . bridges. These stone pilings have claimed a few lives and routinely proven the age-old river runner's equation: current plus obstacles equals potential for disaster. Difficult Bridge and its associated rapid present the first challenge—its abutments are in swift, busy water with a few moves to make above them. The other significant hazard on the run is Red House Hole (near mile marker 114.2), which can be a keeper at higher flows.

Find a sweet ender hole/eddyline combination on river right just above the takeout, a spot known as Bridges Takeout Wave and considered the Poudre's only true park-and-play. The Bridges takeout is also not one to be missed—there is a massive diversion dam less than a mile downstream. This short run is often added to the Poudre Park section for more mileage and popular with the after-work crowd. Due to its propensity to be the only section with water as the summer wears on, Bridges can also become increasingly packed with commercial rafts.

Filter Plant Section

Northern Colorado's classic beginner run.

Nearest city/town: Fort Collins
Start: Highway 14 pulloff below the filter plant (N40 41.458' / W105 14.264')
End: Picnic Rock River Access (N40 40.213' / W105 13.829')
Length: 2.5 miles
Approximate paddling time: 1 to 2 hours
Difficulty rating: Beginner/intermediate
Rapids: Class III (2)
River type: Broad channel
Current: Swift
Environment: Wild and scenic roadside canyon
River gradient: 45 fpm
River gauge: 200 to 1,000 cfs, Cache la Poudre River at Canyon Mouth near Fort Collins
Elevation drop: 105 feet
Hazards: Powerful whitewater features at high water
Season: May through August
Land status: Colorado State Parks
Boats used: Kayaks, rafts, canoes, SUPs
Fees or permits: There is a fee to park at the State Parks-managed access point at Picnic Rock

Maps: *Cache La Poudre National Heritage Area*
Other users: Scantily clad, sometimes inebriated tubers
Contacts: Poudre Paddlers Canoe and Kayak Club, poudrepaddlers.org
Special considerations: Be sure to hit the takeout; there is a low-head dam located just below.
Put-in/takeout information: Use Highway 14, which closely parallels the river, as the primary route for access along this section. The takeout is well marked—look for signs indicating Picnic Rock river access near mile marker 119. To reach the put-in, head upstream (west) on Highway 14 for 3 miles to mile marker 116.8, which is below the actual turnoff for the filter plant. Unload next to the river, and park in the designated parking area across the highway. Watch for fast-moving traffic; most people don't slow down for the corner here, and they don't watch for boaters crossing the road!

The Paddle

Still set in the canyon, with craggy rocks towering above the river, the Filter Plant run sees all types of paddlers and tubers. In part because of its proximity to Fort Collins, it's also popular as an after-work rinse. The river channel is pretty wide open, with a straightforward series of waves and smaller rapids. The first rapid is between the put-in and the bridge. The big one on the run is Mad Dog Rapid (Class II+ to III−), located on a hard right turn. The rest of this run is good to go for just about anyone.

3 St. Vrain River

The St. Vrain drainage begins high up on the flanks of 13,000-plus-foot mountains in the Indian Peaks Wilderness Area, which borders the east side of Rocky Mountain National Park. Falling downhill in various forks, the main stem of the St. Vrain River doesn't completely come together until the quaint foothills town of Lyons.

Upstream of here, the North Fork plummets through a Class V granite canyon choked with logs and boulders. In the last few miles above town, North St. Vrain eases up and offers the best beginner and intermediate paddling. The South Fork drops down a rugged, expert-only canyon local hair boaters use to get their after-work boof fix.

Because of its relatively small drainage and split flow, the St. Vrain's short runnable window is a technical shallow-paddling affair at best. If the water is there and you are in the area, float the lower sections of the river and enjoy some surfing in the park in town.

Shelly's Cottages

A rowdy Class III+ creek with one Class IV drop.

Nearest city/town: Lyons
Start: County Road 80 bridge (N40 14.209' / W105 19.168')
End: Apple Valley Bridge (N40 24.854' / W105 17.418')
Length: 2.7 miles
Approximate paddling time: 1 hour
Difficulty rating: Intermediate
Rapids: Continuous Class III (one Class IV)
River type: Narrow, low-volume creek
Current: Moderate
Environment: Roadside
River gradient: 56 fpm
River gauge: 200 to 400 cfs, North Saint Vrain Creek below Buttonrock (Ralph Price) Reservoir
Elevation drop: 151 feet
Hazards: Strainers
Season: June, July (dam release)
Land status: Private, beware "No Trespassing" signs around first rapid
Boats used: Kayaks, canoes, small rafts
Fees or permits: None

Maps: *US Forest Service, Arapahoe and Roosevelt National Forests*
Other users: Anglers
Contacts: City of Longmont, Public Works and Natural Resources (303-651-8501)
Special considerations: Roads along this entire stretch of river make it possible to scout while driving shuttle.
Put-in/takeout information: From downtown Lyons head north on US Highway 36 a few miles to Apple Valley Road. Turn left (south) and cross the bridge; park in the river access lot just upstream on the right side of the river— this is the takeout. To reach the put-in, continue heading upstream (north) on US 36, look for County Road 80 and turn left (west). Head upstream as the road closely parallels the river and look for a bridge over the river; this is the put-in.

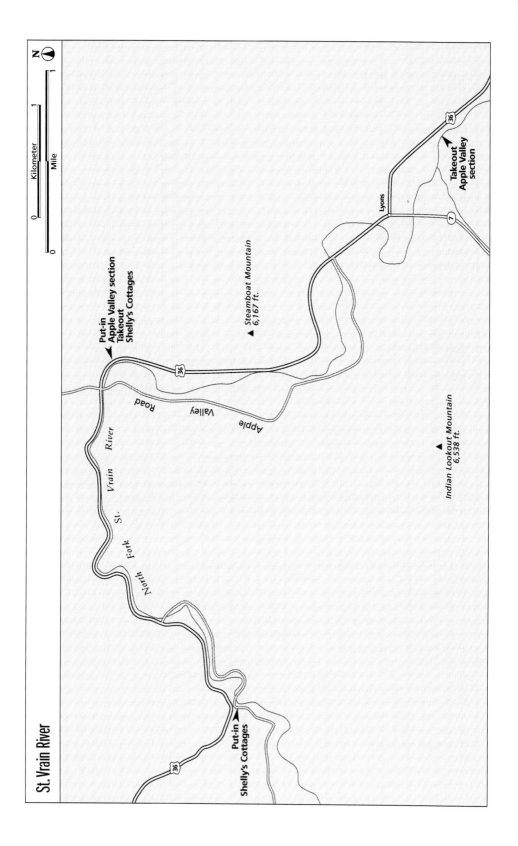

St. Vrain River

The Paddle

In September 2013, huge Front Range floods brought major changes to the riverbed of this short section of the Lower North St. Vrain, once considered a convenient, roadside beginner-intermediate float. Now it's choked with continuous Class III+ creek moves with one Class IV rapid of note, containing a large lateral wave. Enjoy quick boogie moves around mostly small, rounded rocks and some play packed into this short section. When the flow is good, you'll find steady current in a small, sometimes scrapy streambed—beware of occasional downed trees. Flood stage levels should be avoided due to low bridges. This section is also used as a higher put-in for the slightly easier Apple Valley section downstream.

Apple Valley Section

The area "beginner run."

Nearest city/town: Lyons
Start: Apple Valley Bridge (N40 14.854' / W105 17.418')
End: Lyons Park (N40 13.260' / W105 15.811')
Length: 4.2 miles
Approximate paddling time: 1 to 2 hours
Difficulty rating: Advanced beginner/intermediate
Rapids: Class II–III–
River type: Continuous
Current: Moderate to swift
Environment: Rural valley
River gradient: 50 fpm
River gauge: 160 to 300 cfs, North Saint Vrain Creek below Buttonrock (Ralph Price) Reservoir
Elevation drop: 210 feet
Hazards: Rock-pile diversion dam early in the stretch, run or scout on river right
Season: June, July (dam release)
Land status: Mostly private
Boats used: Kayaks, canoes, small rafts
Fees or permits: None

Maps: *US Forest Service, Arapahoe and Roosevelt National Forests*
Other users: Swimmers and tubers within Longmont city limits
Contacts: City of Longmont, Public Works and Natural Resources (303-651-8501)
Special considerations: Be sure to spend some time at the man-made features in Lyons Park. Designed for a range of water levels, high water waves and pocket holes offer up effortless loops and cartwheels while "October Hole" is meant to be a late-season special.
Put-in/takeout information: The traditional takeout is either at the top or bottom of the Lyons Town section. Look for Lyons Park on the south side of US 36 on the east edge of town near the Black Bear Inn. To reach the put-in from downtown Lyons, head north on US 36 a few miles to Apple Valley Road. Turn left (south) and cross the bridge. Park in the river access lot just upstream on the right side of the river. To reach the takeout, return to Lyons on US 36.

The Paddle

The bottom section of the North St. Vrain, Apple Valley meanders through a pleasant rural valley with distant red sandstone cliffs. The river channel snakes and wanders over shallow rocks and passes underneath low branches, featuring continuous, Class II flow with no real flatwater. The last portion of this runs almost doubles in flow as the north and south forks of the St. Vrain join together in the middle of Lyons. Cruise through town and take out at the man-made surfing spots in Lyons Park or head straight to the Oskar Blues brewery.

4 Boulder Creek

This is a relatively small drainage for runoff, but because of the outdoor-oriented nature of the Boulder community, Boulder Creek gets paddled frequently. It literally flows out of the mountains and directly through town.

Draining the Indian Peaks Wilderness Area above Eldora Ski Area, Boulder Creek tumbles through the congested and dramatic scenery of Boulder Canyon. Perhaps better for rock climbing than boating, Boulder Canyon does offer a short window of incredibly technical, expert-only paddling.

As the creek spills out of the canyon on the west side of Boulder, it courses through a section of man-made rapids and surf ledges. The small creek charges through town and eases as it continues heading east onto the plains. Eventually Boulder Creek enters the St. Vrain River, which then flows into the South Platte River.

Town Run

Unbeatable urban creeking.

Nearest city/town: Boulder
Start: Eben G. Fine Park (N40 00.636' / W105 18.181')
End: Colorado University-Boulder Greenhouse (N40 00.714' / W105 15.120')
Length: 3.0 miles or variable
Approximate paddling time: 1 hour or variable
Difficulty rating: Intermediate
Rapids: Man-made drops and holes
River type: Urban creek
Current: Swift
Environment: Bustling outdoor city, complete with tubers, bikers, and rollerbladers
River gradient: 52 fpm
River gauge: 150 to 400 cfs, Boulder Creek at Orodell
Elevation drop: 156 feet
Hazards: Rebar and other man-made debris, low-head dam river left below Library Hole
Season: June through August with night releases in the winter
Land status: City limits
Boats used: Kayaks, inner tubes

Fees or permits: CU requires permits to park between 7:30 a.m. and 7:00 p.m. as of May 2021
Maps: City of Boulder
Other users: Drunken college kids
Contacts: City of Boulder Parks and Recreation (303-441-1880)
Special considerations: Beware the urge to reunite swimmers with their recirculating Walmart-grade craft. Advanced/expert (Class IV-V) runs lie just upstream of the put-in for this run. Head farther up Boulder Canyon on Highway 119 to scout out this action.
Put-in/takeout information: Takeout options abound, including the Boulder Public Library, Boulder High School, the Fish Aquarium, and Scott Carpenter Park upstream of CU. The Eben G. Fine Park can be found on the very western end of Arapahoe Avenue, off Broadway (the main north-south route through town).

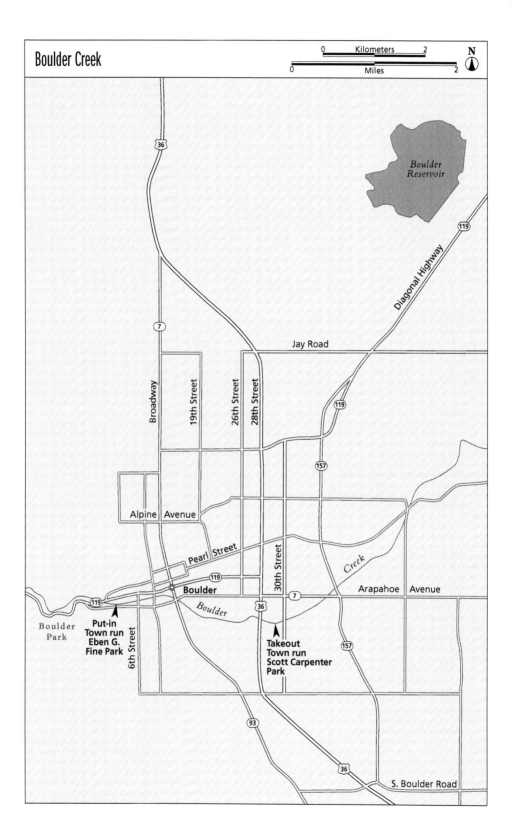

Boulder Creek

The Paddle

A small window of good water for paddling is the hardest part of this run. Once the water is here, a paddle through the heart of Boulder makes for a fun and thrilling urban-creeking experience for intermediate paddlers. Because of its narrow channel, overhanging tree branches in places, and numerous shallow rocks, this is not the nicest beginner zone, even though the actual rapids are not that difficult.

Put in on the west side of town and begin with some fairly continuous small ledges and rocky rapids. When the water is high, it is a nearly nonstop rocket ride. At more reasonable water levels, micro-eddies can be found below some drops. Numerous river modifications have been made to make certain ledges and small diversions more paddling-friendly. The whitewater calms down a bit throughout the length of the run as it heads east.

5 Clear Creek

Draining the east side of the Continental Divide near Loveland Ski Area, Clear Creek is a larger drainage of the Front Range that offers plenty of whitewater action. The river starts off strong and fast as it makes its way rapidly downhill, paralleled by I-70 and Highway 6. Paddlers come to Clear Creek for the action on the water—it is not for those seeking solitude or isolation.

Clear Creek Canyon, however, is a dramatic gash in the granite that pulses with nearly continuous challenging advanced/expert whitewater. As the creek drops out of the mountains, it settles down and offers a gathering spot for Denver-area paddlers with the creation of a whitewater park in the foothills town of Golden. As Clear Creek continues east farther onto the Front Range plains, it flows into the South Platte River on the northern edge of Denver.

Lawson and Dumont

High-quality roadside Class IV.

Nearest city/town: Idaho Springs
Start: Lawson Whitewater Park (N39 45.781' / W105 38.223')
End: Courtney-Riley-Cooper Park in Idaho Springs (N39 44.566' / W105 30.569')
Length: 6.0 miles
Approximate paddling time: 1 to 2 hours
Difficulty rating: Advanced
Rapids: Class IV (Class IV+ above 1,000 cfs)
River type: Ledgy pool-drop
Current: Swift
Environment: Roadside river canyon adjacent to the state's major east-west throughway, Interstate 70
River gradient: 67 feet per mile
River gauge: 200 to 1,200 cfs, Clear Creek near Lawson
Elevation drop: 370 feet
Hazards: Lines of boulders creating narrow drops and some sticky holes
Season: June, July
Land status: Colorado Department of Transportation
Boats used: Kayaks, rafts
Fees or permits: None

Maps: Interstate 70 highway
Other users: Commercial rafters during peak summer
Contacts: Colorado River Outfitters Association (970-260-4135)
Special considerations: The hole at the Lawson put-in is considered one of the best in the region for big air moves and creek-boat loops. Put in here to park-n-play, or to add more continuous Class IV action to the run below. An alternate put-in at Dumont (exit 235) makes for a shorter, slightly easier run.
Put-in/takeout information: While several takeout options exist in Idaho Springs, the easiest to find is the park at 23rd and Colorado Street. Get there via any of the three Idaho Springs exits off I-70. To get to the put-in from Idaho Springs, take I-70 back west and use exit 234 at Downieville. Turn right then left onto the frontage road and continue until you pass under the interstate and cross a bridge over Clear Creek. The Lawson whitewater park is on the right just past a rafting company; this is the put-in.

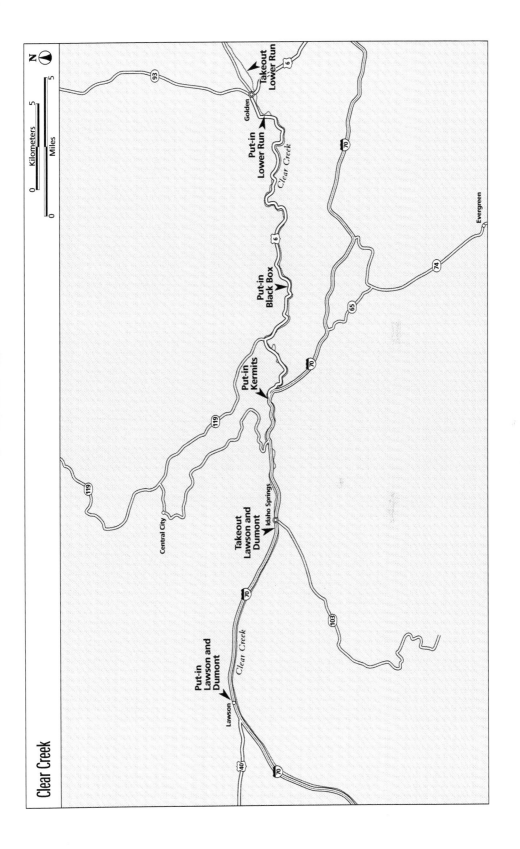

Clear Creek

The Paddle

This section of Upper Clear Creek parallels Interstate 70 for the entirety of the run, and though the water is cold, it hosts hordes of commercial rafters in midsummer. The steepness of the mini-canyon next to the highway lends the current a quick pace, and the first few miles below Lawson are the most continuous. Below here, the rapids become considerably more pool-drop and require good boat scouting above each ledge to find the best exit from the tumultuous hydraulic below. There are also some excellent surf waves; catch them on the fly at flows above 1,200 cfs because there will be few eddies. The main rapid of note is known as Outer Limits, which snakes around a few curves and requires dodging the stickiest holes. Look for it at the I-70 underpass at the west entrance to Idaho Springs (exit 240).

Kermitts

"Not the Numbers Class IV."—Evan Stafford, *Whitewater of the Southern Rockies*. Plus, put-in at a local biker bar!

Nearest city/town: Idaho Springs
Start: Two Bears Tap and Grill—formerly Kermitts Roadhouse (N39 44.779' / W105 26.256')
End: Pulloff below the intersection of Highway 6 and Highway 119 (N39 44.529' / W105 23.433')
Length: 5.4 miles
Approximate paddling time: 1 to 2 hours
Difficulty rating: Advanced
Rapids: Class IV (2), Class III (9)
River type: Steep, rocky mountain stream
Current: Swift
Environment: Mountain highway canyon
River gradient: 110 fpm
River gauge: 200 to 1,000 cfs, Clear Creek near Lawson
Elevation drop: 594 feet
Hazards: Pin spots, undercuts, strainers
Season: May through July

Land status: Colorado Department of Transportation
Boats used: Kayaks, decked canoes, rafts
Fees or permits: None
Maps: Colorado Department of Transportation highway map
Other users: Intrepid commercial rafters
Contacts: Colorado River Outfitters Association (970-260-4135)
Special considerations: Add on couple miles of class III by continuing down "Middle Clear Creek" and taking out at the Mayhem Gulch Trailhead parking lot.
Put-in/takeout information: From Idaho Springs, take the US-6 Golden exit off I-70 and follow this road to the intersection with Highway 119. Park in the Clear Creek Open Space parking lot below the water tank. Take US-6 back toward the interstate; put in across the street from the Two Bears restaurant.

The Paddle

The put-in for the Kermitts run down to Black Rock marks Clear Creek's departure from the I-70 corridor. Though it is fairly straightforward, it certainly isn't very clean. There are pin spots, undercuts, and often wood all over the run. The riverbed here is shallow and sharp, but it does provide some of the best Class IV boof practice around for those looking to step up their creeking game. The Beaver Drops, near the beginning of the run, can be easily scouted from the road before putting. Beaver One is either skirted with a boof on the far left or run down the middle tongue. For Beaver Two, start center then cut left. Then it's a continuous Class IV boogie on down to where the canyon narrows and reveals its first blind horizon line. This drop is known as Guide Ejector, boof right. The boof will land in a medium pool that sits right above Double Knife, the run's signature rapid. Multiple lines exist over a shelf followed by a good-sized hole. Say "Hasta la vista, baby!" to the Terminator Holes before more class IV read-and-run leads to Devil's Elbow, a big left-hand turn in the river marked by a large boulder on the right. After about 5 minutes of flatwater, take out at the Clear Creek Open Space parking lot or continue down the Highway 6 segment of Clear Creek.

Black Rock

The run metro-area boaters use to keep in creeking shape.

Nearest city/town: Denver
Start: Big Easy Trailhead parking area near mile marker 263 on Highway 6 (N39 44.094' / W105 21.942')
End: Downstream side of the bridge directly below Rigor Mortis rapid near mile marker 267 (N39 44.617' / W105 17.845')
Length: 5.5 miles
Approximate paddling time: 1 to 2 hours
Difficulty rating: Expert
Rapids: Class V (2), Class V+ (1)
River type: Tight, fast, shallow creek
Current: Extremely swift
Environment: Roadside
River gradient: 113 feet per mile
River gauge: 250 to 900 cfs, Clear Creek at Golden. At least one Front Range crew has been known to scrape down the Narrows at 107 cfs.
Elevation drop: 620 feet
Hazards: Sharp blast rock and terminal hydraulics
Season: May through July

Land status: Colorado Department of Transportation
Boats used: Kayaks, decked canoes
Fees or permits: None
Maps: US Highway 6
Other users: Class V inner tubers (see sidebar)
Contacts: Colorado River Outfitters Association (970-260-4135)
Special considerations: While in the area, many traveling kayakers (and locals) like to check out Coors Falls, possibly Colorado's easiest park-and-huck, on West Fork Clear Creek. Find it about 3 miles upstream of Empire along Highway 40 heading up Berthoud Pass from I-70. The rest of this hefty 2-mile section is runnable, if you like full-on Class V combat boating.
Put-in/takeout information: The takeout is just downstream of Rigor Mortis after one of several bridges over Clear Creek on Highway 6; this one is at mile marker 267.2. The put-in is at mile 262.9 on Highway 6, at a pullout with large spray-painted rocks.

The Paddle

This is the most challenging run on Clear Creek. A big black rock marks the entrance to the run's namesake rapid, a relatively easy but lengthy boulder garden visible from

TUBER DOWN!

The players: Mikey T, West Virginia Darrick, Dave Bum

The scene: Black Rock section of Clear Creek at Rigor Mortis rapid

The story (as told by Dave "He's Been Everywhere" Bumgarner): It was one of the times I've paddled the Black Rock section of Clear Creek, and everything was going well. We pulled out to set up safety at Rigor Mortis, the area's notorious Class V rapid. Mikey T and West Virginia Darrick went down to the bottom.

I dropped in, got flipped after the first big drop, and rolled up before the big hole. West Virginia Darrick went up, dropped in, styled the first big drop, but was too far right and flipped off a rock. He went past the big hole upside down but didn't get chundered.

Mikey T was walking up a little puckered but still excited. A guy with a raft customer Type V PFD and swim goggles approached us and asked us to set safety. West Virginia Darrick and I looked in awe at what this guy was going to run this with and asked, "Are you going to riverboard?"

"No."

"Are you going to swim it?"

"No."

Then he said, "I'm gonna tube it."

We both recommended against this, but he insisted, listing off all the Colorado gnar he'd run in his tube. Finally, my crew agreed that we loved carnage. So I took his spare throwbag and said, "Good luck!"

As Mikey T was putting on his sprayskirt, the tuber came down to the river. Mikey T looked this aquatic specimen up and down with awe, then shoved off into Rigo. He got flipped in the first part of the drop but quickly rolled up. The water pushed him left, and Mikey T went right into the large hole at the bottom. He was throwing every playboating move he knew. Mikey T looked up at West Virginia Darrick and me, asking what he should do. Our only response was, "Don't. Swim." The last move he tried was an errant splat off the left wall, and Mikey T was luckily flushed out.

He ran up to watch the tuber with the rest of us. As I was setting safety at the bottom, West Virginia Darrick was on a rock and narrating the action from above.

"Tuber in! Tuber in!"

The tuber went off the first drop and disappeared. "Tuber down! Tuber down!" It felt like an eternity, but the tuber popped up upright, with huge eyes, clenching his tube for dear life. He then went into the bottom drop and had the best line he could as the hole ejected him from his tube. As the tube was getting recirculated, its pilot was trying to wade upstream back toward it. We all yelled in unison, "Don't stand up in the river!"

The tube eventually flushed. The three of us turned to the tuber's friend and said, "Your boyfriend is nuts!"

Her response: "He's not my boyfriend, he's my tubing partner."

Highway 6 around mile marker 264. After some boogie water considered mild for those who have the Class V skills for this run, a cliff wall looms on river left signaling the Narrows. A tough entrance leads quickly into Mr. Bill, a munchy hole two-thirds of the way down the rapid. Most sneak it on the far right, but at some levels stout boaters punch it. The Narrows run out provides a quick break before the big one—Rigor Mortis. Here, the walls close in and some big boulders crop up on river right. Swirly rooster tails guard the entrance, which leads into a fast ramp and a subtle pillow move on the right to avoid the meat—a sticky hydraulic that traps boaters, particularly if they end up facing the wall. Go right of the house rock at the end of the rapid, especially if you're swimming, to avoid the large undercut on the left 50 feet downstream from the hole. Take out on river left downstream of the highway bridge.

Tunnel One Down (Below Rigo to Golden Whitewater Park)

A short, easy after-work rinse.

Nearest city/town: Golden
Start: Tunnel #1 Access (N39 44.537' / W105 15.212')
End: Golden Whitewater Park (N39 45.252' / W105 13.693')
Length: 2.1 miles
Approximate paddling time: 1 to 2 hours
Difficulty rating: Advanced beginner/intermediate
Rapids: Class II–III
River type: Roadside canyon to urban walking path
Current: Swift
Environment: Craggy granite, man-made
River gradient: 50 fpm
River gauge: 220 to 1,500 cfs, Clear Creek at Golden, CO
Elevation drop: 180 feet

Hazards: Diversions for irrigation and Coors factory
Season: April through July
Land status: City of Golden
Boats used: Kayaks, canoes, rafts
Fees or permits: None
Maps: Highway 6
Other users: Inner tubers in Golden whitewater park on hot summer days
Contacts: Golden City Hall (303-384-8000)
Special considerations: This is considered the easiest of the whitewater sections on Clear Creek. Put in a little higher, just downstream of Rigor Mortis rapid near mile marker 267.2 for a little Class IV action including a diversion dam. While the dam is runnable, most walk it on river left to avoid flipping and slashing their knuckles on the riverbed's extremely sharp

blast rock. From here, the run becomes Class III until Tunnel #1.

Put-in/takeout information: To reach the takeout from downtown Golden, head north on Washington Street, cross the creek, and turn left (west) at the next traffic light onto 10th Street. Head upstream to the parking area past the baseball fields; this is a higher takeout point.

To reach the put-in, return to the intersection of 10th and Washington streets and turn left (north) onto Washington. Cross over Highway 58 and enter the highway heading west. Highway 58 becomes US Highway 6 as it enters Clear Creek Canyon. Just below the first tunnel and below a diversion dam, look for a dirt pullout on the left; this is the put-in.

The Paddle

Two streams diverged in a canyon . . . Putting on Clear Creek upstream (west of Tunnel 1 provides a handful of Class III rapids on the oxbow around the tunnel. Below east of) Tunnel 1 at the large dirt pullout allows less confident paddlers to bypass the hardest rapids and many crews will split and have newbies wait here. Below the second put-in, near where the river comes back to the road, the Church Ditch diversion pulls about 40 cfs out of the river. Go right at all splits in the river to avoid going down the ditch.

As it approaches the town of Golden, Clear Creek drops over numerous man-made ledges that attract crowds of evening paddlers when flows are good. The ledges are all straightforward charge-on-through affairs for beginners, but also offer good park-and-play.

At the far east edge of the whitewater park, one last hole—aptly named Library Hole—is located next to the library. Shortly below here is the takeout in downtown Golden. Don't miss it or you may end up in a can of Coors beer, is diverted water straight into the factory downstream.

6 South Platte River

Upstream of Denver, the South Platte River consists of two completely separate forks that offer multiple beginner-to-expert sections for paddling.

The North Fork comes to life as it flows off Kenosha Pass and gathers water from the central mountains with the outflow of the Roberts Tunnel Diversion. This diversion saps water from Lake Dillon and the Blue River and diverts it under the mountains to quench Denver's thirst. After most of its flow gets spit out of the tunnel, the North Fork flows through a winding valley, the remote Bailey Canyon, and then through a lower narrow canyon before joining the South Fork.

Meanwhile, the South Fork trickles slowly out of the Buffalo Peaks Wilderness Area. The top of the South Fork slides across the high, open plateau of South Park before getting swallowed by multiple reservoirs. The outflow of Elevenmile Canyon Dam then tumbles through two distinct gorges—Eleven Mile and Cheesman—that offer intermediate/expert creeking with portage options around the gnarliest drops.

The North and South Fork flows finally join in the foothills above Denver, offering up one last short, hikeable section of whitewater in Waterton Canyon before screeching to a halt in Chatfield reservoir. Below this, the South Platte is urban but still offers some paddling options. It then rolls out onto the Front Range plains of eastern Colorado before flowing into Nebraska, where it joins the North Platte River and ultimately flows into the Missouri River.

North Fork

Bailey Canyon
One of Colorado's premier "cut-your-teeth" creek runs.

Nearest city/town: Bailey
Start: McGraw Park (N39 24.277' / W105 28.390')
End: Pine Valley Open Space (N39 24.425' / W105 20.789')
Length: 10.4 miles
Approximate paddling time: 3 to 5 hours
Difficulty rating: Expert
Rapids: Class IV–IV+ (many), Class V (3)
River type: Bedrock littered with large boulders
Current: Extremely swift
Environment: Secluded canyon
River gradient: 85 fpm
River gauge: 165-650 cfs, South Platte at Bailey or Grant, usually similar
Elevation drop: 885 feet

Hazards: Large hydraulics, undercut rocks, occasional wood
Season: April through May, August through September. Off-season flows possible.
Land status: Private land abounds
Boats used: Kayaks, small rafts
Fees or permits: None
Maps: Google maps
Other users: Anglers who pay high-dollar amounts to access the private fishing spots in the upper reaches of the canyon
Contacts: Colorado Whitewater, coloradowhitewater.org
Special considerations: Catch midsummer releases during heat waves when all of Denver simultaneously turns on their air conditioners

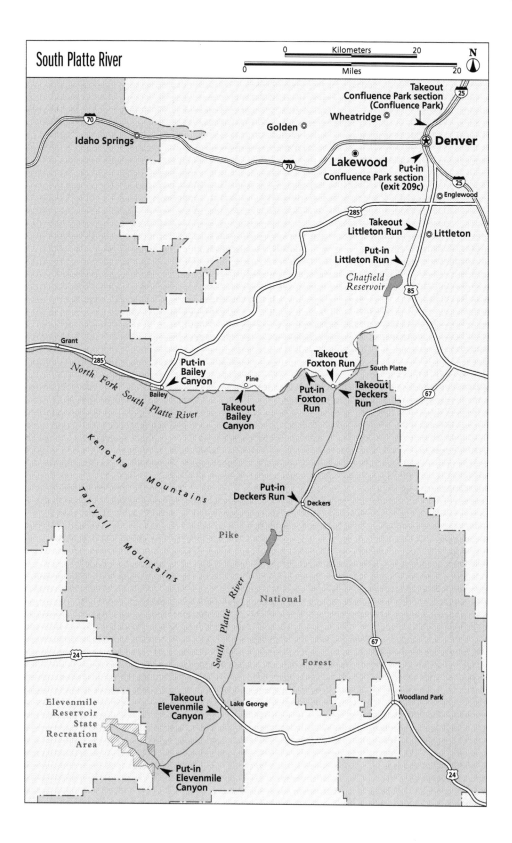

South Platte River

Kilometers
0   20

Miles
0   20

N

70

Idaho Springs

Golden ◎

Wheatridge ◎

Takeout
Confluence Park section
(Confluence Park)
25

★ Denver

70

Lakewood
Confluence Park section
(exit 209c)

Put-in

25

◎ Englewood

285

Takeout
Littleton Run

◎ Littleton

Put-in
Littleton Run

Chatfield Reservoir

85

Grant

285

North Fork South Platte River

Put-in
Bailey
Canyon

Bailey

Pine ○

Takeout
Bailey
Canyon

Takeout
Foxton Run

South Platte

Put-in
Foxton
Run

Takeout
Deckers
Run

67

Kenosha Mountains

Tarryall Mountains

Put-in
Deckers Run

○ Deckers

Pike

South Platte River

National

67

24

Forest

Woodland Park ●

Elevenmile Reservoir State Recreation Area

Takeout
Elevenmile
Canyon

● Lake George

Put-in
Elevenmile
Canyon

24

Put-in/takeout information: To reach the takeout, turn south off Highway 285 at mile 229 onto Pine Valley Road. After 5.9 miles, take a right on Crystal Lake Road. This road ends in 1.3 miles at Pine Valley Ranch Park and a huge paved parking lot right next to the river. The put-in is reached from Highway 285 at mile 222.2 (at the east side of Bailey), where you turn onto Highway 68. After turning south on Highway 68, you will see a feed store, liquor store, and some businesses. The put-in is behind this complex and is called McGraw Park. Since 2019, a new parking lot is being constructed for park access that is to the left (downstream) of these stores. Current parking (limited) is available to the right of the businesses by the old footbridge. Do not park in the store parking spots out front or the feed store operator will try to have you towed. Kayakers previously put-in downstream at a bridge with culverts. The landowners no longer want kayakers using their property to put in, so please put in at the town of Bailey.

The Paddle

Tucked between the mountainous suburbs of Bailey and Pine, Bailey Canyon is a true Colorado gem. Step one: Catch it running. Like everything else in this drainage, flows rely on releases from the Roberts Tunnel. Local boaters have timed these to prove reliable in late summer/early fall, and host an annual BaileyFest over Labor Day weekend.

Step two: Find a Bailey veteran to lead you down. The three Class V rapids are easy to scout (and portage), if you know where they are. A smooth railroad grade runs along river right until the first significant rapid, Four Falls (Class V), after which it picks up on river left. Most mortals carry around the first drop of Four Falls and put back in for the remaining series of drops and maneuvers. This rapid gives way to a mile-long section known as "The Steeps." Here, Bailey noobs will encounter the biggest holes they've ever seen, and hit them, sometimes sideways. The 3 miles between Four Falls and Deer Creek, near the end of the canyon, drop 441 feet. Buckle up and look out for Super Max (Class V), a rollicking S-move into large and sticky hydraulics with a slidey drop at the end. Scout and portage on the left. Alternatively, skip the first half of the rapid containing the biggest undercut hazard, to run the version of this rapid affectionately dubbed "Tampax." Two miles later, Deer Creek tributary comes in above its namesake rapid (Class V), which features a fun launch-pad boof into fluffy whitewater with a shallow run-out. Here the gradient eases into splashy Class III past towering granite domes to the takeout.

Step three: Determine if your guide's definition of runnable is within your acceptable level of risk. While some will go as low as 165 cfs, others need at least 300 to pad out the continuous, heads-up hole-dodging on this run. Then there are those who claim Bailey really only gets going above 600 on the Grant gauge. If you have confidence in your continuous Class V skills, giddy up! If you're hoping to make it more of a Class IV–IV+ affair, offer to run shuttle, grab your mountain bike, and enjoy the trail network surrounding the takeout at Pine Valley Open Space.

Setting safety below Super Max in Bailey Canyon. Credit: Kevin Hoffman

Foxton

The most reliable flows and quality Class III the Front Range has to offer.

Nearest city/town: Pine
Start: Buffalo Creek (N39 24.459' / W105 15.405')
End: Confluence of North and South Forks of the South Platte River (N39 24.475' / W105 10.247')
Length: 10.0 miles (shorter run possible)
Approximate paddling time: 2 to 3 hours
Difficulty rating: Intermediate/advanced
Rapids: Class III+ (numerous), Class IV above 600 cfs
River type: Narrow boulder garden
Current: Swift
Environment: Semi-secluded river canyon
River gradient: 60 fpm
River gauge: 180 to 1,000 cfs (North Fork South Platte River at Bailey)
Elevation drop: 600 feet
Hazards: Strainers
Season: April through September, dam controlled. Off-season flows possible when West Slope water is diverted through Roberts Tunnel from Dillon Reservoir.
Land status: Some private land around put-in
Boats used: Kayaks, small rafts, canoes

Fees or permits: None
Maps: Denver Water, South Platte River Access: Deckers to Buffalo Creek
Other users: Anglers
Contacts: Colorado Whitewater, coloradowhitewater.org
Special considerations: Paddlers looking for a little more action can continue downstream after the confluence into the mile-and-a-half-long Waterton Canyon. This scenic little stretch has four named rapids that approach Class IV in difficulty (S-Turn, Green Bridge, Avalanche, and Vertical Blender) before dumping into the backwaters of Strontia Springs Reservoir. Shoulder your boat and hike back up the river-left trail for this section's "shuttle."
Put-in/takeout information: The put-ins and takeouts for this run are accessed off the dusty, dirt Platte River Road (96 Road). The road closely parallels the river on the left side, making it easy to scout on the way upstream to the put-in. To reach Platte River Road, take Foxton Road downhill off US 285 just outside the town of Conifer.

The Paddle

Just below the put-in in the rundown town of Foxton, the river turns hard to the east and begins getting squeezed into tight, steep drops that channelize well down to 200 cfs. As the river road winds up the canyon, lined by crag climbing areas, narrow flumes of current weave among large granite boulders. Use extra caution through this section—scout and/or portage along the road on the left side of the river. The bottom half settles down and opens up, providing gentler rapids and steady current down to the takeout. Take the half-slice to enjoy play at a decent front-surfing spot near the road junction.

South Fork

Eleven Mile Canyon

Great roadside creeking—in the off chance it is actually running.

Nearest city/town: Lake George
Start: Eleven Mile Reservoir (N38 54.330' / W 105 28.439')
End: Lake George (N38 58.295' / W105 21.899')
Length: 9.3 miles
Approximate paddling time: 2 to 3 hours
Difficulty rating: Intermediate/advanced
Rapids: Class III+, Class IV (1)
River type: Large granite boulder garden
Current: Swift
Environment: Remote
River gradient: 62 fpm
River gauge: 250 to 800 cfs, South Platte River near Lake George, CO
Elevation drop: 577 feet
Hazards: Powerful, river-wide hydraulic at Black Hole rapid
Season: Rare; dam controlled
Land status: Public
Boats used: Kayaks, small rafts
Fees or permits: None

Maps: *National Geographic South Platte River, Eleven Mile Canyon Reservoir to Chatfield Reservoir*
Other users: Anglers
Contacts: Pike-San Isabel National Forests (719-553-1404)
Special considerations: The rarely run, expert-only Cheesman Canyon (Class V) lies downstream. This run requires some very technical paddling/portaging, as well as navigating tricky landowner issues.
Put-in/takeout information: From Colorado Springs, head west on US Highway 24 to Woodland Park and continue heading west to Lake George. Turn left (southwest) onto County Road 97, heading up Eleven Mile Canyon. The takeout is upstream of the bottom Class V rapid, near the Obrien Gulch Picnic Area.

Continue heading upstream along the road, which closely parallels the river and affords great scouting. The put-in is below the top Class V drop, near Cove Campground. Scout and run the aforementioned class V if you can.

The Paddle

This scenic canyon is a top run on the South Fork of the South Platte. The releases coming out of Eleven Mile Reservoir are finicky and rare; if Bailey is not running, this probably is. When there is sufficient water, this is a technical, Class III+ canyon at best if boaters portage the top and final drops (Class V) with one Class IV slide (Black Hole) about a mile in. A relatively out-of-the-way location also plays host to great camping along the river, which can easily be scouted while shuttling.

Deckers

The Denver-area beginner paddler weekend special.

Nearest city/town: Bailey
Start: Deckers (N39 15.415' / W105 13.396')

End: Confluence of North and South Forks of the South Platte River (N39 24.475' / W105 10.247')

Length: 11.0 miles (shorter run possible)
Approximate paddling time: 3 to 4 hours
Difficulty rating: Advanced beginner/
intermediate
Rapids: Class II–III
River type: Open valley
Current: Moderate
Environment: Rural, scenic
River gradient: 20 fpm
River gauge: 250 to 500 cfs, South Platte
below Cheesman Reservoir
Elevation drop: 220 feet
Hazards: Sunburn
Season: April through September; late season
flows more likely due to water project demands
Land status: Some private land around
upstream reaches
Boats used: Kayaks, canoes, rafts
Fees or permits: None
Maps: *National Geographic South Platte River,
Eleven Mile Canyon Reservoir to Chatfield
Reservoir*

Other users: Anglers, tubers
Contacts: Pike-San Isabel National Forests
(719-553-1404)
Special considerations: Ultra beginners/first-
time whitewater boaters who don't want to run
the Chutes can put in a bit upstream at the
Ouzel Campground or Willow Bend Picnic Area
and take out at the parking lot just above the
rapid. There is also a section of intermediate-
friendly Class III whitewater in the 3 miles just
below Cheesman Dam to Deckers, but legal
access for the put-in is challenging. The road
goes away from the river, and there is lots of
private property.
Put-in/takeout information: Use CR 97/
Platte River Road as the primary shuttle route
for this section. To reach CR 97, take Highway
67 north from Woodland Park, just north of
Colorado Springs. The put-in and takeout are
well marked. Other access points can be used
to shorten the overall length of this run.

The Paddle

This lower section of the South Fork of the South Platte offers the best beginner paddling between the big cities of Denver and Colorado Springs. Weekends can be a bit crowded with classes and club groups, but there are plenty of fun river miles for everyone. A road closely parallels the entire section, so it is easy to scout the whole section or to use numerous pullouts to shorten the overall length of this run.

The bottom half of the run contains more Class II whitewater action than the top half. The crux of this entire section is the Chutes Rapid (Class II–III)—a narrow chute between massive boulders located 2 miles above the confluence. The rest of this section is more open, with swift current, good eddylines, and splashy wave trains. This is a great run for budding paddlers or Foxton/Waterton shuttle bunnies, as these two sections share a takeout at the confluence of the North and South Fork.

Littleton Run
Paddle in the shadow of Denver's skyline.

Nearest city/town: Denver
Start: South Platte Park, just below Chatfield
Dam (N39 34.940' / W105 01.844')
End: Bellview Avenue (N39 37.942' / W105
00.898')

Length: 4.0 miles (shorter runs possible)
Approximate paddling time: 1 to 2 hours
Difficulty rating: Intermediate
Rapids: Class II–III

River type: Moving water with man-made features
Current: Moderate
Environment: Urban
River gradient: 13 fpm
River gauge: 400 to 1,500 cfs, South Platte River below Union Avenue, at Englewood; dam controlled
Elevation drop: 52.5 feet
Hazards: Man-made diversions and weirs, questionable water quality
Season: Year-round
Land status: City of Denver and private
Boats used: Kayaks, canoes, rafts, SUPs
Fees or permits: None
Maps: Denver Metro Area
Other users: Denver residents
Contacts: Denver Water (303) 893-2444
Special considerations: Playboaters may wish to spend more time paddling and surfing the ledges at Union Chutes Park—all of which can be scouted and accessed off the trail on river left near Union Avenue off US 85. Flatwater touring enthusiasts can enjoy a tour on Chatfield Reservoir, located just upstream of this section. Refer to the lake-touring section of this guide for further information.

Put-in/takeout information: To reach the takeout from downtown Denver, head south on Interstate 25. At exit 207, veer right (west) onto US Highway 85, also known as Santa Fe Drive. After crossing Hampden and Oxford Avenues, look for Union Avenue; turn right (west) and cross the river. Turn immediately right and park on the eastern edge of the baseball fields next to the river—this is the takeout. To reach the put-in, return to US 85; turn right (south) and continue heading upstream. Just after crossing Mineral Avenue, look for South Platte River Park. Turn right (west) into the park and wind toward the parking area next to the river—this is the put-in.

The Paddle

This section of the South Platte lies just below Chatfield Reservoir as the river makes its way through the urban sprawl of the Mile High City. Riverside restoration and revitalization has taken hold along the South Platte through its metro corridor, so bike trails parallel parts of the river. Numerous once deadly dams have been modified to offer runnable chutes, but care still needs to be taken when approaching all man-made objects, of which there are many, along this section.

The real bonus of this run is that there is some decent surfing at the takeout at Union Chutes. This comprises six or seven modified ledges that are up to Class III at good levels; scout along the trail on river left.

Confluence Park

Wear your nose plugs for a midtown surf sesh next to the REI flagship store.

Nearest city/town: Denver
Start: Confluence Park (N39 45.234' / W105 00.540')
End: Trestle Bridge (N39 45.715' / W104 59.910')
Length: 1.0 mile
Approximate paddling time: Until your eyes start to burn . . .

Difficulty rating: Intermediate playboating
Rapids: Class III
River type: Man-made diversions and weirs in various stages of disrepair, some intentionally formed into whitewater features
Current: Swift
Environment: Urban storm drain
River gradient: 33 fpm

River gauge: 200 to 1,600 cfs, South Platte River at Denver

Elevation drop: 33 feet

Hazards: Discarded needles and other trash

Season: Year-round

Land status: City of Denver

Boats used: Kayaks, canoes, small rafts, pack rafts—grab a demo from nearby Confluence Kayak and Ski, the local metro-area paddle shop

Fees or permits: Parking meters

Maps: Denver Metro Area

Other users: Homeless bridge dwellers

Contacts: Confluence Kayak and Ski (303-433-3676)

Special considerations: Put in at the Eighth Avenue boat launch for 3 miles of cruisey flatwater down to Confluence Park. Try not to be jealous of the tourists on the waterslides at Elitch Gardens amusement park on river right!

Put-in/takeout information: The Confluence Park access area is at the 23rd Avenue exit off I-25. Head north to park along the river next to the REI store. The "takeout" can be found at the 20th Avenue exit; various driving routes and a paved riverside trail system connect the two.

The Paddle

Confluence Park is named for the convergence of the South Platte River and Cherry Creek right in the heart of downtown Denver. Though unoriginal, it is a better name than some that the urban surf spot goes by: Effluence Park, Confluenza, and so on. Located in the middle of a major metropolitan area where all storm drains—as well as various other pollutants—run into the river, the water quality down here can be a bit suspect. Take care to let the sludge clear if paddling immediately after a storm.

The whitewater park itself is a series of ledges and waves that offer good urban surfing or fun crash-on through rapids. Originally constructed as a slalom course, the park's features are tame and the eddies swirly. It's a great place for beginners to hone skills or city-bound paddlers to demo a boat they found on Craigslist. After the main event, which consists of roughly four features fondly referred to as Hepatitis A, B, C, and D—all packed into about 50 yards next to a low-head dam. About 150 yards downstream from here, find the remnants of an old bridge, known to create a better wavehole at most levels than the "playpark" upstream. Finish off the sesh at Trestle Wave below the train bridge at the "takeout."

If you must, scout from the bike trail along the river. The network of manicured parks and trails serves as a gathering spot for tourists and local suits on lunchbreak, complete with viewing decks, and swim spots. The trail is also a way to return to your vehicle without having to fight through downtown traffic for shuttle—bonus points for finding the unmarked, old-school burger- and beer-slinging joint called My Brother's Bar a block from the river-left shore on 15th Street while strolling back up.

7 Arkansas River

Possibly the state's most popular paddling destination, the Arkansas River Valley and its adventure tourism meccas of Buena Vista and Salida attract boaters of all craft and skill level. The Ark drops 4,100 feet over 125 miles of runnable whitewater spanning Chaffee and Fremont counties, with a range of paddling options from Class II to Class V and four world-class whitewater parks. Trickling off the east side of the Continental Divide, the Ark collects snowmelt from Fremont Pass and its surrounding peaks, gaining steam just below the town of Leadville. There it braids itself into a few swift, meandering sections more appealing to wade fishermen than boaters before plunging into Granite Gorge. Then the whitewater action is on, fed by releases from several diversions pumping water through Independence Pass from the West Slope's Fryingpan/Roaring Fork and Eagle River drainages en route to ranches on the eastern plains and other Front Range users. Releases down Lake Creek and Clear Creek, a couple of the Ark's most significant "tributaries," ensure consistent summer flow and fuel a bustling commercial rafting scene.

Flanked by the Saguache Mountains to the west and the Mosquito Range to the east, the Arkansas flows southward in the shadow of snowcapped 14,000-foot peaks. Glacially deposited craggy granite boulders line the banks and create the major obstacles within the river channel. The high-mountain canyons at the headwaters give way to open and rural vistas above Salida. There, the Arkansas bends east and parallels Highway 50 until it funnels into the near-vertical walls of the Royal Gorge just upstream of Canon City. The river then begins its slow journey across the plains to meet the Mississippi in eastern Arkansas, after providing some easy paddling options, a whitewater park, and a reservoir near Pueblo.

This river corridor encompasses private and public land, delineated with official and homemade signage. Access is managed by Colorado Parks and Wildlife, Bureau of Land Management, and a local agency known as the Arkansas Headwaters Recreation Area (AHRA), which has an office in downtown Salida. Many developed (fee-area) boat ramps and roadside whitewater provide for easy, sometimes bikeable shuttles. A yearly state parks pass is available to avoid daily parking fees at AHRA-maintained sites.

Granite Gorge

A forested, high-alpine canyon tucked away from the highway.

Nearest city/town: Buena Vista
Start: Granite bridge (N39 02.580' / W106 15.959')
End: Pine Creek Rapid (N39 00.120' / W106 13.743')
Length: 4.0 miles

Approximate paddling time: 1 to 2 hours
Difficulty rating: Intermediate
Rapids: Class III (multiple)
River type: Boulder garden
Environment: High-alpine canyons
River gradient: 58 fpm

Rowing into Browns Canyon on the Arkansas River. Credit: Rob Hurst

River gauge: 300 to 5,000 cfs, Arkansas River below Granite
Elevation drop: 200 feet
Hazards: Diversion at Clear Creek confluence
Season: May through August
Land status: Colorado Parks and Wildlife, Bureau of Land Management
Boats used: Kayaks, canoes, rafts
Fees or permits: Required at AHRA-managed parking areas and boat ramps
Maps: *RiverMaps, Guide to the Arkansas River*
Other users: Anglers
Contacts: Arkansas Headwaters Recreation Area (719-539-7289)

Special considerations: Don't miss the mandatory takeout for paddlers not wishing to tackle the advanced/expert runs of Pine Creek (Class V) and the Numbers (Class IV) just downstream.
Put-in/takeout information: Use US 24 for both the put-in and takeout. To reach the take-out, head south on US 24 for approximately 4 miles. Look for a large dirt pullout on the east side of the highway. Park here and prepare to hike up a short, rough jeep trail leading to the parking area from railroad tracks that parallel the river. The put-in is in the small town of Granite. Cross the bridge on the east side of the highway to park and put in on river left.

The Paddle

Considered the start to the Arkansas River's runnable whitewater, Granite Gorge delivers Class III wave trains and a few blind horizon lines. Tight riverbanks and

Arkansas River

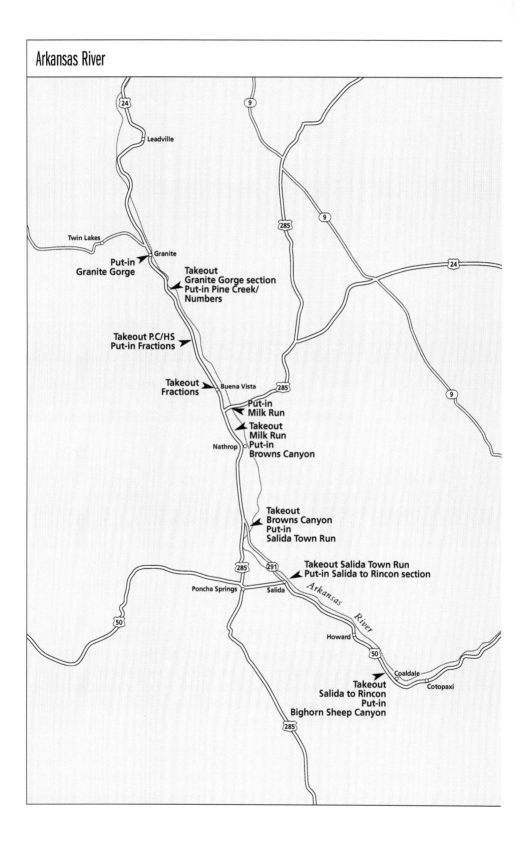

- 24
- 9
- Leadville
- 285
- 9
- Twin Lakes
- Granite
- 24
- **Put-in Granite Gorge**
- **Takeout Granite Gorge section Put-in Pine Creek/Numbers**
- **Takeout P.C/HS Put-in Fractions**
- 9
- **Takeout Fractions**
- Buena Vista
- 285
- **Put-in Milk Run**
- **Takeout Milk Run**
- Nathrop
- **Put-in Browns Canyon**
- **Takeout Browns Canyon Put-in Salida Town Run**
- 285
- 291
- **Takeout Salida Town Run Put-in Salida to Rincon section**
- Poncha Springs
- Salida
- *Arkansas River*
- 50
- Howard
- 50
- Coaldale
- Cotopaxi
- **Takeout Salida to Rincon Put-in Bighorn Sheep Canyon**
- 285

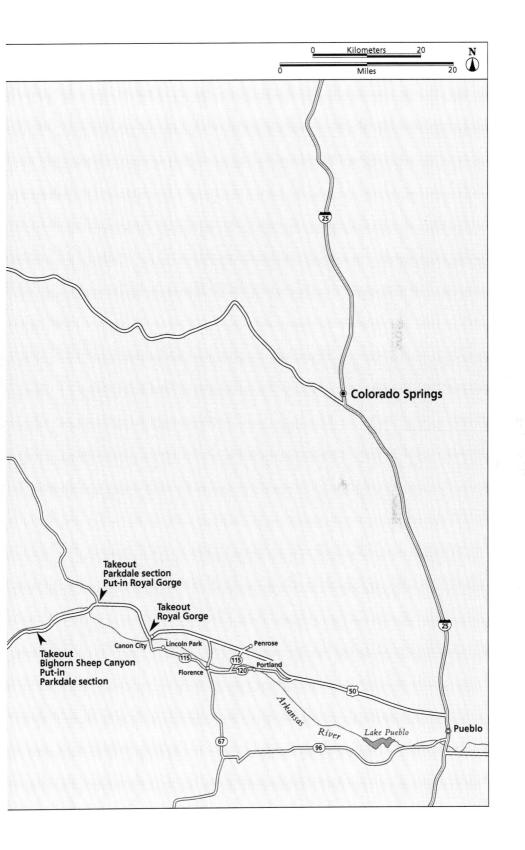

midstream granite boulders choke the current in several places, making low-water maneuvering difficult for commercial rafts and other larger crafts.

Just above the confluence with Clear Creek, where there is a small parking area and alternate river access, boaters encounter a six-tier "boat chute" where a Front Range utility company diverts water destined for Aurora and Colorado Springs. The man-made series of V-waves is sandwiched between recirculating eddies that can get rowdy for kayakers at high flows. The project, completed in winter 2020, eliminates the need to portage what was once a rundown, rebar-laden diversion dam. Below the boat chute, the river squeezes into one more short canyon with good waves and straightforward rapids. A slot between the river-left shore and a house-sized boulder on the right signifies the entrance to Pine Creek Rapid below.

Pine Creek/The Numbers

The steepest, longest, most formidable section of whitewater on the Arkansas, followed by continuous Class IV read-and-run that's considered a western classic.

Nearest city/town: Buena Vista
Start: Pine Creek Rapid or the Numbers recreation site (N38 59.70' / W106 13.20')
End: Railroad Bridge (N38 55.449' / W106 10.199') or other various pullouts along the river road
Length: 6.0 miles or variable
Approximate paddling time: 1 to 3 hours
Difficulty rating: Advanced/expert
Rapids: Class IV (7), Class V (1)
River type: Continuous gradient, boulder garden
Current: Swift
Environment: High-alpine desert
River gradient: 200 fpm Pine Creek, 71 fpm The Numbers
River gauge: 250 to 4,000 cfs, Arkansas River below Granite
Elevation drop: 350 feet
Hazards: Powerful hydraulic at Pine Creek hole
Season: Year-round, ice dependent
Land status: Colorado State Parks, Bureau of Land Management
Boats used: Kayaks, canoes, rafts, expert whitewater SUPs
Fees or permits: Required at AHRA-managed parking areas and boat ramps
Maps: *RiverMaps, Guide to the Arkansas River*

Other users: Anglers, commercial rafters
Contacts: Arkansas Headwaters Recreation Area (719-539-7289)
Special considerations: Local boaters and ELF (extreme low flow) enthusiasts will paddle these sections down to natural flow, sometimes below 200 cfs, year-round. In winter be sure to check for ice dams in the flatter sections either visually or by asking around before putting in.
Put-in/takeout information: Take Highway 24 north out of Buena Vista. To get to the traditional takeout, turn east on County Road 371 at the sign for Railroad Bridge. Cross the river and turn south, and follow the road that parallels the river. Here you will find several AHRA-signed pullouts before arriving at the well-marked, well-maintained boat ramp and recreation site at Railroad Bridge.

The Pine Creek put-in/scouting trail is a dirt pulloff on the east side of Highway 24 about a mile north (upstream) of the Numbers recreation site. Or use the well-marked, AHRA-managed Numbers put-in—the dirt road into this access point was recently regraded along with an upgrade to the boat ramp and put-in area, which now has camping and established pit toilets.

Pine Creek rapid offers one of the most exciting head-to-head whitewater race venues in Colorado. Credit: Kevin Hoffman

The Paddle

Pine Creek Rapid's signature "S-move" is around a nasty hydraulic at the bottom, a hole that infamously traps and retains boaters at flows in the "terrible teens," around 1,600 to 2,000 cfs. At almost a half-mile long, Pine Creek at low to average flows is the perfect training ground for those looking to step up to continuous Class V paddling. High flows (3,000 cfs and above) in this section will delight experts in playboats with towering wave trains and confused currents, with most of the retentive features getting washed out. The whitewater between Pine Creek and the Numbers put-in includes a short, steep bounce through several ledgy holes at Triple Drop rapid and a few other Class IV moves known as "The Zeros."

The Numbers starts off with about a mile of swift flatwater before dropping in to rapid Number 1 just above a private bridge. The next five miles are a creek boating paradise of boofs and slalom moves that change with the slightest increase or decrease in flow. Experts will describe this section as straightforward read-and-run Class IV, with seven named/numbered rapids between the put-in and Railroad Bridge and plenty of busy boogie water in between. Boaters on their first Class IV foray will

A brief respite on a Numbers commercial raft trip on the Arkansas.

benefit from a seasoned guide and mellow flows, though some locals claim the easiest levels are in the 2,000-plus cfs range.

The river between Pine Creek Rapid and Number 6 drops an average of 75 feet per mile. The most dramatic rapid on this stretch is Number 5, located just below the bridge where the county road crosses the river. Here, a twisting drop on a left bend piles current into a large boulder on the outside of the turn, a spot that notoriously flips commercial rafts. Best to scout this rapid from the road while running shuttle; the landowner on the left bank prohibits any access at river level.

The Fractions

Scenic Class II–III whitewater consisting of boulder moves and plenty of eddy-hopping opportunities to test one's future creek-boating mettle.

Nearest city/town: Buena Vista
Start: Railroad Bridge Recreation Site (N38 55.449' / W106 10.199')
End: Buena Vista boat ramp (N38 50.840' / W106 07.388') or the last surf wave in the South Main development
Length: 7.0 miles
Approximate paddling time: 2 to 3 hours
Difficulty rating: Intermediate
Rapids: Class II, III
River type: Continuous boulder garden, man-made features
Current: Swift
Environment: High-alpine desert
River gradient: 44 fpm
River gauge: 200 to 5,000 cfs, Arkansas River below Granite
Elevation drop: 310 feet
Hazards: Sieve at Frog Rock Rapid
Season: May through August
Land status: Colorado Parks and Wildlife, Bureau of Land Management
Boats used: Kayaks, canoes, rafts, SUPs
Fees or permits: Required at AHRA-managed parking areas and boat ramps

Maps: *RiverMaps, Guide to the Arkansas River*
Other users: Anglers, commercial rafters
Contacts: Arkansas Headwaters Recreation Area (719-539-7289)
Special considerations: The Buena Vista Whitewater Park runs the quarter mile from the Barbara Whipple bridge to South Main and provides multiple man-made surf features. Check out the "Staircase Wave" for the best SUP park-n-surf. There is a small boat ramp and parking area at the downstream end of the whitewater park.
Put-in/takeout information: From downtown Buena Vista, follow Main Street east until it dead-ends in a park next to a sports field complex. This boat ramp is the traditional takeout. To get to the put-in, go back west on Main Street and turn right on Colorado Avenue, which becomes County Road 371; take this north out of town. The paved road eventually turns to dirt, crosses the river, and closely parallels the river-left shore. Look for signs for Railroad Bridge Recreation Site; this is the put-in.

The Paddle

Putting in just below the tail end of the Numbers section, the Fractions is a busy intermediate run with considerably mellower gradient than the upstream sections. Steady vertical drop creates constant current and choppy wave trains, especially at the beginning through a section dubbed "The Miracle Mile." The Fractions will keep intermediate paddlers on their toes and delight experts out for a relaxing slalom practice in a stunning, high-alpine environment. Considered one of the deadliest hazards on the Arkansas, the sieve at Frog Rock Rapid becomes a concern at flows above 1,000 cfs. If in doubt, follow the signs to scout or portage on the left. This run ends at the Buena Vista whitewater park, with several surf waves and takeout options.

Milk Run

The Buena Vista local beginner scrape and bash, with stops at a few rafting company bars along the way.

Nearest city/town: Buena Vista
Start: One of the rafting companies in Johnson Village (N38 48.827' / W106 06.241')
End: Ruby Mountain Campground (N38 45.135' / W106 04.249') or Fisherman's Bridge
Length: 5.5 miles (shorter run possible)
Approximate paddling time: 1 to 2 hours
Difficulty rating: Beginner/intermediate
Rapids: Class II, Class III (2)
River type: Shallow, scrapy boulder gardens
Current: Swift
Environment: Mountain-town urban, rural, roadside
River gradient: 32 fpm
River gauge: 250 to 5,000 cfs, Arkansas River near Nathrop
Elevation drop: 176 feet
Hazards: A few strainers, including a junkyard of old cars on a sweeping river-left bend about halfway through the run
Season: May through August
Land status: Colorado Parks and Wildlife, Bureau of Land Management

Boats used: Kayaks, canoes, rafts, SUPs
Fees or permits: Required at AHRA-managed parking areas and boat ramps
Maps: *RiverMaps, Guide to the Arkansas River*
Other users: Anglers, commercial rafters
Contacts: Arkansas Headwaters Recreation Area (719-539-7289)
Special considerations: Proceed to one of several local hot springs after floating.
Put-in/takeout information: To get to the takeout from Buena Vista, head south on US Highway 285, and then turn east and cross the river at the well-marked Fisherman's Bridge. Park here or pass Fish Bridge and turn south at a sign for Ruby Mountain, and follow a narrow dirt road to another AHRA-maintained access point and campground for a longer run. To get to the put-in, go back north on Highway 285 and turn right (east) on Highway 24 at the stoplight in Johnson Village. Check into the office at either Wilderness Aware or American Adventure Expeditions to inquire about parking and fees to use their boat ramps. There is no other public access point here.

The Paddle

Arkansas River boaters will hotly debate the true parameters of what is considered the "Milk Run." Putting in at Johnson Village and floating to Ruby Mountain or one of several access points in between provides a true beginner stretch. This section starts off with busy Class II maneuvering around midstream boulders, until the gradient eases and a more open section of the valley provides swift currents around bends and a few braids into irrigation ditches.

For those who must know what lies between here and the Buena Vista whitewater park upstream, this 2-mile section of river starts with some fun waves and jumbled boulders along the South Main river corridor. The first Class III challenge lies just below the playpark at a rapid known as BV Falls, a slightly steep S-turn with a few

A bird's-eye view of Zoom Flume rapid, at the heart of Browns Canyon. Credit: Rob Hurst

large features known to catch beginner boaters off guard. Heading downstream a mile or so below the put-in, paddlers will encounter an old dam that must be run on the right (Class III with a long, shallow runout). There is a small eddy and established trail to scout or portage here on river right.

Browns Canyon

One of the most popular whitewater runs in the entire United States—or so the raft guides say.

Nearest city/town: Nathrop
Start: Fisherman's Bridge Launch (N38 46.040' / W106 05.693')
End: Hecla Junction Campground (N38 39.110' / W106 03.066') or Stone Bridge (N38 36.693' / W106 03.806')
Length: 13.0 miles (shorter run possible)
Approximate paddling time: 3 to 5 hours

Difficulty rating: Intermediate
Rapids: Class III (9)
River type: Pool-drop boulder garden
Current: Swift
Environment: High-alpine desert
River gradient: 31 fpm
River gauge: 300 to 5,000 cfs, Arkansas River near Nathrop

Elevation drop: 405 feet

Hazards: A few sieves/cracks midriver and along the banks

Season: April through August

Land status: National Monument, managed by Colorado Parks and Wildlife and Bureau of Land Management

Boats used: Kayaks, rafts, canoes, SUPs

Fees or permits: Required at AHRA-managed boat ramps

Maps: *RiverMaps, Guide to the Arkansas River, Colorado*

Other users: Anglers, hikers

Contacts: Arkansas Headwaters Recreation Area (719-539-7289)

Special considerations: Numerous, unpermitted campsites and its relative wilderness atmosphere make Browns Canyon ideal for an intermediate overnighter. To shorten the overall length of the run, paddlers can put in at Ruby Mountain Recreation Site, which is downstream of Fisherman's Bridge and closer to the actual entrance to the canyon. This bypasses a couple of miles of Class II water. Using this and the Hecla Junction takeout, the length of the run is closer to 8 miles. For those short on time or water flow, putting in at Hecla and taking out at Stone Bridge provides a quick 3.5-mile stretch with some of the best whitewater and scenery in Browns Canyon.

Put-in/takeout information: To reach the takeout, head south on US 285 through Nathrop. Shortly after Nathrop, look for a sign for Hecla Junction River Access on the left (east) side of the highway. Follow the dirt road away from the highway and over a hill into the canyon to the most popular takeout. To access the lower takeout, keep heading south on US 285 and turn left (east) onto Highway 291 toward Salida. Just before the highway crosses the river, turn left (north) into a dirt parking lot and access point. To reach the put-in, head north from Nathrop on US 285 and look for signs for Fisherman's Bridge on the east side of the highway. Cross the river, park in the lot on river left, and hike down the steps to launch.

The Paddle

A combination of rugged canyon scenery lined with ponderosa and piñon pines, challenging but not life-threatening pool-drop rapids, and straightforward logistics makes Browns a classic intermediate day trip. One of the only sections of the Ark that deviates from a busy road, Browns provides some of the most "wilderness"-feeling boating in the area and was designated as a National Monument in 2017. Private paddlers will have to share this classic with lines of commercial rafts in the summertime; plan early-morning or evening runs to avoid the masses.

After about 2.5 miles of Class II warm-up, the Ark slides into Canyon Doors and Pinball Rapid (Class III). The Class III action continues below with Zoom Flume, Big Drop, Seven Steps, Widowmaker, and Raft Ripper. Swirly water and strong eddylines can create a hazard for newer paddlers, while intermediate to advanced rafters and kayakers will enjoy crashing through splashy waves with numerous surf and splat spots.

The rapids are frequent, with good pools below each one where paddlers can regroup and clean up any pieces or savor some of the low-walled granite rock formations until the large cement boat ramp at Hecla Junction. For those wishing to complete the canyon, Seidel's Suckhole (Class III+) and Twin Falls (Class III) lay farther downstream. After these big boys, the Arkansas eases down and flows out of Browns

Canyon to the lower takeout at Stone Bridge. Browns is a must-paddle if you're in the area.

Salida Town Run

A family-style float into town, the best true beginner section on the Arkansas.

Nearest city/town: Salida
Start: Stone Bridge (N38 36.693' / W106 03.806')
End: Riverside Park in downtown Salida (N38 32.285' / W105 59.461')
Length: 9.6 miles (shorter run possible)
Approximate paddling time: 2 to 4 hours
Difficulty rating: Beginner
Rapids: Class II (2)
River type: Shallow, meandering
Current: Moderate
Environment: Rural, roadside
River gradient: 20 fpm
River gauge: 300 to 5,000 cfs, Arkansas River near Nathrop
Elevation drop: 230 feet
Hazards: Low-head dam about 2 miles above Salida
Season: May through September
Land status: Colorado Parks and Wildlife, Bureau of Land Management
Boats used: Kayaks, canoes, rafts, SUPs
Fees or permits: Required at AHRA-managed parking areas and boat ramps
Maps: *RiverMaps, Guide to the Arkansas River, Colorado*

Other users: Anglers, inner tubers
Contacts: Arkansas Headwaters Recreation Area (719-539-7289)
Special considerations: A lower put-in can be accessed at Big Bend Access off US 285 south; this will cut 3 miles from the paddle and one of the trickiest shallow rapids, Squaw Creek. As of the time of print, Squaw Creek was undergoing a name change through a statewide initiative to remove racist names from public places.
Put-in/takeout information: Follow Highway 291 into downtown Salida and turn north toward the river at G Street, which dead-ends in a small parking area at the main boat ramp. For an alternate parking area but more rugged takeout trail, head north on F Street until it crosses a bridge to park and access the left side of the river. To reach the put-in, turn around and follow either F or G Street south to First Street. Turn right (west) onto First Street and drive out of town, heading upriver. First Street becomes Highway 291; follow the highway for 8 miles. When Highway 291 crosses over the river, turn right (north) into the Stone Bridge river access parking lot and put-in.

The Paddle

The river channel stays open as it passes ranchland and cruises swiftly downstream from the put-in around smaller rocks and through splashy waves. One small dam marks the only real hazard on this run, and a well-marked runnable channel has been created on the left for paddlers to navigate the drop. At low flows (less than 500 cfs), rafts can hang up on the shallow drops and SUP paddlers with fins may choose the easy portage trail on river left. Local authorities have announced plans to remove the dam, but have not established a timeline for the project. Other than the dam, cruisey paddling takes you right into downtown Salida, where man-made surf features surround the boat ramp just upstream of F Street and offer multiple playboating or SUP

Olympian Scott Shipley runs gates in downtown Salida, where a small slalom scene still thrives.
Credit: Kevin Hoffman

surf options at the takeout. This run is so straightforward the local kayak school uses it and the Salida whitewater park for instruction, and smart locals do too, instead of the Milk Run upstream closer to Buena Vista.

Salida to Rincon

A Class II section punctuated by one long Class III rapid, cliff jumping, and fascinating geology.

Nearest city/town: Salida
Start: Riverside Park in downtown Salida (N38 32.285' / W105 59.461')
End: Rincon Recreation Site (N38 28.350' / W105 51.935')
Length: 9.3 miles (shorter run possible)
Approximate paddling time: 3 to 5 hours

Difficulty rating: Class II–III (advanced beginner/intermediate)
Rapids: Class II, Class III (1)
River type: Shallow, pool-drop with swift bends
Current: Moderate
Environment: Granite canyon, roadside
River gradient: 31 fpm

River gauge: 300 to 5,000 cfs, Arkansas River near Wellsville
Elevation drop: 292 feet
Hazards: Broken-down bridge downstream of Wellsville
Season: May through August
Land status: Colorado Parks and Wildlife, Bureau of Land Management
Boats used: Kayaks, rafts, canoes, SUPs
Fees or permits: Required at AHRA-managed parking areas and boat ramps
Maps: *RiverMaps, Guide to the Arkansas River, Colorado*
Other users: Commercial float fishermen, rafters, and other anglers, especially at low water levels in autumn
Contacts: Arkansas Headwaters Recreation Area (719-539-7289)

Special considerations: Rafters may want to use the well-marked Salida East access point off Highway 50 downstream of Salida town—this cuts off 2 miles but provides easier trailer parking and maneuvering at the boat ramp. Boaters of all craft can add another 9 miles of easy whitewater and a few more Class III rapids, including Badger Creek and Tin Cup, by heading farther downstream to the Vallie Bridge recreation site along Highway 50 near Howard. Both of these sections are popular with float-fishermen, especially in the fall.

Put-in/takeout information: From the put-in at the Salida boat ramp (see Salida Town Run), head south 2 blocks on G Street and turn left (east) onto First Street. Follow First Street out to the junction with US Highway 50; turn left (east) on US 50 and follow it downstream approximately 8 miles to the Rincon takeout.

The Paddle

As the Ark bends to the east, it drops through a nice rural valley just downstream of Salida. Beautiful views of the Sangre de Cristo Mountains fill the southern skyline while open grasslands and cottonwood trees line the riverbanks. Bear Creek Rapid (Class III) is located 3 miles below the put-in, signified by a giant boulder on the river-right bank that funnels the current into confused eddylines and a large pool with a beach on river left.

Bear Creek is long, with several parts, and difficult to scout due to a steep talus field between the river and the railroad tracks above. Start in the wave train just right of center, and then navigate the wide, shallow riffle on an S-curve with some powerful waveholes at the bottom. Regroup in one of several eddies on either side of the river before hitting a bigger wave train and making the crux move left to right between two prominent boulders or holes, depending on the water level. The current then piles into the river-right wall before bouncing through one final wave train with good rescue eddies below. The river-right bank here features nice lunch rocks and the last bit of public land for a break before private land flanks most of the rest of the section.

After Bear Creek, the scenery then becomes increasingly canyon-like, with a fault line near the bridge at Wellsville providing an interesting insight into the river valley's geological formation. Fun Class II wave trains and swirly canyon currents carry paddlers to the takeout. Be sure to check out the local cliff-jumping spot on river left about a mile above Rincon.

Bighorn Sheep Canyon

A craggy, granite-boulder gorge that closely parallels US Highway 50.

Start: Rincon Recreation Site (N38 28.350' / W105 51.935')
End: Pinnacle Rock Recreation Site (N38 26.855' / W105 31.382')
Length: 27.7 miles (shorter runs possible)
Approximate paddling time: Varies with section chosen
Difficulty rating: Advanced beginner/intermediate
Rapids: Class II+, Class III (5)
River type: Granite boulder garden
Current: Moderate to swift
Environment: Desert canyon, roadside
River gradient: 36 fpm
River gauge: 500 to 5,000 cfs, Arkansas River at Wellsville
Elevation drop: 1,000 feet
Hazards: Several rapids that approach Class III in difficulty
Season: May through September

Land status: Colorado Parks and Wildlife, BLM, some private
Boats used: Kayaks, canoes, rafts, SUPs
Fees or permits: Required for parking/camping at AHRA-maintained access points
Maps: *RiverMaps, Guide to the Arkansas River, Colorado*
Other users: Commercial rafters and float fishers
Contacts: Arkansas Headwaters Recreation Area (719-539-7289)
Special considerations: Many access points are well marked on US 50 heading downstream east of Salida. Consider using these, or stringing together their associated AHRA-managed campsites, to do a multi-day on the Arkansas.
Put-in/takeout information: Both the put-in and takeout are well marked on US 50 heading downstream east of Salida.

The Paddle

Most everything on this section can be scouted while running shuttle, so you will see what you're getting into before putting in. Private boaters will have to share this stretch with commercial rafters on midsummer days, and an array of float-fishing craft in the fall. Just downstream of the Rincon boat ramp is Badger Creek Rapid (Class III), formed by debris flushed out of its namesake drainage on river left, which often flash floods during summer thunderstorms.

The river then mellows out between the Lower Ark hamlets of Howard and Swissvale, before veering away from the road and into a mini gorge known as Tin Cup Rapid (Class III). Run this flume starting just left of center, angle to hit the top V-waves, and ride out the exciting wave train into the pool below. Scout from the river right by pulling into a small eddy just above the horizon line—and watch for rattlesnakes.

After the Vallie Bridge access point (signified by a concrete bridge over the river), Cottonwood and Little Cottonwood rapids (Class III) pepper the next section with wave trains, and, at low water, a few slots between boulders just above the town of Cotopaxi. The action picks back up below Texas Creek with Maytag and Devil's Hole (Class III). The takeout at Parkdale is the last access point before the Parkdale section (Class III) and Royal Gorge (Class IV) below.

Parkdale

A splashy roadside intermediate run that is easily added as a Class III warm-up to the Royal Gorge downstream.

Nearest city/town: Canon City
Start: Pinnacle Rock Recreation Site (N38 26.855' / W105 31.382')
End: Parkdale Recreation Site (N38 29.192' / W105 23.408')
Length: 9.0 miles
Approximate paddling time: 2 to 4 hours
Difficulty rating: Intermediate
Rapids: Class III (4)
River type: Pool-drop granite boulder garden
Current: Swift
Environment: Desert canyon, roadside
River gradient: 33 fpm
River gauge: 350 to 3,500 cfs (Arkansas River near Parkdale)
Elevation drop: 285 feet
Hazards: Large boulders form powerful holes in Three Rocks Rapid at high water (>2,000 cfs)

Season: April through August, year-round possible
Land status: Colorado Parks and Wildlife, Bureau of Land Management
Fees or permits: Required at AHRA-managed parking areas and boat ramps
Maps: *RiverMaps, Guide to the Arkansas River, Colorado*
Other users: Commercial rafters
Contacts: Arkansas Headwaters Recreation Area (719-539-7289)
Special considerations: The roadside nature and less technical whitewater lend this section a slightly less demanding Class III feel than Browns Canyon 60 miles upstream.
Put-in/takeout information: Both the put-in and takeout are well marked on US 50 heading downstream east of Salida.

The Paddle

This section retains the canyon character of the sections upstream, but with steeper, more condensed whitewater. Once again, U.S. 50 offers easy scouting opportunities while shuttling. The big ones on this section are Three Rocks (Class III), Five Points (Class III), Spikebuck (Class III+), and Sharks Tooth (Class III). You don't want to miss the giant commercial boat ramp at the takeout—just downstream lies the grand entrance into the advanced/expert Royal Gorge (Class IV) below.

The Royal Gorge

High-quality whitewater set in the warmer climate and slightly juicier flows of the downstream end of the Arkansas Valley—the area's most viable year-round paddling option.

Nearest city/town: Canon City
Start: Parkdale Recreation Site (N38 29.192' / W105 23.408')
End: Centennial Park in Canon City (N38 26.170' / W105 14.603')
Length: 10.0 miles

Approximate paddling time: 3 to 5 hours
Difficulty rating: Advanced
Rapids: Class IV (4), Class III (numerous)
River type: Pool-drop, railroad blast rock
Current: Swift
Environment: Walled-in gorge

Rafters maneuver around the many obstacles of Sunshine Rapid in the Royal Gorge.
Credit: Kevin Hoffman

River gradient: 46 fpm
River gauge: 300 to 3,500 cfs, Arkansas River near Parkdale
Elevation drop: 400 feet
Hazards: Rebar, other man-made debris
Season: April through September, year-round depending on ice
Land status: Colorado Parks and Wildlife, Bureau of Land Management
Boats used: Kayaks, rafts, canoes
Fees or permits: Required at AHRA-managed parking areas and boat ramps
Maps: *RiverMaps, Guide to the Arkansas River, Colorado*
Other users: Scenic train riders

Contacts: Arkansas River Headwaters Recreation Area (719-539-7289)
Special considerations: Continue downstream to surf the remaining features in the small whitewater park in Canon City.
Put-in/takeout information: To reach the takeout, follow US Highway 50 east to Canon City and turn right (south) on Fourth Street. Cross a bridge to river right, turn right on Griffin Street, then immediately right into Centennial Park, where there is a boat ramp and newly renovated trail along the man-made whitewater park. Access the well-marked Parkdale recreation site west of Canon City near mile marker 267 on Highway 50.

The Paddle

Vertical walls and limited access lend the Royal Gorge a remote feel, until paddlers encounter the throngs of tourists ogling from the open cars of a scenic train ride and peering down from a sightseeing bridge 950 feet above the river. Add strings of commercial rafts in the summer months, with their associated photography business, and the place becomes a veritable amusement park. Sunlight in the Gorge is limited to a few hours a day, so plan accordingly, especially in the darker months. The rapids on this stretch, considered a stepping stone to the busier Class IV Numbers section 80 miles upstream, are pool-drop with most of the gradient concentrated in the 5 miles between Sunshine Rapid, Sledgehammer, the Narrows, and Wall Slammer (Class IV).

Most first-timers will scout Sunshine, a series of drops and slots with a hole at the bottom right at which it helps to have planned ahead. The scout/portage is along a rusted-out pipe running along river right marked by a broken-down building. The rest of the river is littered with man-made debris from the railroad, abandoned bridge projects, and a now-defunct water-pumping system.

The next series of horizon lines encompass Sledgehammer, featuring several steep ledges at low water and powerful hydraulics at flows above 1,500 cfs. A large cement structure that shunts a side creek over the railroad tracks signifies the start of the Narrows, where boaters must dodge a few holes hidden among otherwise clean, rollicking wave trains. Maneuver around small boulders while hugging the inside of the left bend at Wall Slammer to avoid the rapid's eponymous consequences. After Corner Pocket (Class III), the gradient eases and the Gorge spills out into a valley above Canon City. Just upstream of town and its man-made whitewater park, boaters must navigate several ledgy irrigation diversions including one dam with a boat chute river left, which provides some surfy play of its own.

The Fryingpan River valley above Basalt. Water from this river's headwaters gets diverted to the east side of the Continental Divide.

COLORADO, THE WILD WEST OF WATER RIGHTS

The late 1950s and early 1960s saw a heyday of dam building, highway construction, and other engineering feats across the country. It was the era in which the Bureau of Reclamation "beavers" (as Edward Abbey so fondly refers to them in his acclaimed conservation-minded tome *Desert Solitaire*) were busy impeding the Colorado River behind Glen Canyon dam to form Lake Powell (1964) and stuffing the San Juan River into the backwaters of Navajo Dam (1962).

Prior to this postwar building frenzy, fueled by the optimism of real estate developers on Colorado's Front Range and "rain follows the plow" farmers on the arid plains, federal engineers saw the 14,000-foot Sawatch Range as a small bump on their road to watering the burgeoning communities and ranches on the east side of the Continental Divide. The beavers had already set their sights high in the Rocky Mountains above a little town called Aspen, and squarely on the Roaring Fork River and its most significant tributary, the Fryingpan.

Transmontane diversion projects were once a source of bitter dispute in Colorado. Residents on the western slope resented the Front Range's insatiable appetite for their water, which the eastern city dwellers claimed just flowed "unused" down the Colorado River. West–east diversion efforts became a target of government and private enterprise. Denver and Colorado Springs undertook the Blue River project; Denver also built Dillon Reservoir, the Moffat Tunnel, the Vasquez Tunnel, and others for the purpose of conveying water from western Colorado to the state's capital. Private companies financed the Otero Canal, Clear Creek Reservoir, and the Busk-Ivanhoe Tunnel.

The "appropriation" of Colorado's water, and its associated industry, is predicated on rights set forth in many western state constitutions. In the landmark water law case *Coffin vs. Left Hand Ditch Co.* (1882), the Colorado Supreme Court ruling upheld these statutes, stating that when it comes to running water, use it or lose it. At least, the first person to put flowing water to use for a "beneficial purpose" will never lose it. First come, first served. Finders, keepers; losers, weepers.

This was in contrast to the "riparian rights" of the Old World—farmers from England, old and new, with naturally moist lands, gave little thought to water rights. The people living along the shores of a waterway had a right to use the water as needed, as long as they returned enough flow through groundwater discharge to sustain their neighbors downstream.

Arid Colorado, on the other hand, sought out a more "equitable" solution. The state's constitution provided such a solution by drowning out riparian law with public ownership. With this law in place, farmers need not own land adjacent to a creek or river to use the water; everyone had an equal chance to claim the unused resource.

Furthermore, the constitution allowed users the right to remove the water from its source and transport it across "public, private, or corporate lands" in "ditches, canals and flumes" (Constitution of the State of Colorado 1876, section 7), and stated that "the right to divert the unappropriated waters of any natural stream to beneficial uses shall never be denied."

The statutes seemed to stem from the frontier-minded prospectors/settlers, who regarded "first in time, first in right" as the binding code of Colorado's early gold mines. Prior to that, Arkansas River users followed the acequias tradition of Spanish settlers, in which all water belonged to the community.

It seems fitting that water literally became Colorado's new gold and acquired "a value unknown in moister climates" (Coffin et al. 1882, 446). Acknowledging the value of water in the desert, the court praised and predicted the entrepreneurial and engineering spirit of the American West. Many of the interior western states followed suit, with Arizona, Idaho, Utah, and Wyoming adopting the "Colorado doctrine" of water rights.

The Fryingpan-Arkansas Project put it all into play. In the 1930s, the Bureau of Reclamation began investigating a way to supplement the Arkansas River's flow with Western Slope water. At the same time, it began work on the multi-purpose Colorado-Big Thompson Project (CBT), designed to generate hydropower and deliver water for irrigation, municipal, and industrial use. The largest transmontane project in Colorado, CBT pumps snowmelt from the headwaters of the Colorado River, stored in Grand Lake, through a 13-mile tunnel to the million people and 615,000 acres of irrigated farmland surrounding Boulder and Fort Collins in the northeastern part of the state. The project was a major artery to the economy and growth of the Front Range.

With its arable farmland and topography more suited to support a large population than its neighboring, water-rich west slope, the east slope thirsted on. While the Front Range (and the area along the Arkansas River) had flourished, the mountainous mining towns west of the Continental Divide had endured a cyclical, boom-and-bust economic history.

So why not build a series of dams, tunnels, and 8-foot-diameter conduit that sucks spring runoff from the headwaters of the Roaring Fork and Fryingpan Rivers and spits it out on the east side of the Continental Divide onto semi-arid fields, municipalities, and industries of the Arkansas River valley? Consisting of 6 storage dams; 17 diversion dams and structures; hundreds of miles of combined canals, conduits, tunnels, and transmission lines; and two power plants, switchyards, and substations, the Fry-Ark project took almost 50 years from idea to completion.

Embattled politically at the local and federal level, the project went through several revisions and was eventually approved by Congress in 1962. Contractors used a state-of-the-art, German-engineered boring machine to pierce through the granite undercarriage of the Continental Divide. Thirty feet long, 10 feet in diameter, and hydraulically powered by three 200-horsepower motors, the machine drilled through rock with a compressive strength of up to 33,500 psi. The hardness of the rock presented few problems for the boring machine, but soft sections at faulted zones, blocky ground, and areas of decomposed rock caused delays in operation.

Across the Divide about 15 miles southwest of Leadville on the upper reaches of the Arkansas River was the chosen site for Sugar Loaf Dam and Turquoise Lake. It was at this point that the water from the Boustead Tunnel emptied into the first of several storage facilities on the Eastern Slope.

From the Twin Lakes just to the south, the diverted water makes its way downstream into the agricultural regions of the Arkansas River Valley, where it comes to rest in the terminal storage reservoir located 6 miles west of Pueblo.

At Pueblo Reservoir, crews delayed placing concrete until April 1973 due to severe weather conditions, but by year's end the dam had risen to a point that filling the 30,000 acre-feet of permanent pool in Pueblo Reservoir could begin. In early 1974, the Fry-Ark project released water from Twin Lakes and Turquoise Lake for this purpose.

By the 1980s, intrepid rafters and kayakers, as well as fishermen, had discovered the white-water riches of the Arkansas. The 100 miles of runnable river, also hailed as a Gold Medal trout stream, have become a mecca of outdoor tourism and its related cash flow.

Subsequently, some river enthusiasts found an arguably more valuable business opportunity than farming in Colorado: tourism. The list of Arkansas River stakeholders now included whitewater rafting and fly-fishing outfitters, and the small towns that thrive on these industries' flock of summer tourists. By the late 1990s, these parties found a way to ensure they kept getting their piece of Colorado's water, the Voluntary Flow Management Program (VFMP).

The agreement argues that, other than evaporative losses, the VFMP is considered a non-consumptive use of water. It simply states that when those with "senior water rights"—the ranchers of the eastern plains and Front Range cities—"call" for their water, it will be released from Twin Lakes Reservoir and flow southeast to Pueblo Reservoir during the summer rafting season. The target flow is 700 cfs at the Wellsville Gauge east of Salida, from July 1 to August

15 each year. Year-round, the VFMP helps manage flows to support the trout-fishing industry. Water flows down the Arkansas, and cash flows from rafters' pockets into local hotels, shops, and restaurants.

Legendary Civil War general and river runner John Wesley Powell, a geologist by trade but perhaps best known for his daring explorations of the Colorado and Green Rivers via handmade boats, published his findings on these waterways in 1875. He then cautioned that the federal government should consider watersheds, instead of neat square shapes, when drawing state lines. This warning was a precursor to the "water wars" that would, and still, ensue as the nation continues to settle and develop based on American idealism instead of topography and environmental conditions. Think about that the next time your paddle plies the waters of the Arkansas or a raft guide shouts, "All forward!"

8 Rio Grande

Perhaps one of the most famous rivers in the West, the river that eventually forms the border between Texas and Mexico starts high up in the southwest corner of Colorado. At 1,887 miles, the second-longest river in the United States, it drains the north side of the San Juan Mountains and makes a wide southeastern arc as it eventually tumbles out of the mountains. It then cuts through the plateaus of New Mexico before snaking its way into the Gulf of Mexico.

Up here in Colorado, the Rio Grande offers good beginner/intermediate sections for canoes, kayaks, rafts, and SUPs. The top section is a short, remote canyon lined with jagged rocks and burned forest. Then it eases downstream through a broad valley, and the river passes willow and cottonwood trees amid Yellowstone-esque ranch lands. As the Rio Grande drops into the broad San Luis Valley, the gradient drops to next to nothing and the flow begins to get sucked through irrigation diversions for bean farming.

Stay west of the valley to find the boating goods—and to say you paddled the headwaters of the Rio Grande. A plethora of riverside camping and other outdoor attractions in this area make for a fun weekend getaway.

Headwaters Box Canyon

One of the highest paddled sections of the Rio Grande, a stunning canyon at the bottom of the burn-scarred Weminuche Wilderness.

Nearest city/town: Creede
Start: River Hill Campground (N37 43.755' / W 107 13.841')
End: Fern Creek Bridge (N37 46.471' / W 107 08.400')
Length: 8.1 miles
Approximate paddling time: 2 to 4 hours
Difficulty rating: Intermediate/advanced
Rapids: Class III
River type: Continuous Class III that can be pushy at high water (>1,100 cfs)
Current: Swift
Environment: Once forested, burn scar canyon
River gradient: 50 fpm
River gauge: 350 to 2,250 cfs, Rio Grande at Thirty Mile Bridge near Creede
Elevation drop: 40.5 feet
Hazards: A low bridge at the takeout can be very hazardous to different crafts. If it looks too low to pass under, take out above the bridge.

Specific flows for passing under the bridge haven't been determined.
Season: May to early June. The Forest Service campground at the put-in does not open until Memorial Day each year.
Land status: US Forest Service
Boats used: Kayaks, canoes, rafts
Fees or permits: Day use and camping fees at the USFS put-in
Maps: USFS Creede quadrangle
Other users: Anglers
Contacts: US Forest Service Rio Grande National Forest (719-852-5941)
Special considerations: This run is doable starting in late April if temps are warm enough to trigger an early snowmelt (see "Epic Class II Adventures," pages xv-xvi) or if downstream farmers have called for releases from the Rio Grande Reservoir just above it. Park outside River Hill campground being careful not to

Rio Grande

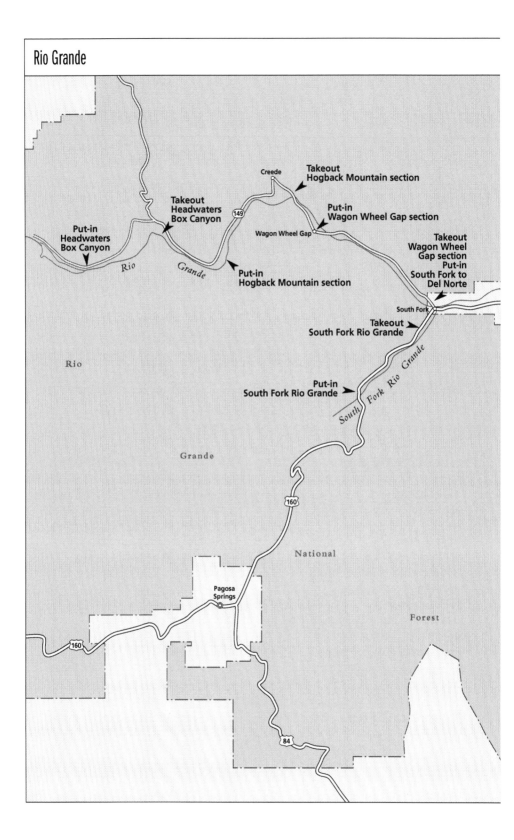

Creede

Takeout
Hogback Mountain section

Takeout
Headwaters
Box Canyon

Put-in
Wagon Wheel Gap section

Put-in
Headwaters
Box Canyon

149

Wagon Wheel Gap

Takeout
Wagon Wheel
Gap section
Put-in
South Fork to
Del Norte

Rio   Grande

Put-in
Hogback Mountain section

South Fork

Rio

Takeout
South Fork Rio Grande

South Fork Rio Grande

Put-in
South Fork Rio Grande

Grande

160

National

Pagosa
Springs

Forest

160

84

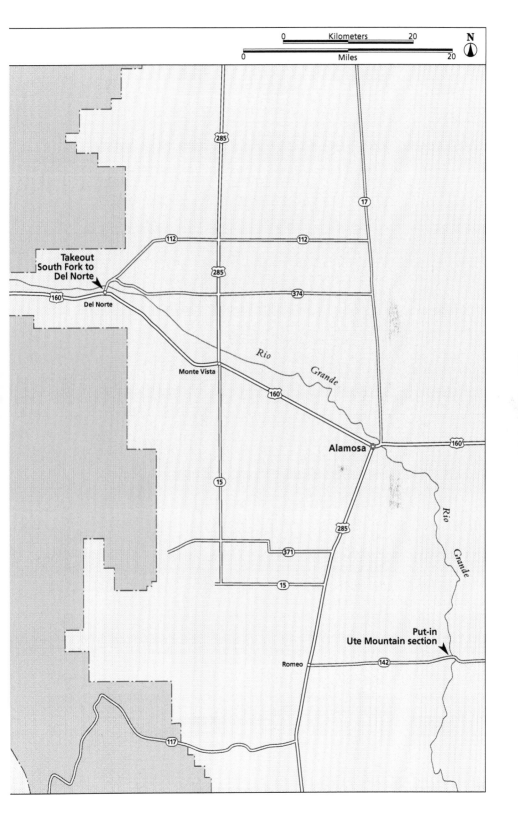

N

Takeout
South Fork to
Del Norte

Del Norte

Monte Vista

Rio Grande

Alamosa

Romeo

Put-in
Ute Mountain section

Rio Grande

A springtime paddle into the Rio Grande's Headwater Box Canyon. Credit: Scott Link

block the entrance, or better yet, get dropped off and walk around the gate to the river. There is also a seldom-run Class IV–V section of the Rio Grande above the reservoir.

Put-in/takeout Information: Head west out of the town of Creede on Highway 149 for approximately 31 miles. Turn left (south) onto Forest Service Road 520 just after mile marker 41. Follow this for 1.7 miles, then turn left again on County Road 38, passing under a sign for the new Crooked Creek housing development. The next mile of dirt road gets increasingly narrow, rutted, and looking like it could wash out or become muddy with rain. Continue to a bridge crossing the river; this is the takeout. To get to the put-in, return to FSR 520 and turn left (west). Climb uphill, passing Road Canyon Reservoir. Look for signs for River Hill Campground; this is the put-in.

The Paddle

Just 2 miles below the Rio Grande Reservoir, the river cuts into a jagged, vertical-walled canyon with some quality technical whitewater. This committing little gorge is almost 1,000 feet deep between hillsides once lush with spruce and fir forest. A series of fires in 2013 burned 179 square miles from here almost to South Fork, and charred tree trunks dangle precariously above the riverbanks for the length of this run, just waiting to fall and obstruct the current below. By midsummer, some area guide services float fish here so new wood is removed regularly, but heads-up during the early season.

Take care navigating the rocky rapids down in here—you are a long way away from a road. Below the put-in, the river braids out in a few places that can be scrapy at low flow. There is one steep drop in the bedrock before the river constricts and creates a few Class III horizon lines. Once through the canyon, paddlers drop out onto a broad open valley for the last 3.0 miles down to the takeout.

Due to the irregular releases of the dam just upstream, finding this section with enough flow can be the biggest challenge of the whole run.

Hogback Mountain

A nice fir-lined canyon with some fun technical Class II whitewater that can swell to easy Class III in highest flows.

Nearest city/town: Creede
Start: Pullout off FSR 523 (N37 47.578' / W106 58.878')
End: Creede State Wildlife Area (N37 49.014' / W106 54.891')
Length: 15.0 miles, shorter and longer runs possible
Approximate paddling time: 4 to 6 hours
Difficulty rating: Advanced beginner/ intermediate
Rapids: Class II–III
River type: Medium-volume mountain stream
Current: Swift
Environment: Small canyon, rural valley
River gradient: 24 fpm
River gauge: 350 to 2,000 cfs, Rio Grande at Thirty Mile Bridge near Creede
Elevation drop: 360 feet
Hazards: Multiple bridges for private ranches and fishing clubs
Season: April through July
Land status: US Forest Service, Colorado Parks and Wildlife, private
Boats used: Kayaks, canoes, rafts, SUPs
Fees or permits: Check for current information at Creede SWA
Maps: USFS Creede quadrangle
Other users: Anglers, drift boats

Contacts: USFS Divide Ranger District–Creede Office (719-658-2556)
Special considerations: Beginner whitewater paddlers, canoeists, and SUPers may enjoy the Class I section above this known as Antelope Park, a pleasant meandering float through a lush valley lined with volcanic cliffs and rock formations. There is little of interest in terms of whitewater here, and private ranches line much of the riverbanks through this section.
Put-in/takeout information: To reach the takeout from Creede, head west on Highway 149. Turn left (south) on Airport Road/County Road 806 just outside town. Follow this to the Creede State Wildlife Area parking and boat ramp on the upstream side of a bridge crossing the river. To get to the put-in, return to Highway 149 and follow it west. Turn left (south) on Middle Creek Road/FSR 523 just before crossing the river near highway mile marker 27. The boat ramp is on the south side of the river (river right) located between the Highway 149 bridge and the bridge going to the campground. You are unable to park in the boat ramp so make sure to turn around and park at the top of the hill near pavement.

The Paddle

This section of the Rio Grande cuts into a shallow canyon as it drops out of the broad open valley upstream. There is a slightly remote feeling in here, despite the numerous vacation homes popping up all around the drainage. The upper portion of this run features rolling wave trains and pleasant scenery away from the road. Downstream, the river mostly parallels Highway 149, and the run becomes less secluded. If you want to opt out of this section, intermediate access points can be used to shorten your paddle. Several bridges create most of the hazards on this run, particularly for rafts with frames and oars.

Wagon Wheel Gap Section

A scenic float with historical significance.

Nearest city/town: South Fork
Start: Wagon Wheel Gap (N37 46.528' / W106 49.968')
End: Highway 149 Bridge, South Fork (N37 40.554' / W106 39.262')
Length: 11.4 miles
Approximate paddling time: 3 to 4 hours
Difficulty rating: Easy
Rapids: Class II
River type: Broad river valley
Current: Moderate
Environment: High-alpine desert
River gradient: 21 fpm
River gauge: 200 to 2,800 cfs, Rio Grande at Wagon Wheel Gap
Elevation drop: 239.4 feet
Hazards: Several railroad trestles and private bridges
Season: Anytime
Land status: US Forest Service, Colorado Parks and Wildlife, and private
Boats used: Rafts, kayaks, canoes, SUPs, driftboats

Fees or permits: None
Maps: *National Geographic: South San Juan, Del Norte*
Other users: Commercial rafters and anglers
Contacts: Colorado Parks and Wildlife, Monte Vista Office (719-587-6900)
Special considerations: The 5-mile section of the Rio Grande above this is another wide-open pastoral paddle like the Antelope Park section farther upstream. The river settles down through this broad, flat valley with swift current but no whitewater of any kind. Multiple access points from here to South Fork provide options for shorter or longer floats.
Put-in/takeout information: Highway 149 parallels the length of this section. On the way upstream out of South Fork, drop a vehicle at the dirt parking area river right above the bridge just outside town; this is the takeout. The put-in is on river left, at a pullout just downstream of a bridge. Park up near the highway and carry your boat the short distance to the small boat ramp.

The Paddle

This nice little section of paddling begins in a steep V-shaped valley that is almost 2,000 feet deep. According to the interpretive site near the put-in, native peoples in this area would lie in wait here for passing wagon trains. They would then hang the wagon wheels from the cliff walls to warn oncoming white settlers. The tighter valley walls squeeze the river, and the current picks up speed and offers fine Class

II whitewater in the top half of this run. A railroad trestle shortly below the put-in presents the section's biggest hazard—the pylons are narrowly spaced, at an off angle to the current flowing around a sharp bend. This area collects debris at higher water.

As the valley opens, the current settles down a bit and eases toward South Fork. Highway 149 closely parallels the length of this section, so paddlers can scout while doing the shuttle.

South Fork to Del Norte

A long section of worthy beginner paddling—plus a playwave and brewery!

Nearest city/town: South Fork or Del Norte
Start: South Fork (N37 40.554' / W106 39.262')
End: Del Norte (N37 41.111' / W106 21.086')
Length: 18.0 miles (shorter runs possible)
Approximate paddling time: 4 to 6 hours
Difficulty rating: Beginner
Rapids: Class I-II–
River type: Prime trout habitat
Current: Moderate
Environment: High-mountain ranching valley
River gradient: 17 fpm
River gauge: 350 to 3,000 cfs, Rio Grande near Del Norte
Elevation drop: 335 feet
Hazards: Diversion dam that presents a hazard at all flows (N37 41.245' / W106 22.059'), bridge at Hanna Lane/County Road 17 that presents a hazard at flows above 4,000 cfs (N37 41.330' / W106 27.600'), Flying W Bridge that presents a hazard at flows above 2,500 cfs (N37 41.031' / W106 22.803')
Season: April through September
Land status: Mostly private

Boats used: Rafts, canoes, kayaks, drift boats
Fees or permits: None
Maps: *National Geographic: South San Juan, Del Norte*
Other users: Even more float-fishing trips per river mile than in the upstream sections
Contacts: southwestpaddler.com
Special considerations: An alternate launch site at the Hanna Lane (CR 17) Bridge, about 16 miles downstream of South Fork, can shorten this run. Find it on the south side of the river (river right) just after the concrete bridge.
Put-in/takeout information: From the junction of Highway 149 and US 160, head east on US 160 to Del Norte. In the middle of town, turn left (north) at the traffic light onto Highway 112. Just after crossing some railroad tracks, look for a park off to the left (west). Pull in here and park next to the river and its newly constructed playwave; this is the takeout. To get back to the put-in, take Highway 160 west to South Fork. Head west on Highway 149 to the first bridge over the river; this is the put-in.

The Paddle

As the Rio Grande drops out of the upstream mountains into the flat valley below, this section offers nice current and riffles with small waves. The Class I-II rapids scattered throughout the run are suitable for fishing dories, of which there are many. This section is also noted by the Colorado Division of Wildlife for its gold-medal trout (mostly browns) fishing. But, with a robust fishing industry often come dependable recreational flows—you know, for the fish habitat. Catch a surf on the newly engineered wave at the takeout, then tell your fish stories at the Three Barrel Brewery in Del Norte after this float!

Ute Mountain Section

An awesome canoe or beginner overnighter on the Colorado–New Mexico border.

Nearest city/town: Fort Garland
Start: Lobatos Bridge (N37 04.703' / W105 45.381')
End: Lee Trail, New Mexico (N36 48.765' / W105 41.765')
Length: 24.0 miles
Difficulty rating: Beginner
Rapids: Class I-II–
River type: Moving water
Current: Moderate
Environment: High desert
River gradient: 2.6 fpm
River gauge: 300 to 3,250 cfs, Rio Grande near Lobatos
Elevation drop: 164 feet
Hazards: Erratic winds, fences
Season: Potential year-round. Boating is not permitted from Lobatos Bridge to Lee Trail (New Mexico) from April 1st to May 31st to protect sensitive wildlife breeding areas, including nesting raptors.
Land status: Costilla County, Colorado; Taos County, New Mexico
Boats used: Kayaks, canoes, rafts, SUPs
Fees or permits: Free, permit required
Maps: *The Rio Grande, A River Guide to the Geology and Landscapes of Northern New Mexico*

Other users: Few
Contacts: southwestpaddler.com
Special considerations: Though this section provides relative solitude and ample wildlife, interesting geology, and side canyon hikes, campsites are small and may require a hike to the canyon rim. This, paired with the steep takeout trail, make it unsuitable for large craft.
Put-in/takeout information: To reach the takeout, take Highway 159 south into New Mexico. Colorado Highway 159 becomes New Mexico Highway 522. Ten miles south of the border, turn right (west) onto Sunshine Valley Road. Follow this dirt road underneath power lines for 6 miles toward the canyon rim. Next to the canyon rim, turn left (south) and go 4 miles to the trailhead for Lee Trail. Lee Trail requires a grueling 500-yard-long, 200+-foot climb, and paddlers must carry all their gear and boats up the trail to the actual takeout. To reach the put-in, head back north on Highway 159 through the town of San Luis. Look for H Road 11.2 miles north of the Colorado border. Turn left (west) on H Road toward the town of Mesita. Pass through town and turn left (south) onto 7 Road. Shortly turn right (west) onto G Road and follow it to the bridge that crosses the river; this is the put-in.

The Paddle

Just before the Rio Grande crosses from Colorado into New Mexico, the river begins cutting its way down into the northern edge of the Taos Plateau and offers a fine beginning-level overnight trip. At the southern edge of the San Luis Valley, the Rio Grande picks up some once-diverted flow from irrigation in the form of numerous side streams. There is adequate water for paddling, as well as a high-desert canyon worth exploring.

Below the put-in, a beautiful basalt rock gorge rises up 200+ feet as the river drops down beneath the walls. This section is considered the northern part of the Taos Gorge Wild and Scenic River. Abundant birdlife can be spotted throughout the run—the canyon is home to eagles, falcons, owls, mergansers, and Canada geese.

Numerous fun Class II rapids are scattered throughout this run, but they tend to increase as paddlers make their way downstream.

Two days is ample time to float through this section; most campsites can be found on narrow beaches among the piñons and juniper. This out-of-the-way segment is seldom run, so paddlers will most likely have this section of river all to themselves. Just downstream from this run lies the expert-only Upper Taos Box Run (Class V), followed by the popular in early spring Lower Taos Box Run (Class III–IV).

South Fork Rio Grande

A tight, technical little tributary to the Rio Grande offering an easy creek run when the water levels are right.

Nearest city/town: South Fork
Start: Park Creek Campground (N37 35.542' / W106 43.719')
End: Beaver Creek Road Bridge (N37 39.151' / W106 39.251')
Length: 9.0 miles
Approximate paddling time: 2 to 3 hours
Difficulty rating: Intermediate
Rapids: Class II–III–
River type: Shallow creek
Current: Swift
Environment: Forested mountain pass
River gradient: 27 fpm
River gauge: 250 to 400 cfs, South Fork Rio Grande at South Fork
Elevation drop: 246.5 feet
Hazards: Shallow obstacles and low bridges
Season: May through June
Land status: US Forest Service, private

Boats used: Whitewater kayaks, canoes
Fees or permits: None
Maps: *Avenza Maps: Wolf Creek Pass, Colorado*
Other users: Anglers
Contacts: US Forest Service, Rio Grande National Forest (719-657-3321)
Special considerations: Catch it if you can!
Put-in/takeout information: Use US 160, which parallels the majority of this section, for both the put-in and the takeout access points. Heading west out of South Fork, you'll see a sign for Beaver Creek Road off to the left (east) next to a bridge crossing the river; this is the takeout. To reach the put-in, continue heading west on US 160 for 9 miles, looking for a Forest Service sign for Park Creek Campground. Turn left (east) into the campground; this is the put-in.

The Paddle

This whole run can be scouted while driving down US Highway 160 from Wolf Creek Pass heading east. Heavily forested hillsides cloak a nice section of paddling that also offers busy, technical, and shallow whitewater. Because of its small riverbed, this one has a short flow window.

9 Conejos River

The Conejos River (*conejos* means "rabbit" in Spanish) flows in a relatively isolated part of the state on the east side of the South San Juan Mountains below the Continental Divide. Largely draining the mountains to the south of Wolf Creek Pass, the Conejos does not lack for ample flows come snowmelt time of year. After that, it may run as late as August due to releases from Platoro Reservoir or if the drainage receives significant rainfall. If the Upper Rio Chama and Rio Brazos are flowing, then the Conejos will likely be runnable.

The river begins with the outflow of Platoro Reservoir near its headwaters; this dam is largely used for flood control and irrigation. Below here the river courses steeply and tightly through some expert whitewater before easing down into a short intermediate canyon, finally settling down into milder sections as it eases out of the mountains and into the flat San Luis Valley before joining the Rio Grande.

The Conejos River corridor is an isolated area of the state surrounded by national forest. Paddlers will find heavily forested hillsides and little traffic when paddling and camping in the area. This area is indeed worthy of wild and scenic status. This little-disturbed pocket of the state is home to pristine forests and abundant wildlife, including bald eagles, peregrine falcons, and bighorn sheep.

Pinnacle Gorge

A brief isolated section of technical river running through a deep grotto of fluted volcanic ash spires.

Nearest city/town: Antonito
Start: Bridge on Lake Fork Road (N37 18.494' / W106 28.708'), or Saddle Creek
End: Bridge above South Fork Confluence (N37 14.080' / W106 28.275')
Length: 5.0 miles
Approximate paddling time: 2 to 3 hours
Difficulty rating: Intermediate
Rapids: Class II–III (Class IV)
River type: Low volume
Current: Swift
Environment: Desert canyon
River gradient: 75 fpm
River gauge: 250 to 600 cfs, Conejos below Platoro
Elevation drop: 480 feet
Hazards: Steep, rocky drops with occasional wood

Season: April through June, later flows possible due to irrigation releases from Platoro Reservoir
Land status: US Forest Service
Boats used: Kayaks, canoes, rafts
Fees or permits: None
Maps: *Rio Grande National Forest*
Other users: Few
Contacts: USFS Rio Grande National Forest (719-657-3321)
Special considerations: Find miles of Class II family-floatable boating, fishing, and camping below the takeout. Watch for barbed wire and private property here.
Put-in/takeout information: On the east edge of the San Juan Wilderness just north of the New Mexico state line, dirt CR 250 parallels the course of the river. Parking for the takeout is at the footbridge just above the confluence

Conejos River

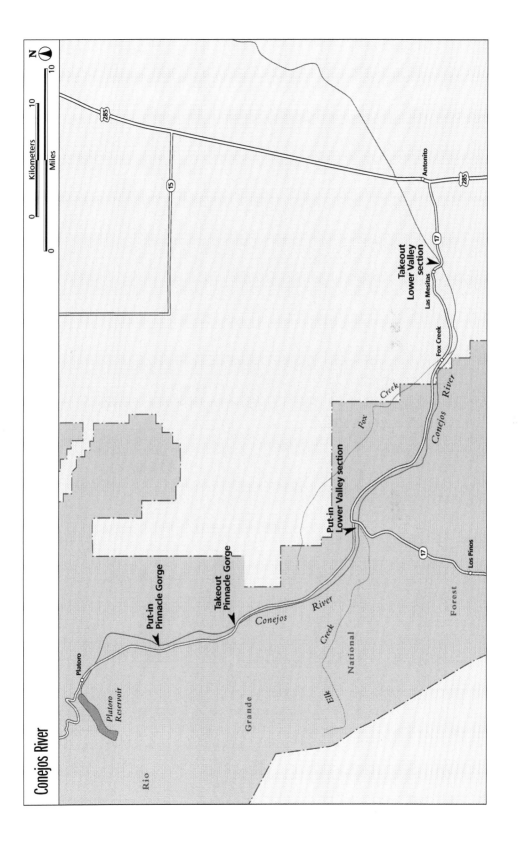

with the South Fork Conejos, at a well-marked trailhead about 200 yards above the river. The put-in is upstream of the Pinnacles at the Trail Creek crossing. For a longer run put in near Saddle Creek on FR105.

The Paddle

This short and obscure canyon is located where the road climbs up and away from the river. The crux of the run is found at the base of the largest spires—this is Pinnacle Rapid (Class III). At higher flows, it can approach Class IV in difficulty. Two miles below the rapid, the canyon walls settle back, and the river eases out of the gorge. The takeout is located at the mouth of the canyon.

Lower Valley Section

Another whitewaterish section of the Conejos worth doing.

Nearest city/town: Antonito
Start: Highway 17 Bridge (N37 07.671' / W106 21.436')
End: Mogote Campground (N37 03.796' / W106 14.134')
Length: 7.0 miles
Approximate paddling time: 2 to 4 hours
Difficulty rating: Beginner/intermediate
Rapids: Class I–II
River type: Medium volume
Current: Swift
Environment: Desert canyon
River gradient: 20 fpm
River gauge: 300 to 2,700 cfs, Conejos near Mogote
Elevation drop: 282 feet
Hazards: Few

Season: April through July
Land status: US Forest Service
Boats used: Kayaks, canoes, rafts
Fees or permits: None
Maps: *Rio Grande National Forest*
Other users: A few more
Contacts: USFS Rio Grande National Forest (719-657-3321)
Special considerations: Aspen Glade Campground can be used as an intermediate access point. The river at this campground is also the site of S-Turn Rapid, the largest scoutable rapids on this section.
Put-in/takeout information: Use Highway 17, which parallels the length of this section, for both the put-in and takeout. All access points are well marked.

The Paddle

Gaining a good bit of flow from the entrance of Elk Creek just upstream of the put-in, this lower section of the Conejos holds more water longer into the summer. Here, paddlers will find a mellow float through ranchland, paralleled by Highway 17 for the length of the run. Good water and current push paddlers downstream with little effort.

The crux of this run is S-Turn Rapid, just upstream of Aspen Glade Campground. Paddlers may wish to scout this rapid while running shuttle. Except for this larger rapid, the rest of the run is straightforward, offering one last section of pleasant paddling on the Conejos before it flattens out into the valley below.

Western Slope Paddles (North-South)

A scenic float through Ruby/Horsethief canyons. Credit: Rob Hurst

10 Yampa River

The Yampa River is the longest free-flowing tributary in the Colorado River Basin. The Yampa flows out of the east side of the Flat Tops and the northern flank of the Gore Range before eventually joining the Green River along the Colorado-Utah border. Dropping out of the mountains in this northern part of the state, the Yampa flows strong with snowmelt in late spring/early summer and settles down as lower flows in mid- to late summer continue dropping.

The highest runs on the Yampa are set in a pastoral open valley before cutting through the ski town of Steamboat Springs. Downstream of town, the Yampa collects the Elk River and meanders lazily downstream through more ranchland toward the town of Craig. Downstream of Craig, the river slides into isolated and scenic Duffy Canyon and the short Juniper Canyon; both offer some fine canoeing. Downstream of these canyons, the Yampa lazes through another open valley before getting a dramatic pinch through the expert-only Cross Mountain Gorge. After exiting this slice of a canyon, the Yampa cruises through Lily Park and the Little Snake River enters, further increasing the flow.

Below Lily Park, the Yampa drifts into a gem of a multi-day trip through the impressive Yampa Canyon. This section does not disappoint desert wilderness lovers also seeking a little bit of whitewater. At its confluence with the Green River in Echo Park, the Yampa is officially swallowed up beneath a prominent outcropping known as Steamboat Rock. This trip often ends on the Green, which proceeds downstream into Whirlpool Canyon in Dinosaur National Park.

Steamboat Town

A river-restoration success story.

Nearest city/town: Steamboat Springs
Start: Yampa River Park, Rich Weiss Memorial Park (N40 28.524' / W106 49.860')
End: 20 Mile Road Bridge near the library (N40 29.362' / W106 50.497')
Length: Up to 2.0 miles, or park-n-play
Approximate paddling time: 1 to 3 hours
Difficulty rating: Beginner/intermediate
Rapids: Class II-III–
River type: Man-made whitewater park
Current: Swift
Environment: Off-season ski town
River gradient: 25 fpm
River gauge: 700 to 5,000 cfs, Yampa at Steamboat Springs

Elevation drop: 45 feet
Hazards: Unintentional rodeo moves at high water
Season: May through August
Land status: Town of Steamboat Springs
Boats used: Playboats, SUPs, canoes, rafts
Fees or permits: None
Maps: Steamboat walking trail
Other users: Tubers and anything else that floats
Contacts: friendsoftheyampa.com
Special considerations: A bike path and paved streets make for an easy bike shuttle.
Put-in/takeout information: Use US 40 as the main shuttle route on this section. On the

west side of town, turn left (south) onto 20 Mile Road, looking for signs for the library. A parking area is located on the downstream side of the bridge; this is the takeout. To get to the put-in, head south through the middle of town to the Yampa River Park.

The Paddle

The Yampa River Improvement Project was implemented in 1981 to revamp the river corridor and the paddling quality by placing boulders in various locations in the river channels. What was once a mellow section has now become a playful and enjoyable run for the after-work crowd. More recent river improvements include construction of a permanent slalom course and man-made play features. The most notable are C-Hole and D-Hole, near the takeout.

Elk River

Lower Elk

Nearest city/town: Steamboat Springs
Start: Box Canyon Campground (N40 46.158')
End: Glen Eden Bridge (N40 43.007' / W106 54.841')
Length: 8.4 miles
Approximate paddling time: 2 to 3 hours
Difficulty rating: Intermediate
Rapids: Class III
River type: Continuous
Current: Swift
Environment: Scenic forest service road
River gradient: 65 fpm
River gauge: 500 to 3,000 cfs, Elk near Milner
Elevation drop: 540 feet
Hazards: Fast, cold water with occasional wood
Season: May through July
Land status: US Forest Service, contentiously private
Boats used: Kayaks

Fees or permits: None
Maps: *Routt National Forest*
Other users: Anglers
Contacts: southwestpaddler.com
Special considerations: Colorado's most recent hotbed of river access issues with surrounding private fishing lodge owners. Stay in your boat.
Put-in/takeout information: From downtown Steamboat Springs, head west on US 40 past the library. Look for signs for County Road 129; turn right (north) onto CR 129 and travel upstream to the town of Clark. Just above town, CR 129 crosses the river; this is the takeout. To reach the put-in, turn right (east) onto Forest Service Road 400 (dirt) and follow it upstream along the river. Look for sings for Box Canyon Campground; this is the put-in.

The Paddle

Just downstream of Steamboat Springs, the Elk River flows out of the Mount Zirkel Wilderness Area and heads to the south before joining the Yampa on the west side of town. Another swift, free-flowing, snowmelt-fed river, the Elk tumbles in a more continuous character over boulders in a heavily wooded canyon. This canyon's short accessible upper reaches are a Class V, expert-only affair. Below that, on the Lower Elk, there are no major drops, just fast eddyless boogie boating in higher water.

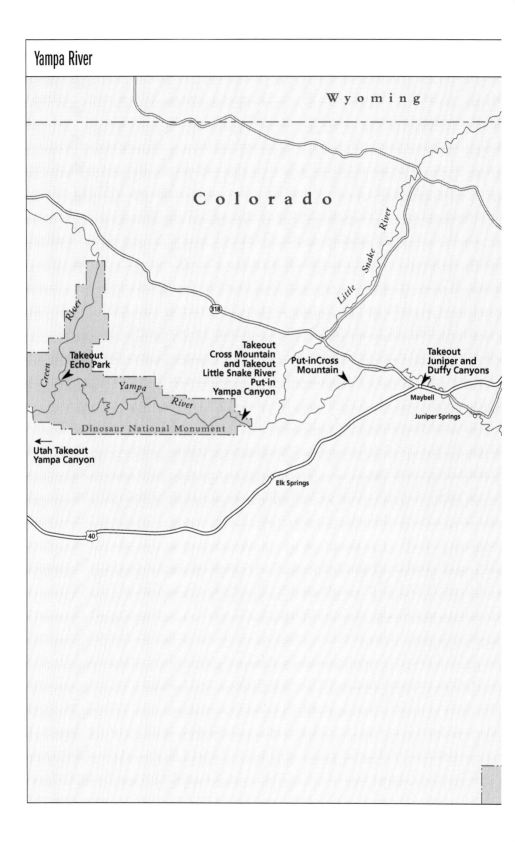

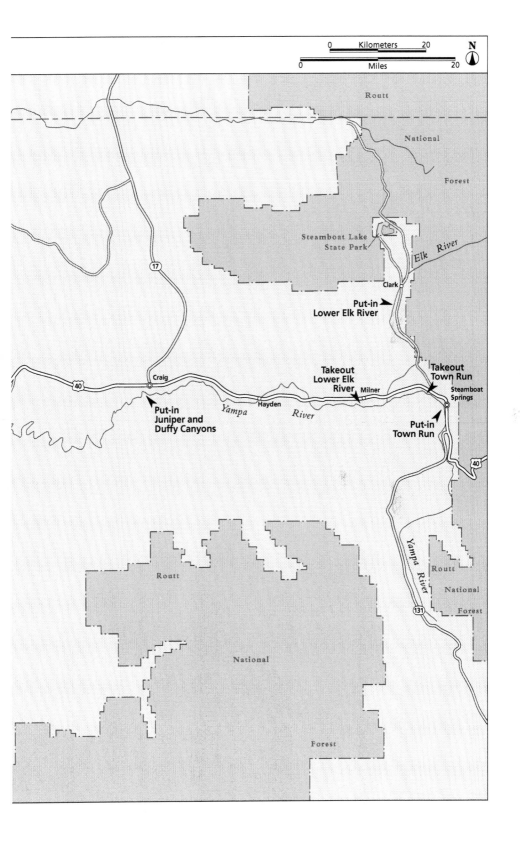

Little Yampa (Duffy) Canyon and Juniper Canyon

A gem of a run for desert-loving, multi-day-seeking canoeists set in a 500+-foot-deep canyon.

Nearest city/town: Craig
Start: South Beach River Access
(N40 28.799' / W107 36.840')
End: Maybell Bridge River Access
(N40 30.071' / W108 01.983')
Length: 50.0 miles (shorter runs possible)
Approximate paddling time: 2 to 4 days
Difficulty rating: Beginner
Rapids: Class I
River type: Moving water
Current: Moderate
Environment: Steep-walled sandstone canyon
River gradient: 7 fpm
River gauge: 1,100 to 10,000 cfs, Yampa below Craig
Elevation drop: 233 feet
Hazards: None
Season: April through August
Land status: Bureau of Land Management
Boats used: Kayaks, rafts, canoes, SUPs
Fees or permits: None
Maps: BLM Little Yampa Canyon Special Recreation Management Area
Other users: Anglers

Contacts: BLM Little Snake Field Office (970-826-5000)
Special considerations: Unlike the Yampa Canyon proper, no permit is needed to float or camp in this stretch. Please use minimum-impact camping skills (toilet system and fire pan) to help protect the river corridor from future degradation.
Put-in/takeout information: From the junction of Highway 13 and US 40, head west on US 40, looking for a sign for County Road 53. Turn left (south) onto this dirt road and drive until you reach a bridge over the river at abandoned Juniper Springs; this is the takeout. A higher takeout is often used at the Duffy river access off County Road 17 (located off US 40), which is located upstream on river right from Government Bridge. To reach the put-in, head east on US 40 upstream to the town of Craig. Just west of town, look for signs for Highway 13. Turn right (south) onto Highway 13 and head downstream toward the put-in at the South Beach river access site.

The Paddle

This section offers beginning paddlers a fine remote segment of river that cuts into steep-walled sandstone canyons. Below the put-in, the river eases past numerous cottonwood flatlands that provide excellent campsites. Wildlife abounds, with numerous sightings of mule deer, bighorn sheep, nesting eagles, ospreys, and waterfowl.

The river through the canyon meanders beneath steep walls but offers no whitewater and is a rare canyon section with no real threat. The river slides out of the canyon and for the last 10 miles flows through open, barren lands before the first takeout at the bridge in the now abandoned town of Juniper Springs. Then the Yampa cuts a V-shaped slot through Juniper Mountain. Measuring 1,500 feet deep, Juniper is another little-known but rewarding beginner-level paddling run, which can be done as a 5-mile day section. Squeezed between canyon walls, numerous small Class II rapids are found in the bottom of this canyon. Previous blasting has formed a Class

III rapid 2 miles into the run. This short, attractive canyon is far from any people; it is seldom paddled and will offer a fine, remote day on the water.

Cross Mountain Gorge

Good for a muddy high-water frolic in spring, or a craggy creek boat scraper in late summer.

Nearest city/town: Craig
Start: East Cross Mountain Public Access (N40 29.160' / W108 19.440')
End: Deerlodge Park River Access (N40 27.193' / W108 22.931')
Length: 6.4 miles (1.6 flatwater)
Approximate paddling time: 1 to 3 hours
Difficulty rating: Advanced
Rapids: Class IV+ (3)
River type: Muddy desert water flowing over broken sandstone
Current: Swift
Environment: High-mountain desert
River gradient: 60 fpm
River gauge: 600 to 6,000 cfs (Class V at this level), Yampa near Maybell
Elevation drop: 574 feet
Hazards: Large, powerful whitewater features at high water; sharp, scrapy sandstone at low water
Season: April through August

Land status: Bureau of Land Management
Boats used: Kayaks, rafts
Fees or permits: Parking fee at put-in
Maps: *Bureau of Land Management Cross Mountain Wilderness Study Area*
Other users: None
Contacts: BLM Cross Mountain WSA, blm.gov/visit/cross-mountain-wsa
Special considerations: Camping at the put-in can make for several quick laps in a few days.
Put-in/takeout information: To reach the takeout, turn off Highway 40 about 16 miles west of Maybell at the sign for Deerlodge Park. Drive in 4 miles to a small parking area at the canyon mouth. To get to the put-in, head east on Highway 40 back toward Maybell, and go 1.5 miles to a dirt road turnoff (Moffat 85 Road) marked by the only large tree near the road. Drive 2.5 miles and bear left over a cattle guard, and continue to the East Cross Mountain Public Access (fee area).

The Paddle

A far drive for most Colorado boaters (with the exception of Steamboat locals), Cross Mountain Gorge is often some of the state's first runnable whitewater in early spring. It draws a fair amount of expert paddlers out of winter hibernation, jonesing for a high-water fix. Cross Mountain also goes down to surprisingly low flows (600 cfs or lower) and can be a late season stop once other mountain drainages have dried up. This short, craggy sandstone gorge offers superb desert scenery and high-quality, manageable Class IV whitewater, particularly at flows above 1,300 cfs. At 2,800, the high-water juice is loose, and many experts choose to take a playboat for the surfing and downriver play—or to easier escape the clutches of its massive holes. After a 1.5-mile flatwater paddle in, the first of the notable hydraulic features is found at Osterizer (IV+). This rapid is usually scouted or portaged on river right; note the sneak line to the right of the meat. High flows may necessitate scouting/portaging from the left.

The next rapid, Snake Pit (IV+), is the longest and usually most difficult rapid on the run. Quick zigzag action around ugly sharp boulders ends with a large curler perfect for catching air. Scout from the left. Between here and the takeout, the rapids mellow out but remain generally Class IV⁻ there is one riverwide ledge hole lying in wait that can be snuck against the left wall.

Little Snake River

The most unknown beginner river in the whole state of Colorado.

Nearest city/town: Craig
Start: County road bridge southwest of Baggs, Wyoming (N40 59.545' / W107 46.518')
End: Deerlodge Park River Access (N40 27.193' / W108 22.931')
Length: 60.0 miles (shorter runs possible)
Approximate paddling time: 2 to 4 days
Difficulty rating: Beginner
Rapids: Class I
River type: Flat, meandering
Current: Moderate
Environment: Rural mountain west
River gradient: 8 fpm
River gauge: 500 to 1,500 cfs
Elevation drop: 502 feet
Hazards: None
Season: May through June
Land status: Bureau of Land Management, private
Boats used: Canoes, kayaks
Fees or permits: None

Maps: *Bureau of Land Management Little Snake Travel Management Area*
Other users: Few
Contacts: BLM Little Snake Field Office (970-826-5000)
Special considerations: Another intermediate and more-used access point is the Highway 318 bridge, just west of Maybell.
Put-in/takeout information: To reach the takeout from the town of Craig, head west on US 40, continuing through the town of Maybell. Sixteen miles west of Maybell, turn right (north) onto Deerlodge Park Road. Follow Deerlodge Park Road to its end and look for signs for the Deerlodge Park launch site; this is the takeout. To reach the put-in, return to Craig and head north on Highway 13. Just before the Wyoming–Colorado state line, south of Baggs, turn left (west) onto County Road 430. Follow CR 430 downstream as it parallels the river for 26 miles until it crosses the river; this is the put-in.

The Paddle

Tucked way up in the northwest corner away from everybody, and with only a narrow window of good flows because it's free flowing, the Little Snake hardly sees paddlers. That is the very reason to go. Not only does the river lack people but it is also relatively remote in terms of a scenic multi-day paddling experience for canoeists.

Flowing south through the Little Snake State Wildlife Area in its upper reaches, the river eventually joins the Yampa in the middle of Lily Park. It largely meanders peacefully through a lush, fertile bottomland lined with willows and cottonwoods set beneath rolling sagebrush hills. Out-of-the-way ranches can be seen along the banks, and rough dirt roads somewhat parallel sections of the river. This is a fine, isolated little river for adventurous canoeists seeking to explore a little-known treasure.

Yampa Canyon–Dinosaur National Monument

A quintessential western multi-day: easy whitewater and stunning geology that comes with a short season, questionable flows, and competitive permit system.

Nearest city/town: Dinosaur

Start: Deerlodge Park (N40 27.193' / W108 22.931')

End: Split Mountain Boat Ramp (N40 26.728' / W109 15.155')

Length: 72.0 miles

Approximate paddling time: 3 to 5 days

Difficulty rating: Advanced beginner/ intermediate

Rapids: Class II-III+ (1)

River type: Muddy, free-flowing western classic

Current: Moderate

Environment: Desert canyon

River gradient: 12 fpm

River gauge: 1,300 to 4,500 cfs, Yampa at Deerlodge Park

Elevation drop: 564 feet

Hazards: Raft flips can cause wet, soggy camping gear on cold nights.

Season: April through June

Land status: Dinosaur National Monument, permitted

Boats used: Kayaks, canoes, rafts, SUPs

Fees or permits: Permits required year-round. Lottery for high-use season (second weekend in May to second weekend in July); applications due January 31 each year—recreation.gov.

Maps: RiverMaps, Guide to the Green and Yampa Rivers in Dinosaur National Monument

Other users: Commercial raft trips, outdoor leadership schools in canoes

Contacts: Dinosaur National Monument River Office (970-374-2468)

Special considerations: Have a permit party for this one!

Put-in/takeout information: Use US 40 as the primary route for access on this section. To reach the takeout, head west out of the town of Dinosaur, cross into Utah, and look for signs for Dinosaur National Monument in the town of Jensen. Turn right (north) onto Highway 149 into the park. Pay the entrance fee and follow signs for the Split Mountain Boat Ramp; this is the takeout. To reach the put-in, head back east on US 40. Turn left (north) onto Deerlodge Park Road about 40 miles east of Dinosaur. Follow this dirt road to its end and look for signs for the Deerlodge Park launch site; this is the put-in. River Runners Transport out of Vernal, Utah, can rent gear or provide shuttle (435-781-4919, riverrunnerstransport.com).

The Paddle

Yampa Canyon offers the beginner/intermediate an ideal combination of paddling characteristics—an incredibly beautiful canyon setting, numerous days of paddling, low gradient, gentle straightforward rapids, and great camping. The only problem with paddling this section of river is actually getting permission to put in. A river permit is required, as assigned by the Dinosaur National Park Service River Permits Office. The permit process is a lottery that must be applied for well before the intended launch date. Get many folks in your group to apply and hope for the best.

Once you've obtained a permit, settle in for a wilderness paddling experience like that of only a few other rivers in the entire United States. The Yampa is one of the last major rivers in Colorado to remain undammed and free flowing, which can make it tricky to predict summer flows. Most boaters plan for a 3- to 5-day trip in this stunning canyon, which is more than 2,000 feet deep and filled with twists and turns between sheer-walled cliffs.

The river cruises away from the put-in and drops into the canyon just below. The whitewater found here includes Tepee (Class II+) and Big Joe Rapids (Class II+). The big one of the trip is Warm Springs Rapid (Class III+), which can be scouted, or portaged, on the right. Numerous side canyons offer nice hiking options, and assigned camping usually ensures a great campsite for the evening. At the confluence with the Green River in Echo Park, the Yampa officially ends. A remote takeout is located just below here on the left, though most parties finish the trip at Split Mountain boat ramp (Utah) 26 miles downstream.

After the Yampa River confluence, the Green drops into deep, dark Whirlpool Canyon. As the name implies, swirly water and eddylines bounce off the canyon walls forming unstable paddling through numerous Class II rapids and Greasy Pliers Rapid (Class III).

As the Green slides abruptly out of this canyon, it enters the lazy, open valley known as Island Park. After 7 miles of open, tranquil water, the Green suddenly plummets straight into a mountain, thus cutting Split Mountain Gorge. Down here the whitewater picks up with straightforward rapids with big waves in the form of Moonshine (Class III), S.O.B. (Class III−), School Boy (Class II+), and Inglesby Rapids (Class III−). The canyon rim towers above the river, and all too soon paddlers are spit out onto the boat ramp that is the takeout. It is possible to paddle just the 8-mile-long Split Mountain Canyon as a day trip. A permit is still required to launch on this section of the Green River, located entirely in Utah (recreation.gov).

11 Green River

The Green River is a western classic first explored by John Wesley Powell in the late 1800s. Flowing southward out of the impressive Wind River Mountain Range—a beautiful, relatively little-known mountain landscape in southwestern Wyoming—the Green is unfortunately stopped in its tracks by Flaming Gorge Dam. The outflow of Flaming Gorge offers paddlers a stretch of good beginner/intermediate water as the Green slides into Red and Swallow Canyons and eventually out through the broad plains of Browns Park.

There the Green slices back into the rugged mountainside by forming the beautiful and geologically unique Lodore, Whirlpool, and Split Mountain Canyons. These high-desert multi-day trips can be linked together for an intermediate paddling trip with stellar canyon scenery, weaving across the Utah-Colorado state line twice in its path. The Green makes a transition as it begins a due-south course, flowing through the more barren canyons of Desolation, Grey, Stillwater, and Labyrinth, all in Utah, before ultimately joining the Colorado River in the heart of Canyonlands National Park.

Fault line geology rises above the river in Lodore Canyon.

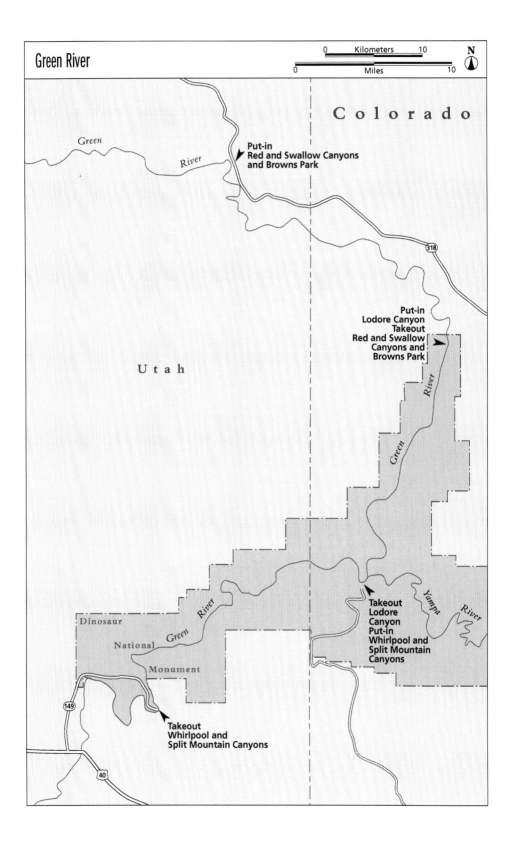

Red and Swallow Canyons and Browns Park

A fantastic beginner-intermediate section set in the Flaming Gorge and the tailwaters of its infamous dam.

Nearest city/town: Dutch John
Start: Spillway boat ramp below Flaming Gorge Dam, Utah (N40 54.546' / W109 25.327')
End: Lodore boat launch (N40 43.618' / W108 53.284')
Length: 46.0 miles (shorter runs possible)
Approximate paddling time: 1 to 3 days
Difficulty rating: Beginner
Rapids: Class II–III (1)
River type: Easy wave trains and boulder maneuvers
Current: Moderate
Environment: Heavily used desert waterway with roadless sections
River gradient: 6 fpm
River gauge: 200 to 5,000 cfs, Green River near Greendale, UT
Elevation drop: 285 feet
Hazards: Fish hooks
Season: April through October
Land status: US Forest Service, Bureau of Land Management
Boats used: Kayaks, rafts, canoes, dories, SUPs
Fees or permits: Parking/launch fees
Maps: *National Geographic Flaming Gorge National Recreation Area*

Other users: Commercial float anglers, wade fishermen
Contacts: Ashley National Forest (435-789-1181); BLM Vernal Field Office (435-781-4400)
Special considerations: Shorter runs can be done by using the Little Hole boat ramp (mile 7), Bridge Hollow access point (mile 16), Swallow Canyon boat ramp (mile 26), or the full distance down to Lodore.
Put-in/takeout information: From Maybell head west on Highway 318, crossing over the Little Snake River. Eventually come to the turn-off on County Road 34N for the Lodore boat launch area; this is the takeout.

To reach the put-in and additional upstream access points, continue heading west on Highway 318. At the Utah-Colorado state line, the road turns to dirt. Continue upstream, passing the Swallow Canyon boat launch area (either a put-in or lower takeout). Five miles farther up the road is the Bridge Hollow access point. Go 9 more miles upstream through the town of Dutch John to signs for the river access below Flaming Gorge Dam; this is the highest put-in.

The Paddle

These stretches are known as the A, B, and C sections of the Green. Good fishing, easy access, and plenty of camping make them popular, especially with late season dam-controlled flows that keep them running well into the fall. From the base of Flaming Gorge Dam in Utah, the river swiftly cruises between steep iron oxide–colored walls that stand over 1,500 feet above the river. Its gentle flow is punctuated with Class II horizon lines and wave trains. Below here the river opens up a bit and then drops back between the walls of Swallow Canyon. Here paddlers encounter Red Creek Rapid (Class III), the rowdiest whitewater found upstream of Lodore Canyon. Below Swallow Canyon, the river eases into a broad plain and mellows out to Class I all the way to the lowest access point. The cold water of the Flaming Gorge (because of the outflow from the bottom of the reservoir) offers optimal float-fishing and can become quite crowded with commercial dory boats.

Lodore Canyon

Challenging intermediate paddling in the bottom of an incredibly beautiful, remote, and deep sandstone-walled river canyon—a classic Colorado multi-day.

Nearest city/town: Maybell
Start: Lodore boat launch (N40 43.618' / W108 53.284')
End: Split Mountain Boat Ramp (N40 26.728' / W109 15.155')
Length: 44.0 miles
Approximate paddling time: 3 to 5 days
Difficulty rating: Intermediate
Rapids: Class III (3)
River type: Pool-drop, boulder garden
Current: Swift
Environment: Desert sandstone canyon
River gradient: 13 fpm
River gauge: 800 to 6,000 cfs, Green River near Greendale, UT
Elevation drop: 555 feet
Hazards: Low water and large boulders create notorious pin spots for rafts.
Season: Year-round is possible.
Land status: Dinosaur National Monument, permitted
Boats used: Kayaks, rafts, canoes, SUPs
Fees or permits: Permits required year-round. Lottery for high-use season (second weekend in May to second weekend in September); applications due January 31 each year—recreation.gov.

Maps: *RiverMaps, Guide to the Green and Yampa Rivers in Dinosaur National Monument*
Other users: Commercial rafters, outdoor leadership schools
Contacts: Dinosaur National Monument River Office (970-374-2468)
Special considerations: "Low-dore" skinny water descents are possible, and easier to obtain permits for, during the off-season—especially in small crafts.
Put-in/takeout information: To reach the takeout, head west out of the town of Dinosaur on Highway 40, cross into Utah, and look for signs for Dinosaur National Monument in the town of Jensen. Turn right (north) onto Highway 149 into the park. Pay the entrance fee and follow signs for the Split Mountain Boat Ramp; this is the takeout.

To reach the put-in, return to Highway 40 and travel east to the town of Maybell. Turn left (west) on Highway 318 for approximately 45 miles. Look for County Road 34N (dirt) off to the left (south) and signs for the Lodore Canyon launch site. Follow this road down to the river, look for a boat ramp and campground; this is the put-in. River Runners Transport out of Vernal, Utah, can rent gear or provide shuttle (435-781-4919, riverrunnerstransport.com).

The Paddle

Lodore Canyon offers some of the most challenging whitewater on the entire Green River—look up "raft pin at Winnie's Rock" on YouTube for proof. Unfortunately, its power has largely been controlled and regulated by Flaming Gorge Dam 50 miles upstream. Nonetheless, the canyon scenery and still-thrilling rapids make Lodore a hotly sought-after multi-day permit.

Sunshine on the walls of Lodore Canyon.

The canyon walls jump up just below the launch site and squeeze paddlers throughout this trip down to the confluence with the Yampa River. Side canyons offer intimate little grottos tucked away from the main canyon. Through the canyon the whitewater provides good short rapids such as Upper Disaster Falls, Lower Disaster, and Triplet Falls (all Class III) and Hell's Half Mile (Class III+). Most of these rapids require technical rock maneuvering at lower water levels, with good recovery pools below. Hell's Half Mile, as the name implies, is a longer rapid with a shallow run out.

Below here the canyon walls still stand tall, but the river swiftly heads downstream beneath Steamboat Rock and takes in the Yampa River tributary in the Echo Park area of Dinosaur National Park. A remote takeout is located just below here on the left, though most parties finish the trip at Split Mountain boat ramp (Utah) 26 miles downstream. After the swirlies of Whirlpool Canyon, the Green meanders and braids around a few islands before pouring into Split Mountain Canyon, a Class II-III day section accessed at Rainbow Park, for the last 8 miles of the trip. (See Yampa River: Yampa Canyon for more information.)

12 Colorado River

The headwater tributaries to the mighty Colorado River start high in the snow-capped peaks within Rocky Mountain National Park. Just outside the western border of the park, the outflow of Lake Granby marks the official start of the Colorado. The Colorado River cuts a relatively straight westward route through the state as it makes its descent toward the most famous section of river in the world farther downstream—the Grand Canyon.

Within the state borders, the Colorado River lazes its way through prime fishing waters near Hot Sulphur Springs and then suddenly tumbles downhill in a cold, swift torrent of expert-only whitewater through Gore Canyon. It then settles down throughout a rural valley in its upper sections, passing State Bridge, McCoy, and Dotsero.

The Colorado swallows up the Eagle River and makes another rush of expert whitewater through Barrel Springs, followed by the intermediate-friendly Shoshone Canyon. Downstream of this section, the river meanders and cruises along, paralleling Interstate 70 to the Colorado–Utah border. Just as the Colorado leaves the state, it enters the remote sandstone landscape of Ruby/Horsethief Canyon.

Gore Canyon

If surviving this quintessential Colorado Class V isn't enough, do it as fast as you can, solo (with safety in place), at the annual Gore Race in late August—or do it in a commercial raft.

Nearest city/town: Kremmling
Start: Colorado and Blue confluence (N40 02.554' / W106 23.733')
End: Pumphouse Campground (N39 59.344' / W106 30.532')
Length: 9.2 miles
Approximate paddling time: 3 to 4 hours
Difficulty rating: Expert
Rapids: Class V (2), Class IV+ (4)
River type: Pool-drop (?)
Current: Extremely swift
Environment: High-mountain railroad cut
River gradient: 115 fpm in canyon proper, with 3.9-mile flatwater paddle in
River gauge: 600 to 2,500 cfs (Colorado River near Kremmling)
Elevation drop: 358 feet
Hazards: Sieves, powerful hydraulics, sharp blast rock in riverbed

Season: Year-round, ice dependent
Land status: Bureau of Land Management, mostly private before the canyon
Boats used: Kayaks, rafts, decked canoes
Fees or permits: Parking and camping fees at the takeout
Maps: *RiverMaps, Guide to the Upper Colorado River, Kremmling to Dotsero, Colorado*
Other users: Commercial rafters
Contacts: Upper Colorado River–Gore Canyon, BLM (970-724-3000)
Special considerations: Releases down the Blue River water this stretch well before the Colorado snowmelt season and into the fall, making it optimal for an off-season romp. Plan to bring the family for excellent camping and a newly constructed, SUP-surfable whitewater park at the takeout.

Eddying out for warm springs (upstream, not pictured) on the Upper Colorado River.
Credit: Rob Hurst

Put-in/takeout information: From Kremmling, head south on Colorado Highway 9 for 2.3 miles. Turn right onto County Road 1, also called Trough Road. Follow this for 10.3 miles and then turn right on CR 106. Drive 1.6 more miles the Pumphouse Recreation Area; this is the takeout. To get to the put-in, head back out to CR1 toward Highway 9. After 9.8 miles, just after the road crosses the Blue River, turn left on the only road before hitting Highway 9, and follow this to the dirt parking area by the river; this is the put-in.

The Paddle

A sweet seal-slide at the put-in and four miles of flatwater guard the entrance to Gore Canyon, whose flanks rise like the gates of Mordor out of northern Colorado ranchlands. After this meandering slog, paddlers often stop at "Dress Rock" to layer up against the river's cold waters and sharp blast rock lying in wait below. Applesauce (Class IV+) offers up the canyon's signature test piece—a short, bouncy drop with a nice pool below. After that, the action becomes more continuous at Gore Rapid (Class V) and its myriad line choices, including a Class IV sneak. Scout from the active railroad tracks on river right. After this, the river steamrolls through Scissors, Pyrite, Tunnel, and Toilet Bowl (all Class IV–IV+ with Class IV boogie water in between) with a brief respite before the long and demanding Kirschbaum's (Class IV+). Another mile and a half of flatwater interspersed with a few Class III rapids

Colorado River

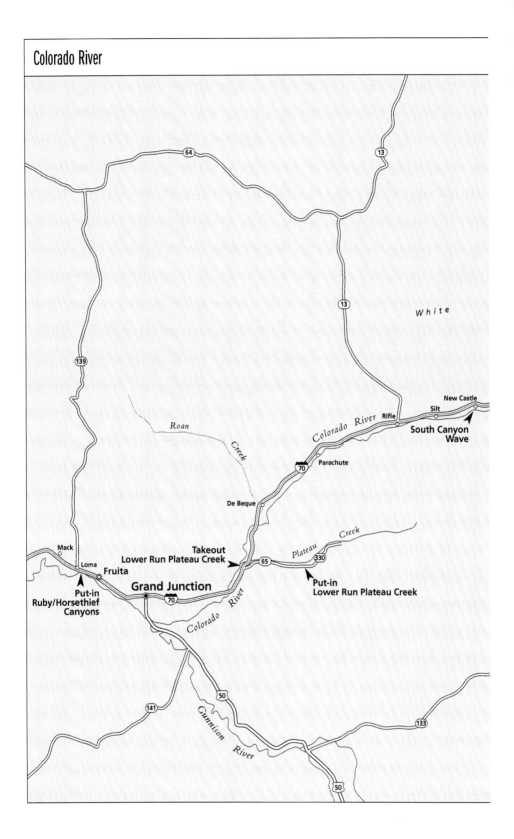

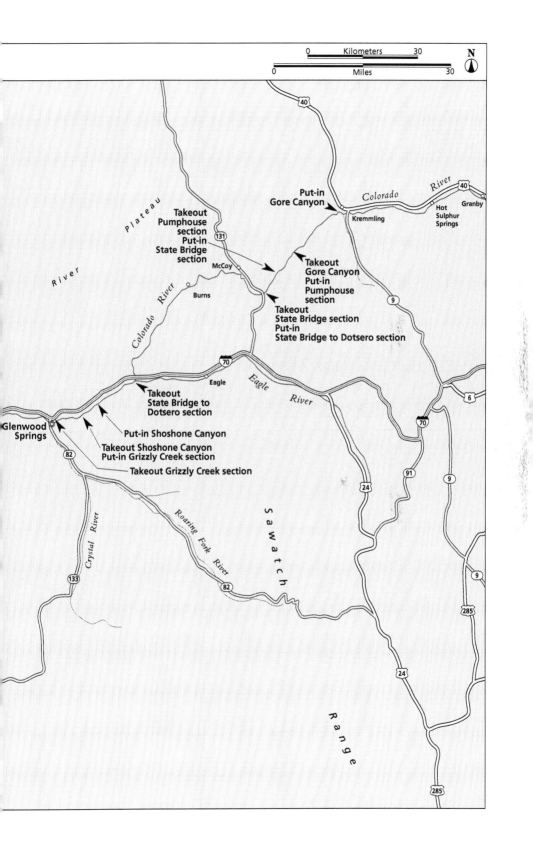

0 Kilometers 30

0 Miles 30

N

Put-in
Gore Canyon

Colorado River 40

Granby

Hot
Sulphur
Springs

Kremmling

Takeout
Pumphouse
section
Put-in
State Bridge
section

River

Plateau

131

McCoy

Takeout
Gore Canyon
Put-in
Pumphouse
section

Takeout
State Bridge section
Put-in
State Bridge to Dotsero section

Burns

Colorado River

9

70

Eagle

Eagle River

Takeout
State Bridge to
Dotsero section

6

70

Glenwood
Springs

Put-in Shoshone Canyon

Takeout Shoshone Canyon
Put-in Grizzly Creek section

Takeout Grizzly Creek section

82

91

9

24

S
a
w
a
t
c
h

Crystal River

133

Roaring Fork River

82

9

285

R
a
n
g
e

24

285

A team of rafters charges into Applesauce, the first rapid in Gore Canyon. Credit: Rob Hurst

lands at the takeout, a popular campground where man-made surf waves provide eve-ning, kid-friendly entertainment. American Whitewater hosts the annual "Gorefest" fundraiser in late August—but recently lost their insurance policy for Class V racing, making a fast descent down Gore even scarier.

Pumphouse Section

It can be a crazy zoo of all types of craft at the put-in and takeout of this section, with slightly more whitewater and canyon feel than the State Bridge stretch below.

Nearest city/town: Kremmling
Start: Pumphouse Campground (N39 59.344' / W106 30.532')
End: Rancho Del Rio (N39 53.748' / W106 36.558') or Yarmony Bridge (N39 53.445' / W106 37.009')
Length: 11.0 miles (shorter run possible)
Approximate paddling time: 3 to 5 hours

Difficulty rating: Class II-III (advanced beginner/intermediate)
Rapids: Class III (2), Class II (numerous)
River type: Open valley, short canyons
Current: Moderate to swift
Environment: High desert
River gradient: 15 fpm
River gauge: 500 to 5,000 cfs (Colorado River near Kremmling)

Elevation drop: 165 feet

Hazards: Large boulders, swift current, and strong wave features at high water

Season: Year-round

Land status: Bureau of Land Management

Boats used: Kayaks, rafts, canoes, SUPs

Fees or permits: Required at BLM and private access points

Maps: *RiverMaps, Guide to the Upper Colorado River, Kremmling to Dotsero, Colorado*

Other users: Anglers, hike-in hot springs partiers

Contacts: Bureau of Land Management Upper Colorado River Recreation Area (970-876-8000)

Special considerations: Pair this float with the State Bridge or other sections downstream for an overnighter or lodge-assisted multi-day.

Put-in/takeout information: All access is off County Road 1, which is located off Highway 9 just south of the town of Kremmling. All access points are well marked. Use Radium Recreation Site (off CR 11) as an intermediate access point to shorten this run.

The Paddle

Ah, summer weekends on the Upper C—seems every family in Denver has bought themselves a raft and considers this their "local" float trip. Paired with reliable flow from the releases down the Blue, a lukewarm hot spring, and cliff jumping midrun, Pumphouse becomes a true Colorado party!

Paddlers start out with a short valley float perfect for spotting bald eagles and other birdlife before entering Little Gore Canyon. Eye of the Needle Rapid (Class III), the crux of the run, is found in the middle of the canyon. At high water, good waves form here while low water brings pin and flip potential off the large boulder in the center. Flows above 4,000 cfs cause two holes to form over said boulder.

All too soon, the canyon opens up and a bridge crosses over the river at Radium Recreation Site; this can be used as an access point. Below this bridge, the river again bends away from the road and cuts into Red Gorge, which contains continuous Class II–III rapids. Yarmony Rapid is marked by a riverside sign; it has a large wave hole best negotiated by moving from left to center. Below this canyon, rural paddling and gentle waves bring paddlers down to the takeout.

State Bridge

Short, roadside, with huge eddies and predictable wave trains up to insane water levels make this the most beginner-friendly raft or kayak run in the state.

Start: Rancho Del Rio (N39 53.757' / W106 36.528')

End: State Bridge (N39 51.466' / W106 38.985')

Length: 3.9 miles

Approximate paddling time: 1 to 2 hours

Difficulty rating: Class II (beginner)

Rapids: Class II

River type: Desert high-volume

Environment: Roadside

River gradient: 15 fpm

River gauge: 500 to 5,000 cfs (Colorado River near Kremmling)

Elevation drop: 58.5 feet

Hazards: Boats have been known to flip or wrap on the Yarmony bridge pylon river center.

Season: Year-round

Land status: Bureau of Land Management

Boats used: Kayaks, rafts, canoes, SUPs, inflatable unicorn pool toys

Fees or permits: Required at BLM and some private access points

Maps: *RiverMaps, Guide to the Upper Colorado River, Kremmling to Dotsero, Colorado*

Other users: Anglers, tubers

Contacts: Bureau of Land Management Upper Colorado River Recreation Area (970) 876-8000

Special considerations: The small outfitter at the put-in at Rancho Del Rio offers gear rentals and a shuttle service. As you drive in, avoid the packs of three-legged dogs, brush past the porch dwellers sleeping off last night's party, and duck into the rustic cabin office. Rest assured, they will deliver your shuttle rig intact and on time. Plus, they have ice. ranchodelrio .com (970-653-4431)

Put-in/takeout information: The takeout is on river left, just upstream of the historic State Bridge across the river on Highway 131. Look for a large dirt pullout and parking area. To get to the put-in, head upstream on CR 1. Rancho Del Rio is a fee access area to put in. Just downstream, the Yarmony Bridge is a free alternative put-in point.

The Paddle

What can be said about State Bridge? Once a hopping venue for local music and eclectic yurt-style accommodations, surrounded by BLM campsites, this quaint little hippie haven burned down in 2007. Efforts to restore the "resort" on the west end of the highway bridge have come in fits and starts, and the place has yet to come fully back to life. However, the classic beginner section of whitewater that bears its name remains the same: perfect. Straightforward wave trains, easy river maneuvers with minor consequences, and pools below every rapid invite those just learning any type of paddlecraft. Though we will miss ducking under the road underpass and bellying up to State Bridge Resort's huge wooden bar next to ranch hands and fellow soggy river runners, this section is often added to the upstream run or used as a bit higher put-in for a lower run.

State Bridge to Dotsero

A meandering, lazy paddle interspersed with fun Class II rapids between flat sections of moving current.

Nearest town: Dotsero

Start: State Bridge (N39 51.466' / W106 38.985')

End: Dotsero boat ramp at the confluence of the Colorado and Eagle Rivers (N39 39.008' / W107 03.626')

Length: 45.0 miles (shorter runs possible)

Approximate paddling time: Varies based on length of run, multi-days possible

Difficulty rating: Beginner/ intermediate

Rapids: Class II (8), Class II+ (2)

River type: Wide and largely unobstructed

Current: Moderate

Environment: Rural valley

River gradient: 5.5 fpm

River gauge: 500 to 9,000 cfs, Colorado River at Catamount Bridge

Elevation drop: 246 feet

Hazards: Multiple bridge abutments can be dangerous at high water.

Season: Year-round; best flows May through July

Land status: Bureau of Land Management, private, Eagle County

Boats used: Kayaks, canoes, rafts, drift boats, SUPs

Fees or permits: Day use and parking fees at some access points

Maps: *RiverMaps, Guide to the Upper Colorado, Kremmling to Dotsero, Colorado*

Other users: Anglers

Contacts: BLM Kremmling Field Office (970-724-3000), kfo_webmail@co.blm.gov

Special considerations: The 7.5-mile stretch between Sweetwater River access and Dotsero, near the confluence with the Eagle River, is one of the state's premier first-time paddler runs. The current is calm but swift enough to form practice eddies interspersed with Class II rapids and a beginner surf sport near the Deep Creek confluence. Bring your partner or budding paddling crew for a weekend with sweet car camping spots along the river or off Coffee Pot Road that parallels Deep Creek.

Put-in/Takeout information: The Dotsero boat ramp is just on the south side of I-70 at the confluence of the Colorado and Eagle Rivers. To get to the put-in, follow the Colorado River Road (CR 30) upstream. Just before the town of McCoy, turn right (east) onto Highway 131, which leads to State Bridge. Intermediate access points include Catamount Bridge Recreation Site, Burns and Pinball river access sites, and Cottonwood Island Recreation Site.

The Paddle

A rural road parallels this section of the Upper Colorado, making shorter runs easily possible. You can also scout the majority of the river while setting shuttle. This zone is great for open canoeists and family raft trips, as well as beginning kayakers. BLM camping options abound, making it one of the most underrated, and as yet unpermitted, multi-day paddling trips in Colorado. The largest rapid, and most viable playspot, on this section—Rodeo Rapid/Burns Hole (Class III)—is located just downstream of the little town of Bond.

Shoshone Canyon

The most-used, year-round, intermediate section of river in the state.

Nearest city/town: Glenwood Springs

Start: Exit 123 of I-70 East (N39 34.134' / W107 13.680')

End: Grizzly Creek boat ramp, exit 121 off I-70 West (N39 33.618' / W107 15.060')

Length: 1.7 miles

Difficulty rating: Intermediate

Rapids: Class III (4)

River type: Pool-drop, boulder garden

Current: Swift

Environment: Scenic interstate corridor

River gradient: 39 fpm

River gauge: 500 to 5,000 cfs, Colorado River near Dotsero

Elevation drop: 65.6 feet

Hazards: Powerful hydraulics at high water (above 3,000 cfs)

Season: Year-round

Land status: Colorado Department of Transportation

Boats used: Kayaks, canoes, rafts, SUPs

Fees or permits: None

Maps: I-70 highway map

Other users: Commercial rafters, anglers

Contacts: Colorado Department of Transportation, Region 3 office (970-243-2368)

Special considerations: Reliable access may be the most difficult aspect of Shoshone. Glenwood

Canyon is notoriously plagued by wildfires, avalanches, and floods, all of which can close the highway indefinitely. The burn scar from the most recent fire in 2020 caused a landslide that covered the interstate and rerouted the river. As of summer 2022, with heavy rains and flood warnings, CDOT officials intermittently closed the Grizzly Creek boat ramp and other access points to private boaters to allow only commercial raft traffic. Check with a local boater or area paddling Facebook groups for up-to-date access information in Glenwood Canyon, or check codot.gov/travel/glenwoodcanyon or cotrip.org for road closures.

Put-in/takeout information: From the town of Glenwood Springs, head east on I-70 to the takeout at Grizzly Creek (exit 121). Leave a vehicle at the takeout or follow the river trail upstream. The put-in (exit 123) allows only westward entry back onto I-70.

The Paddle

This run combines the ideal factors of reliable water, easy access, good rapids, and a variety of play spots—as well as the site of an annual locals' New Year's Day paddle.

All the rapids can be seen from the river-right paved trail for scouting the run, and numerous eddies can be caught to break apart each rapid. The rapids of note in downstream order are Entrance Exam, Wall, Tombstone, Superstition, and Maneater. Play this section hard for longer runs or do numerous runs—bonus points for biking the shuttle.

Grizzly Creek and Glenwood Wave

An added "cool-down" for Shoshone just upstream or a learning section for budding whitewater paddlers.

Nearest city/town: Glenwood Springs
Start: Grizzly Creek boat ramp, exit 121 off I-70 (N39 33.618' / W107 15.060')
End: Two Rivers Park, just below the Roaring Fork confluence (N39 33.060' / W107 20.040')
Length: 5.8 miles
Approximate paddling time: 2 to 3 hours
Difficulty rating: Advanced beginner/intermediate
Rapids: Class II+ (III)
River type: Flatwater with obvious whitewater features
Current: Moderate
Environment: Scenic interstate corridor
River gradient: 23 fpm
River gauge: 500 to 5,000 cfs, Colorado River near Dotsero
Elevation drop: 131.24 feet

Hazards: Punchy, obvious holes and large waves at high water (above 3,000 cfs)
Season: Year-round
Land status: Colorado Department of Transportation
Boats used: Kayaks, canoes, rafts, SUPs, driftboats
Fees or permits: None
Maps: I-70 highway map
Other users: Many commercial rafters and float fishing trips
Contacts: Colorado Department of Transportation, Region 3 office (970-243-2368)
Special considerations: See information about road closures in the Shoshone description.
Put-in/takeout information: To reach the takeout, take exit 116 off I-70 for Glenwood Springs. Turn right off the exit ramp and drive

to a traffic light. Turn left at the light onto US Highway 6. Head downstream less than a mile, looking for signs for Two Rivers Park (restrooms and park facilities); this is the takeout. To reach the put-in, return to I-70 East and take exit 121 for the Grizzly Creek boat ramp.

The Paddle

The Grizzly Creek run marks the end of Glenwood Canyon's steep-walled scenery as the Colorado River flows into the town of Glenwood Springs. Numerous straightforward rapids mark the first half of the trip down to No Name (exit 119); the second half of the trip eases down into town. Year-round water offers a reliable section for paddlers to get out and hone their skills. There is an optional lower put-in at the No Name exit. After that the river bends back to I-70 downstream of the tunnel. About a half mile below here, find a natural hot spring on river left, a special treat on winter paddles!

For a little extra excitement, float past the takeout to the Glenwood Wave (and another access point), a much hyped man-made whitewater feature known for its glassy face and surfability at a variety of flows. At high water (above 5,000 cfs), watch out for shortboard surfers dropping in off the rocky shore!

South Canyon Wave

When it's in, exit here for some of the state's best park-n-play.

Nearest city/town: Glenwood Springs
Start: Exit 111 (South Canyon) off Interstate 70 (N39 33.698' / W107 24.452')
End: Same
Length: 0.0 miles
Approximate paddling time: As many blunts as desired
Difficulty rating: Advanced playboating
Rapids: Class III+ (1)
River type: High-volume surf wave
Current: Swift
Environment: Scenic interstate corridor
River gradient: Not applicable
River gauge: 3,000 to 3,600 cfs, Colorado River below Glenwood Springs
Elevation drop: How high can you pop?
Hazards: Flushing off the wave into the Class I section down to New Castle
Season: Before and after peak flow

Land status: Colorado Department of Transportation
Boats used: Stubby playboats for best aerial maneuvers, or bring the half-slice for endless soul surfing
Fees or permits: None
Maps: I-70 highway map
Other users: Commercial rafters and float-fishing trips
Contacts: Colorado Department of Transportation, Region 3 office (970-243-2368)
Special considerations: Find an undeveloped hot spring about a mile up the road and on the right for a post-surf soak.
Put-in/takeout information: Take the South Canyon ramp (exit 111) off I-70. Instead of bearing right for the developed boat access here, turn left and cross the bridge. Find the wave on river left.

The Paddle

If you're looking for a bit more paddling in the Glenwood area, the South Canyon section offers another piece of quality paddling on the Colorado River just west of Glenwood Springs. As they leave the put-in, paddlers will find swift current and gentle wave trains that carry them downstream to the major whitewater of this section—South Canyon Rapid (Class II–II+). This rapid is located near mile 5 of the trip, just upstream of a bridge accessed off I-70 (exit 111). This rapid also forms a great eddy-accessed surf wave when the flow is around 2,000 cfs. Below this point, the river clips along with good eddylines and smaller waves to the takeout at the town of New Castle.

Ruby/Horsethief Canyons

The quintessential first-ever overnight river trip for many regional paddlers.

Nearest city/town: Fruita
Start: Loma Boat Ramp (N39 10.440' / W108 48.462')
End: Westwater Canyon Launch Site, Utah (N39 05.197' / W109 06.094')
Length: 25.0 miles
Difficulty rating: Beginner
Rapids: Class I-II–
River type: High-volume desert artery
Current: Moderate
Environment: Dry, sandy hills and red rock cliffs
River gradient: 7 fpm
River gauge: 2,500 to 50,000 cfs, Colorado near Colorado-Utah state line
Elevation drop: 155 feet
Hazards: Swirly eddylines can trip up open canoes.
Season: Year-round, ice-dependent
Land status: Bureau of Land Management
Boats used: Rafts, kayaks, canoes, SUPs, inflatable dinosaurs
Fees or permits: Overnight camping permits are required and can be secured within 60 days of a trip launch. During the months of May through September, there is a fee for the overnight camping permit and reservation, although children 16 years old and under

camp for free year-round. From November through April, an overnight camping permit is required; however, a fee is charged for the reservation only (there is no fee for the overnight camping permit). There is a maximum of 25 heartbeats per group, including adults, children, and dogs (two dogs per group). No permit is required for day use in Ruby/Horsethief. Use website recreation.gov to apply for permits and pay fees.
Maps: *RiverMaps, Guide to the Colorado and Green Rivers in the Canyonlands of Utah and Colorado*
Other users: Some motorized craft
Contacts: BLM/McInnis Canyons National Conservation Area (970-244-3000)
Special considerations: This section is often added on to the more whitewater-oriented Westwater Canyon below, a 17-mile day or overnighter section located entirely in Utah.
Put-in/takeout information: To reach the takeout, head west on I-70 out of the city of Grand Junction to exit 225 (Westwater) and head southwest to the boat ramp area. To reach the put-in, get back on and head east to exit 15 (Loma). Head south off the exit ramp and follow a short road to the put-in beach.

Small riffles make up the only whitewater on Ruby/Horsethief Canyons. Credit: Rob Hurst

The Paddle

Ruby/Horsethief is often the first-ever paddling experience for the next generation of young paddlers—sometimes in utero. This is not a dramatic steep-walled raging river canyon; it's more of a gentle float beneath sandstone cliff walls, with nice and open sagebrush-filled camping.

Bring the SUP or open canoe, and the little ones, on this trip! A wide-open river channel is punctuated with swift, steady current; nice eddies; and occasional waves at certain water levels. Desert enthusiasts will find good hiking up the side canyons of Rattlesnake (near mile 3.5) and Mee (near mile 14) Canyons.

The most popular overnight site is in the Black Rocks area (near mile 16). With confused currents around river-level volcanic cliffs, the Black Rocks area contains perhaps the run's most stressful features of swirly water and smaller waves.

Plateau Creek

A little gem of a Class III creek when it is flowing.

Nearest city/town: Grand Junction
Start: Mile marker 53 on Highway 65 (N39 11.334' / W108 04.922')

End: Canyon mouth on Highway 65 at exit 49 on I-70 (N39 10.990' / W108 16.860')
Length: 8.3 miles (shorter run possible)
Approximate paddling time: 2 to 3 hours

Difficulty rating: Intermediate/advanced
Rapids: Class III, IV (2 at flows above 800 cfs)
River type: Low volume, continuous
Current: Swift
Environment: Forested state highway
River gradient: 72 fpm
River gauge: 300 to 800 cfs, Plateau Creek near Cameo
Elevation drop: 594 feet
Hazards: A few low bridges, some ropes, and a cable hanging across the river can be dangerous at high flows.
Season: April through June
Land status: Colorado Parks and Wildlife, private
Boats used: Kayaks, canoes, small rafts

Fees or permits: None
Maps: Highway 65 road map
Other users: Few
Contacts: CPW Office (Grand Junction) (970-255-6100)
Special considerations: The steep, fast-flowing nature of Plateau Creek can belie its creeky character—and make it more than an intermediate paddling endeavor. Heads-up for strainers and other hazards, particularly at higher flows.
Put-in/takeout information: Use Highway 65 as the primary access route for this section. Both the put-in and takeout are well marked and easy to find. To reach Highway 65, take exit 49 off I-70 and head east toward the town of Collbran.

The Paddle

One of the largest drainages off the flat-topped Grand Mesa, Plateau Creek flows fast and continuously downhill due west until it drops into the Colorado River just upstream of Grand Junction. Entirely free-flowing and springing to life during snowmelt, the Plateau Creek Valley is a nice tucked-away area of relative tranquility set beneath dry sandstone-cliff walls.

Upper Plateau Creek

The top section, starting near mile marker 53, features more exciting Class III with a continuous feel. Expect a handful of small ledge holes and maneuvering around rocks. There is a private bridge trestle that can collect wood. Toward the end, it steepens at a shallow straightaway next to the road. A house-sized boulder on river right, with a large pullout and cottonwood tree, marks the start to the lower "Racecourse" section.

Lower Plateau Creek

This bottom section of Plateau Creek—where the creek drops steadily into a sandstone canyon—is where the intermediate paddling lies. Constant flow carries paddlers downstream before the last mile or so of the run offers up the more challenging whitewater. Below the highway bridge on the last portion of this run, the action really heats up. The whitewater climbs to good Class III, with the narrow, steeper channel presenting a risk of strainers and wood debris. Scout as best as possible while running shuttle and put in for a good little intermediate creek run to break up the drive along I-70.

13 Blue River

The swift-flowing Blue River flows out of Dillon Reservoir in the heart of Summit County. Fed from high-mountain tributaries flowing off numerous adjacent ski areas (Breckenridge, Keystone, Arapaho Basin, and Copper Mountain), the Blue fills up Dillon Reservoir and then flows downstream, making a swift journey northward before joining the Colorado River. Its rocky course is punctuated by erratic releases from Dillon and Green Mountain Dams. The dams release water from the bottom of their reservoirs, making the Blue an always cold water paddling affair.

Upper Blue River

A short but sweet burst of Class II–III rapids between Summit County and Green Mountain Reservoir.

Nearest city/town: Silverthorne
Start: Blue River Campground (N39 43.440' / W106 07.620')
End: Columbine Landing (N39 45.600' / W106 08.101')
Length: 3.0 miles
Approximate paddling time: 1 to 3 hours
Difficulty rating: Intermediate
Rapids: Class II, Class III– (Class IV– above 600 cfs)
River type: High elevation, cold mountain fishing stream
Current: Swift
Environment: Secluded, forested canyon
River gradient: 47 fpm
River gauge: 200 to 2,000 cfs, Blue River below Dillon
Elevation drop: 177 feet
Hazards: Continuous, cold water
Season: Dam controlled, April through late June
Land status: US Forest Service
Boats used: Kayaks, canoes, rafts, SUPs

Fees or permits: None
Maps: *USFS Dillon Ranger District, White River National Forest, Special Uses, Route/Use Designation Maps*
Other users: Anglers
Contacts: USFS Dillon Ranger District (970-468-5400)
Special considerations: Another possible paddle is from the town of Silverthorne to the put-in of this run (9 miles, Class I-II), with access along Highway 9. Or put in at the Columbine Landing and continue down into Green Mountain Reservoir (8 miles, Class I-II), with a takeout at the Blue River fishing access point off Highway 9.
Put-in/takeout information: To reach the takeout from Silverthorne, travel downstream (north) on Highway 9 to the well-marked Columbine Landing access point where a bridge spans the river and FR 2400 ducks off to the right. To reach the put-in, head back south on Highway 9 to Blue River Campground.

The Paddle

This section of the Blue contains the best whitewater. With Highway 9 paralleling most of the river for easy access, the Upper Blue drops down away from the road to offer a secluded, heavily wooded canyon.

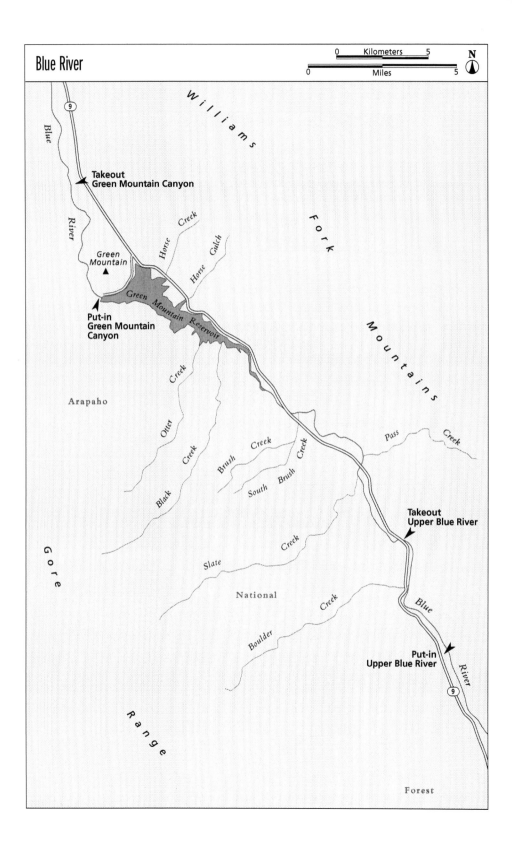

Blue River

Kilometers 5

Miles 5

N

Williams Fork Mountains

Blue River

9

Takeout
Green Mountain Canyon

Creek

Horse

Horse Gulch

Green Mountain

Green Mountain Reservoir

Put-in
Green Mountain
Canyon

Arapaho

Creek

Otter

Creek

Black

Brush

Creek

South Brush

Creek

Creek

Pass

Creek

Takeout
Upper Blue River

Slate

National

Creek

Blue

Creek

Put-in
Upper Blue River

Gore

Boulder

Range

River

9

Forest

Down here paddlers will encounter the crux whitewater of the run at Boulder Creek Rapid, which is marked by Boulder Creek tumbling into the river on river left. Paddlers who don't notice the creek come upon the rapid unexpectedly on a relatively blind corner. Below this rapid, more continuous Class II–III whitewater carries paddlers swiftly out of the canyon toward the takeout back out by the highway.

Green Mountain Canyon

A desirable day outing with better scenery than anywhere else on the Blue River.

Nearest city/town: Kremmling
Start: Below Green Mountain Dam (N39 52.686' / W106 20.041')
End: Spring Creek Bridge on 10 Road (N39 55.334' / W106 20.880')
Length: 3.8 miles
Approximate paddling time: 1 to 3 hours
Difficulty rating: Intermediate
Rapids: Class II (II+ above 800 cfs)
River type: Pool-drop, boulder garden
Current: Swift
Environment: Forested river canyon
River gradient: 50 fpm
River gauge: 300 to 10,000 cfs, Green River below Green Mountain Reservoir
Elevation drop: 321 feet
Hazards: Two fish ladders near the end of the run
Season: Late-summer/early-fall dam releases
Land status: US Forest Service
Boats used: Kayaks, canoes, rafts, SUPs, drift boats
Fees or permits: None
Maps: USFS, White River National Forest

Other users: Anglers
Contacts: White River National Forest Supervisor's Office (970-945-2521)
Special considerations: Below this takeout, the Blue River lazes 9 miles northward to its confluence with the Colorado River. This beginner section contains gentle current flowing past private ranches and farmland. Put-in is at the Spring Creek Bridge. To reach the takeout, head north on Highway 9 to County Road 1 (Trough Road) and head west. Just before crossing the Blue River, turn north on County Road 21 and use the fishing access at the confluence as a takeout.
Put-in/takeout information: To reach the takeout, head south from Kremmling or north from Silverthorne to Spring Creek Road (10 Road). Turn west and take out at the bridge over the river. The put-in is at the base of the dam on the north side of Green Mountain Reservoir off Highway 9. Turn west on Heeney Road (30 Road) and drive over the dam. The put-in is just across the dam on river left; a rope is recommended to lower boats here.

The Paddle

Once released from the bottom of Green Mountain Reservoir, the chilly water speeds along at a steady pace with tight eddies, wave trains, and a few Class II–III rapids. The biggest is called the Wall Rapid, followed by two fish ladders. It is recommended to portage the fish ladders at low water; they are easily scouted with large pools on either side but carrying on river right is best. With steep hillsides lined with pines and fir, this is a nice intermediate run with the seclusion of a pleasant river canyon.

14 Eagle River

The Eagle is a swift, free-flowing tributary to the Colorado River. Flowing westward out of Vail Valley with Interstate 70 and US Highway 6 paralleling its course, the Eagle is a lively river with a few intermediate paddling sections, but it is not a wilderness run by any means. The Eagle River is a welcome retreat from a land marked by high-speed interstates and conspicuous wealth. Busy and action packed near the top and lazy near the bottom, the Eagle has a section for both beginner and intermediate paddlers.

Gilman Gorge

The Vail-area creek boating standard, with a ghost town at the bottom!

Nearest city/town: Minturn
Start: Red Cliff suspension bridge (N39 30.459' / W106 22.690')
End: Tigawan Road/FR 707 (N39 33.133' / W106 24.323')
Length: 4.0 miles
Approximate paddling time: 1 to 3 hours
Difficulty rating: Difficult
Rapids: Class IV+ (4), Class V− at flows above 400 cfs
River type: High-mountain headwaters
Current: Swift
Environment: Designated Super Fund site
River gradient: 120 fpm
River gauge: 250 to 700 cfs, Eagle River near Minturn
Elevation drop: 459 feet
Hazards: Blast rock and man-made debris from the old Gilman mine
Season: May, June, early July
Land status: Abandoned ghost town
Boats used: Kayaks, nothing inflatable

Fees or permits: None
Maps: paddlingmaps.com
Other users: None
Contacts: southwestpaddler.com
Special considerations: Bring a camera, and plenty of time, to check out the ruins of the once-bustling Gilman mine and its surrounding ghost town—the Vail Valley's next affordable housing option? Rumor also had it that a developer wanted to build a private ski area here.
Put-in/takeout information: To get to the takeout, exit I-70 at Minturn and head south on Highway 24. Pass through Minturn and turn right (south) on Tigawan Road just outside the city limits. Follow this to a large dirt parking area on river right; this is the takeout. To reach the put-in, take Highway 24 south over Battle Mountain Pass, across the massive suspension bridge, and past the turnoff for Red Cliff. Turn right toward the river, and then left onto a small dirt road and parking area near the confluence with Homestake Creek; this is the put-in.

The Paddle

Gilman Gorge, like its neighbor the Royal Gorge on the Arkansas River, suffers from an environmental paradox. Its steep, creeky nature and dramatic, lush forested walls draw any expert river adventurer. But the remains of mining operations, including suspect-looking tailings ponds and man-made debris, litter its continuous rapids and signature drops.

Eagle River

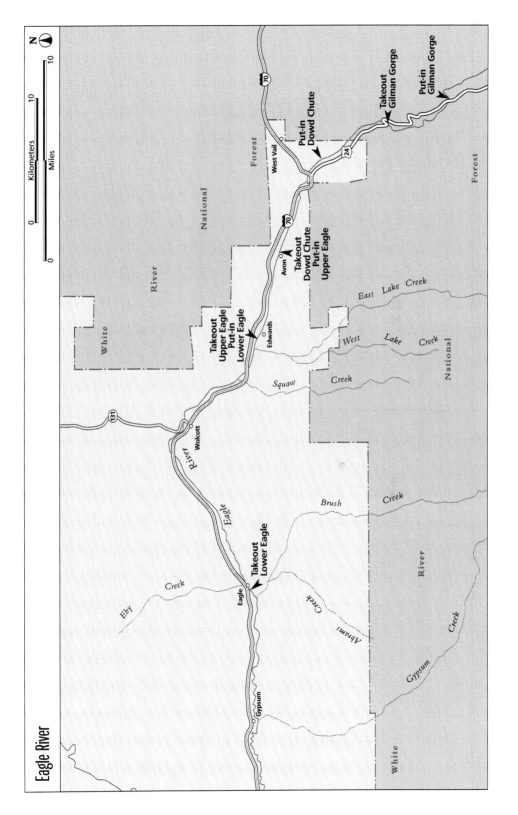

The author readies her boof stroke at Tower Rapid in Gilman Gorge. Credit: Rob Hurst

From the put-in at the confluence with Homestake Creek, also considered an area Class V classic, the seemingly small mountain stream rushes past willows before tipping into some Class III–IV read-and-run. The first rapid of note is Fall Creek (IV+), where the obvious side creek tumbles down to river level and paddlers pass under a railroad bridge. Quickly catch a small eddy on river right after a sharp right turn to scout. The rapid's crux hole maneuver can become sticky at high flows, and there is pin potential on the flat face of a postage stamp boulder in the runout. This leads into the heart of the run, a series of fun drops and slides. They are aptly named S-Turn, Mega Boof, and Tower rapids, all considered Class IV+ at most water levels. A local guide is recommended—or just scout this short action-packed section in its entirety from the mining access road.

After that, the river calms to continuous Class II until the second railroad bridge. Slurry Pipe Rapid is a difficult rapid with jagged Class V consequences. It should be scouted thoroughly from the overpass and both sides of the river, taking note of bridge pilings and rebar among a few really big holes. Boaters who wish to make this run more of a Class IV+ outing often do the easy portage here and put back in to float to the takeout just downstream.

Dowd Chute/Avon Whitewater Park

How many laps can you do?

Nearest city/town: Minturn
Start: Forest Service Visitor Center (N39 36.454' / W106 26.727')
End: Avon Whitewater Park (N39 37.938' / W106 31.323')
Length: 4.8 miles
Approximate paddling time: 1 to 3 hours, multiple laps possible
Difficulty rating: Difficult
Rapids: Class IV (1)
River type: Steep and punchy pool-drop leading into shallow, continuous Class II
Current: Swift
Environment: Roadside
River gradient: 70 fpm
River gauge: 250 to 4,000 cfs, Eagle River near Minturn
Elevation drop: 295 feet
Hazards: Fast, cold water over shallow obstacles
Season: May, June, early July
Land status: Colorado Department of Transportation, Town of Avon

Boats used: Kayaks, rafts
Fees or permits: None
Maps: "Middle Colorado and Eagle Rivers," Colorado Parks and Wildlife
Other users: Commercial rafters, anglers
Contacts: southwestpaddler.com
Special considerations: Multiple laps possible using the Eagle County bus system for shuttle!
Put-in/takeout information: Exit I-70 at Minturn (exit 171) and turn left (north) on Highway 6 toward Avon. To take out just below Dowd Chute, find the Riverbend bus stop on the right in the town of Eagle-Vail. If taking out in Avon (recommended for enjoying the surf features there), follow Highway 6 to the Avon roundabout, take the first exit toward town, then make the first right on Hurd Lane; this is the takeout. To get back to the put-in, return to Highway 6 and drive west back to Minturn. The Forest Service Visitor Center and bus stop is on the right just past the I-70 ramps; this is the put-in.

The Paddle

Another of Colorado's rivers squeezed between a railroad and highway, Dowd Chute produces a short but rowdy mile or so of Class IV whitewater. The action starts just below the put-in after the river intercepts Gore Creek flowing out of Vail and crosses under the interstate. Dowd Chute's namesake rapid produces powerful laterals and holes most paddlers prefer to miss; these holes become sticky and more consequential at flows above 1,200 cfs.

After Dowd Chute, the river widens and makes a hard right turn under a railroad bridge before another quarter mile of Class IV. Then it mellows to very continuous Class II until Avon, where the town constructed three surf features in 2006.

A group of kayakers splash through the lead-in to Dowd Chute. Credit: Rob Hurst

Upper Eagle

A fast-paced, nearly continuous section of intermediate whitewater flowing past fir trees in a heavily vegetated shallow canyon.

Nearest city/town: Avon, Edwards
Start: Avon Whitewater Park Avon Whitewater Park (N39 37.938' / W106 31.323')
End: Water treatment plant downstream of the town of Edwards (N39 38.717' / W106 35.475')
Length: 4.9 miles
Approximate paddling time: 1 to 3 hours
Difficulty rating: Intermediate
Rapids: Class III (multiple)
River type: Shallow and continuous
Current: Swift
Environment: Mountain town suburbia
River gradient: 50 fpm
River gauge: 500 to 3,000 cfs, Eagle below Wastewater Treatment Plant at Avon
Elevation drop: 250 feet
Hazards: Cold, shallow whitewater with few eddies, not suitable for beginners
Season: May, June, July
Land status: Town of Avon, Town of Edwards, private

Boats used: Kayaks, canoes, rafts
Fees or permits: None
Maps: *"Middle Colorado and Eagle Rivers," Colorado Parks and Wildlife*
Other users: Commercial rafters, anglers
Contacts: southwestpaddler.com
Special considerations: Though this run lacks many defined features or maneuvering, its cold water and continuous nature can lead to bruising swims and exhausting gear rescues.
Put-in/takeout information: The fastest route for shuttling on this run is I-70. Take exit 163 at the town of Edwards. Head south from the exit to a junction with US 6. Turn right (west) on US 6 and travel 1 mile from the lights to the next bridge over the river. Park on the north side of the river near the water treatment plant; this is the takeout. Get back on I-70 and head east to Avon (exit 167). At the roundabout, take the first exit toward town then make the first right on Hurd Lane; this is the put in.

The Paddle

The Upper Eagle between the Vail suburbs of Avon and Edwards is a local favorite—splashy, fun, and not to be taken lightly. After the Avon Whitewater park, the river tumbles downstream through a busy maze of more continuous Class III rapids. At higher flows, it's a series of crashing waves. As the water level drops a bit more, rocks poke out for good maneuvering, and eddies become more inviting.

Lower Eagle

The most popular with Vail Valley commercial raft trips, anglers, and newer paddlers.

Nearest city/town: Edwards
Start: Water treatment plant downstream of the town of Edwards (N39 38.717' / W106 35.475')

End: Chambers Park, next to the fairgrounds in the town of Eagle (N39 39.336' / W106 49.966')
Length: 15.8 miles, shorter runs possible
Approximate paddling time: 3 to 5 hours

Difficulty rating: Intermediate
Rapids: Class II–III
River type: More cold, continuous Colorado Class II
Current: Swift
Environment: Western Slope sandstone plateaus
River gradient: 36 fpm
River gauge: 700 to 5,000 cfs, Eagle River below Milk Creek near Wolcott
Elevation drop: 646 feet
Hazards: Continuous cold water flowing over shallow features
Season: Free flowing, with high-water runoff May through June; lower water levels into July and August
Land status: Town of Edwards, Town of Eagle, private
Boats used: Kayaks, canoes, rafts
Fees or permits: None
Maps: *"Middle Colorado and Eagle Rivers,"* Colorado Parks and Wildlife

Other users: Commercial rafters, anglers
Contacts: southwestpaddler.com
Special considerations: The BLM access located 0.5 mile downstream of Wolcott (I-70 exit 157) can be used as a midway access point.
Put-in/takeout information: Use US Highway 6 for the best roadside scouting along the shuttle. The small frontage highway closely parallels the river between Edwards and Avon. Those looking for a more high-speed shuttle can use I-70. Find the takeout off the Eagle exit (exit 147) at Chambers Park, near the fairgrounds on the west side of the town of Eagle. To get to the put-in, take exit 163 at the town of Edwards. Head south from the exit to a junction with US 6. Turn right (west) on US 6 and travel 1 mile from the lights to the next bridge over the river. Park on the north side of the river near the water treatment plant; this is the put in.

The Paddle

A step down in difficulty from the upstream runs, this section offers mostly Class II rapids, with a few very manageable Class IIIs thrown in. Larger rapids of note on this run include Trestle Bridge, Interstate, and Dead Cow Rapids. This popular section of the Eagle offers a quality early summer paddling experience as the river tumbles its way out of the mountains and into sandstone plateaus characteristic of the Western Slope.

15 Roaring Fork River

Tumbling off the western side of the Sawatch Mountain Range and Independence Pass through the famously ritzy mountain town of Aspen, the free-flowing Roaring Fork races 60 miles northward to its confluence with the Colorado River in the town of Glenwood Springs. Multiple quality paddling sections, good access, and a nice river valley setting combine to make the Roaring Fork River a sought-after destination for intermediate paddlers.

Slaughterhouse

The West Slope's premier Class IV slides and boulder gardens.

Nearest city/town: Aspen
Start: Henry Stein Park (N39 12.716' / W106 50.407')
End: Upper Woody Creek Bridge (N39 15.412' / W106 52.881')
Length: 4.5 miles
Approximate paddling time: 1.5 to 3 hours, depending on how much downriver play your party prefers
Difficulty rating: Advanced/expert
Rapids: Class IV (3), Class IV–V– at flows above 2,500 cfs
River type: Channelized boulder garden
Current: Swift
Environment: Rich and famous high-alpine forest
River gradient: 80 fpm
River gauge: Roaring Fork River below Maroon Creek near Aspen
Elevation drop: 308.5 feet
Hazards: Potential for early-season and post-flood wood
Season: May through July
Land status: Mostly private, though the Rio Grande trail runs along the river-right bank most of the way before veering away from the river toward the end of the run
Boats used: Kayaks, decked canoes, rafts
Fees or permits: None
Maps: *National Geographic, Roaring Fork and Fryingpan Rivers*
Other users: Commercial rafters

Contacts: Aspen Kayak and SUP (970-618-2295)
Special considerations: Optional for Class V crews: If Slaughterhouse is running about 1,000 cfs or better, put in on Castle Creek, one of the Roaring Fork's tiny but significant tributaries. From the roundabout west of town, drive south on Castle Creek Road (the road up to Aspen Highlands ski resort), turn left after 1 mile, and park in one of the lower lots of the Aspen Music School. Then enjoy a steep, twisting tour of multimillion-dollar mansions and their associated backyard art. Creeky in nature and fairly continuous, numerous well-defined eddies make for efficient boat scouting; be discrete if you must step out for a quick look or portage new wood. As with all Colorado creeks, take care in times of muddy water and recent floods. When you float under the Highway 82 bridge just outside town, you'll soon be at the confluence with the Roaring Fork.
Put-in/takeout information: Take the Woody Creek Canyon exit off Highway 82 about 7 miles south of Aspen. Park at large dirt pulloff on river right known as Wilton Jaffe Senior Park, just downstream of Upper Woody Creek Bridge; this is the takeout. To get to the put-in, return to the town of Aspen on Highway 82, turn right (north) on Cemetery Lane, and follow it over the speed bumps to a small park. This road can also be used to connect the two access points.

Dropping in to Slaughterhouse Falls at low water. Credit: Rob Hurst

The Paddle

Channelized and technical, this paddles much like the Numbers section of the Arkansas just on the other side of Independence Pass. Despite its east-slope counterpart stealing most of its flow (see "Colorado the Wild West of Water Rights," pages 61–64), Slaughterhouse is a little steeper, and more channelized, which make for a juicier feel with similar volume. A quick 90-minute drive over one of the country's most scenic high-mountain passes separates the two after Memorial Day when the road is open, which makes this run a necessary stop on any spring Colorado paddling trip. That would also be the time to catch its short runnable window, due to the abovementioned diversion of the Roaring Fork headwaters after July 1. The highlight is the slidey, 6-foot Slaughterhouse Falls (Class IV) about a half mile in. Before that, eddy-hop through Entrance Exam (Class IV), which starts about 200 yards down from the put-in, and have a scout of the falls from river right. Run just left of center at low to medium flows, hitting the "V" in current over this riverwide bedrock ledge. At higher flows consider a far-right line under the branches. Afterward, bebop down S-Turn, the longest rapid of the run. Next is Triple Drop, which has a sticky hole at the bottom river-center. Then take out at Upper Woody Creek.

Roaring Fork River

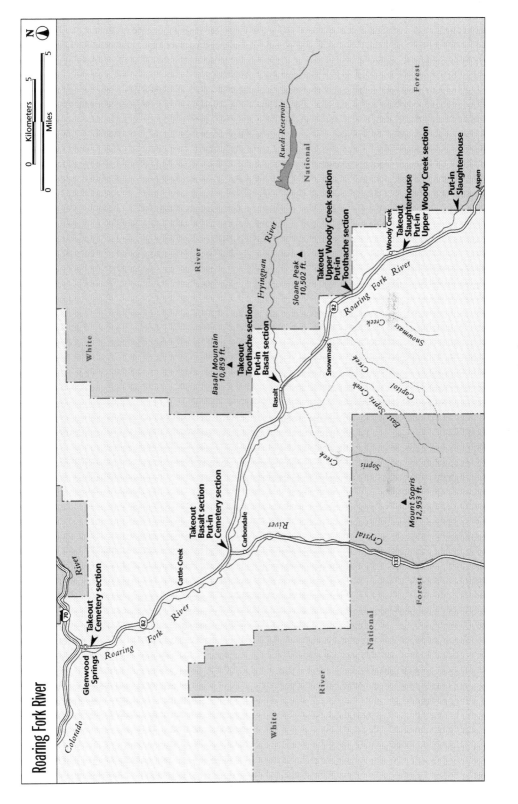

Upper Woody Creek Section

Strong intermediate territory, more for its fast pace than for its technical difficulty or individual rapids.

Nearest city/town: Aspen
Start: Upper Woody Creek Bridge (N39 15.412' / W106 52.881')
End: Lower Woody Creek Bridge (N39 17.890' / W106 55.322')
Length: 4.0 miles
Approximate paddling time: 1 to 2 hours
Difficulty rating: Intermediate
Rapids: Class III (multiple)
River type: Continuous, shallow mountain stream
Current: Swift
Environment: Populated high-alpine forest
River gradient: 62 fpm
River gauge: 200 to 1,400 cfs, Roaring Fork below Maroon Creek near Aspen
Elevation drop: 236 feet
Hazards: Deceptively continuous, cold whitewater
Season: May through July
Land status: Private, Woody Creek town
Boats used: Rafts, kayaks, canoes, SUPs

Fees or permits: None
Maps: *National Geographic, Roaring Fork and Fryingpan Rivers*
Other users: Commercial rafters, anglers
Contacts: Aspen Kayak and SUP (970-618-2295)
Special considerations: Take out at Lower Woody Creek Bridge in its namesake town with its namesake tavern—the famous watering hole of the late Hunter S. Thompson, who was known to carouse, and write, in the Aspen area.
Put-in/takeout information: Use 17 Road, also known as Upper River Road, on river right to avoid highway traffic. The takeout is at the 16 Road bridge off Highway 82 at Old Snowmass near mile marker 27.5. To reach the put-in, return upstream on 17 Road. Drive through the trailer park community of Woody Creek and park in the large dirt pulloff on river right known as Wilton Jaffe Senior Park, just downstream of Upper Woody Creek Bridge; this is the put-in.

The Paddle

This section of the Roaring Fork churns downstream on a steady, continuous course through Class II–III whitewater. Though it is often considered the easiest section of the Roaring Fork, Upper Woody Creek is fast, cold, and shallow. Locals love it for high-water springtime romps, or for its defined eddies at low to medium flows, and often consider it the Aspen area "beginner" run.

Lower Woody Creek/Toothache

A quick, blast-downstream run.

Nearest city/town: Basalt
Start: Lower Woody Creek Bridge (N39 17.890' / W106 55.322')
End: Highway 82 Bridge at mile marker 25 (N39 20.552' / W107 00.379')

Length: 6.2 miles
Approximate paddling time: 2 to 3 hours
Difficulty rating: Intermediate
Rapids: Class III (multiple)

River type: Continuous, shallow mountain stream
Current: Swift
Environment: Populated high-alpine forest
River gradient: 59 fpm, 88 fpm at Toothache rapid
River gauge: 200 to 1,400 cfs, Roaring Fork below Maroon Creek near Aspen
Elevation drop: 370 feet
Hazards: Some continuous, technical whitewater
Season: May through July
Land status: Private, town owned
Boats used: Kayaks, rafts, canoes, SUPs (?)
Fees or permits: None
Maps: *National Geographic, Roaring Fork and Fryingpan Rivers*

Other users: Commercial rafters, anglers
Contacts: Aspen Kayak and SUP (970-618-2295)
Special considerations: Study the local Roaring Fork Transit Authority bus schedule for a possible shuttle option
Put-in/takeout information: Use Highway 82 for shuttle, which offers glimpses of the river for en-route scouting. Find the Highway 82 bridge over the river near mile marker 25; this is the takeout, also known as Wingo Junction river access. To reach the put-in, head southeast on Highway 82 toward Aspen and turn left on Gerbaz Way. Park at the road bridge (Lower Woody Creek Bridge); this is the put-in.

The Paddle

The name Toothache comes from the largest rapid on this run: Toothache Rapid (Class III). This section of river flows into Woody Creek Canyon, and a series of Class III wave trains fill the heart of the run. Toothache is the largest of the straight-forward waves.

Cemetery Section

The lowest section of the Roaring Fork with the longest season and most reliable flows.

Nearest city/town: Glenwood Springs
Start: Highway 133 bridge in Carbondale (N39 28.812' / W1078 17.219')
End: Veltus Park (N39 32.693' / W107 19.874')
Length: 6.2 miles
Approximate paddling time: 2 to 3 hours
Difficulty rating: Advanced beginner/intermediate
Rapids: Class III (1), Class II (multiple)
River type: Continuous, shallow mountain stream
Current: Swift
Environment: Mountain-town suburbia
River gradient: 29 fpm
River gauge: 450 to 5,000 cfs, Roaring Fork at Glenwood Springs

Elevation drop: 140 feet
Hazards: Eddyline at the confluence is a guaranteed flip for new kayakers.
Season: April through August, fall when the Fryingpan is releasing for fish habitat
Land status: Private and city-managed
Boats used: Rafts, kayaks, canoes, SUPs
Fees or permits: None
Maps: *National Geographic, Roaring Fork and Fryingpan Rivers*
Other users: Commercial rafters, anglers
Contacts: Aspen Kayak and SUP (970-618-2295)
Special considerations: The 12 miles upstream of here, between Basalt and Carbondale, is also a runnable, mostly continuous Class II section. Put in at the Highway 82

bridge (the takeout for the Lower Woody Creek section) and take out at the bridge in Carbondale. There is a man-made whitewater park in Basalt, constructed in the late 20-teens, that has been known to produce some raft-flipping holes at high flows.

Put-in/takeout information: To reach the takeout, take Highway 82 into Glenwood Springs. Once in town, Highway 82 becomes Grand Avenue. Turn west onto Eighth Street, cross the river, and then turn left (south) and drive for one block to Veltus Park. To reach the put-in, turn south onto Highway 133 from Highway 82, heading into Carbondale. The immediate bridge across the river is the put-in. A midway access point can be used at the Iron Bridge (at the 6-mile point of the run), just below Highway 82. Down to this bridge is excellent beginner paddling (Class I–II). Another possible downstream takeout is located below the confluence with the Colorado River at Two Rivers Park on river right.

The Paddle

Set beneath the beautiful Mount Sopris and collecting the Crystal River at its confluence just below the put-in, this lowest section typically has the most volume and gentle whitewater of the Roaring Fork Valley. It is the most suitable section for beginner kayakers and rafters or for SUPers.

The gradient drops down as the river flows through private ranches and open farmland on both sides of the river. As it approaches its confluence with the Colorado, the Roaring Fork makes a final flexing of its whitewater muscles at Cemetery Rapid—0.25 mile of Class II–II+ whitewater. Below this rapid, paddlers enter the backstreets of Glenwood Springs.

16 Crystal River

The Crystal tumbles out of the West Elk Mountains hard and fast and, yes, crystal clear. The headwaters of the Crystal rip through some of the most committing and expert-only gorges in the whole state. The midreaches of the Crystal create a technical onslaught of challenging advanced/expert-level whitewater.

It is in the lower reaches that intermediate paddlers will find fitting sections on the Crystal. Flowing northward around the western flank of towering Mount Sopris, the Crystal is paralleled by Highway 133, which offers mostly unobstructed views of the riverbed and the majority of the rapids through this pristine river canyon.

Avalanche Section

The first easier section below the tumultuous upstream runs, while still offering a canyonlike setting.

Nearest city/town: Carbondale
Start: Avalanche Creek pullout (N39 15.249' / W107 14.044')
End: BRB Campground (N39 19.102' / W107 12.592')
Length: 5.1 miles
Approximate paddling time: 1 to 2 hours
Difficulty rating: Intermediate
Rapids: Class III (1)
River type: Fast, cold mountain stream
Current: Swift
Environment: Scenic canyon
River gradient: 64 fpm
River gauge: 500 to 3,000 cfs, Crystal River above Avalanche Creek, near Redstone
Elevation drop: 325 feet
Hazards: Continuous, cold whitewater; constant potential for wood
Season: May through August
Land status: USFS (upper reaches), highway, and private
Boats used: Kayaks, canoes, rafts
Fees or permits: None
Maps: *White River National Forest*
Other users: Anglers

Contacts: Glenwood Area Boaters Facebook page
Special considerations: The two river miles upstream of here include the doable-at-average-flows Class IV Narrows section, with the zero-margin-for-error Meatgrinder (Class V) above that. Scout these from the highway for kicks or put in higher up to add these rapids. The Narrows is a quarter mile of steep, shallow, rocky whitewater that's not a place to be upside down in a kayak. It requires at least 500 cfs, it becomes Class IV at about 600, and it's considered a V– at flows above 1,000—swims here are ugly with the potential for getting trapped in a sieve or undercut.
Put-in/takeout information: Highway 133 provides a quick, easy shuttle as well as scouting opportunities while shuttling. Parking for the takeout is just off Highway 133 near mile marker 62, at a road intersection upstream of the KOA; the campground owners have asked that boaters park/access the river here rather than on their property. Find the Avalanche Creek pulloff on the east side of the highway near mile marker 57; this is the put-in.

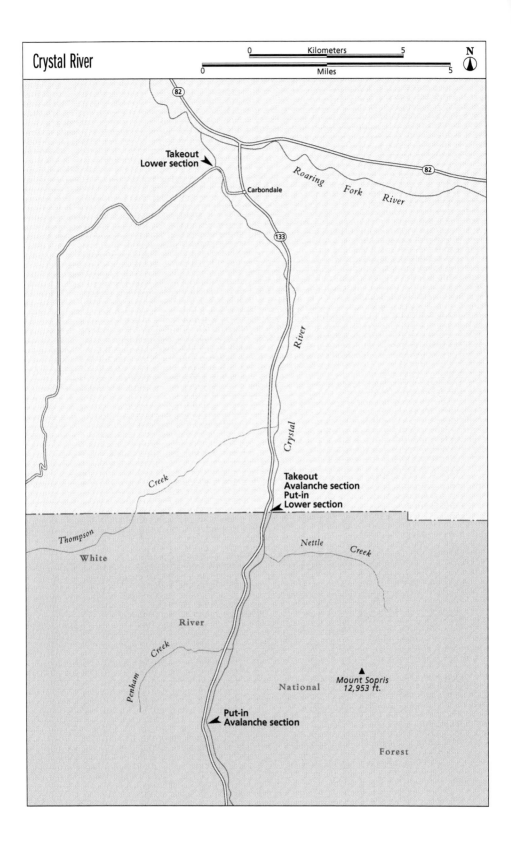

Crystal River

N

0 Kilometers 5
0 Miles 5

82

Takeout
Lower section

Carbondale

Roaring Fork River

82

133

River

Crystal

Creek

Takeout
Avalanche section
Put-in
Lower section

Thompson

White

Nettle Creek

River

Penham Creek

National

Mount Sopris
12,953 ft.

Put-in
Avalanche section

Forest

The Paddle

Semicontinuous, mellow whitewater continues to wind through the picturesque Crystal Valley along Highway 133. Like most of Colorado's high-alpine runs that are considered Class III, this one can require Class IV awareness with fast, cold water; shallow rapids; and few eddies. It also requires navigating a few braided channels with wood that moves around. There are several bridges to gated communities; when you see one, expect a rapid. "The Big One" (Class III) is about midway through—a narrow chute with large straightforward waves. The scenery here makes nearby Roaring Fork seem almost urban in comparison, which makes for a nice afternoon paddle or advanced beginner training session—for those with a reliable whitewater roll.

Lower Crystal

The Crystal's easiest paddling, best for SUPs.

Nearest city/town: Carbondale
Start: BRB Campground (N39 19.102' / W107 12.592')
End: Bridge over the Crystal River next to the Colorado Rocky Mountain School (N39 24.480' / W107 13.767')
Length: 8.3 miles
Approximate paddling time: 2 to 3 hours
Difficulty rating: Advanced beginner/ intermediate
Rapids: Class II+
River type: Continuous, cold water mountain stream
Current: Swift
Environment: Rural mountain valley
River gradient: 39 fpm
River gauge: 300 to 1,000 cfs, Crystal River above Avalanche Creek, near Redstone
Elevation drop: 38.7 feet
Hazards: Shallow, sharp rocks and cold water
Season: May through early July
Land status: Mostly private

Boats used: Kayaks, canoes, rafts, SUPs
Fees or permits: None
Maps: Carbondale town
Other users: Anglers, teenage slalom boaters practicing on the CRMS gates
Contacts: Colorado Rocky Mountain School (970-963-2562); Glenwood Area Paddlers Facebook group
Special considerations: Consider adding the Cemetery section of the Roaring Fork for more Class II action.
Put-in/takeout information: In the quaint mountain town of Carbondale, turn west on Main Street (Colorado 106) at the roundabout by 7-Eleven. Follow this to the river and bear left (west) on Colorado 108 and park at the bridge over the Crystal; this is the takeout. To get to the put-in, return to Highway 133 and drive south about 7 miles to the Avalanche pulloff on the west side of the road just upstream of the KOA.

The Paddle

From the canyon mouth down to the confluence with the Roaring Fork River next to Carbondale, the river meanders with steady current through open pastureland and past ranches. Use caution passing underneath numerous bridges, and dodge flying golf balls around the River Valley Ranch Course. High water forms eddyless action. Catch views of 12,000-foot Mount Sopris, often snowcapped during the Crystal's paddling season. This is the area's ultimate beginner section, and it's best for SUPs.

17 Taylor River

Dam controlled and flowing out of Taylor Park Reservoir, the Taylor begins its southwestern route toward the East River by dropping through a pleasant pine- and fir-forested canyon while dancing around numerous granite boulders and rocks. The overall nature of the Taylor is of a swift-flowing technical river that is fairly straightforward and forgiving. A rural Forest Service road parallels the entire river to allow for easy access and scouting.

The Taylor was a semi-secluded little river until the state finished paving Cottonwood Pass in 2019, rerouting the highway's hairpins to better accommodate mondo luxury RVs and toy haulers. Still, its scenic canyon, busy but forgiving whitewater, easy access, and abundant camping are sought after by advanced beginner/intermediate travelers and locals alike.

The Taylor River and its canyon are treasured for whitewater goods and, like most other high-elevation, cold water mountain streams, supreme trout habitat. It has a storied history of run-ins with hostile locals, mostly the owners of private fishing lodges looking to keep boaters from disturbing the fish, or their affluent guests. Still, it maintains a small commercial rafting industry and local paddling scene. Catch the Western State paddling club here on summer evenings for Taylor Tuesdays.

Taylor Canyon

Colorado NIMBY ("not in my backyard") boating at its finest.

Nearest city/town: Almont, Buena Vista
Start: Upper Taylor commercial raft put-in (N38 44.935' / W106 42.169')
End: South Bank River Access (N38 43.530' / W106 46.161')
Length: 5.2 miles
Approximate paddling time: 2 to 3 hours
Difficulty rating: Intermediate
Rapids: Class III
River type: Granite boulder garden
Current: Swift
Environment: Fir-lined mountain canyon
Hazards: Strainers
Season: May through July, dam controlled
Land status: Bureau of Land Management, private
Boats used: Kayaks, rafts
Fees or permits: None
Maps: *Gunnison National Forest*

Other users: Anglers
Contacts: BLM Gunnison Field Office (970-641-4435)
Special considerations: For those looking for a little more action on this section, put in a little higher at the old New Generation river access. Here you will find the Slot, the only drop considered Class IV on this run. The "Middle Taylor" refers to the 2.5 miles between here and 5-Mile Bridge. This section is generally regarded as not suitable for beginner/intermediate paddlers due to man-made obstructions and access issues—the surrounding private property makes rescue difficult.
Put-in/takeout information: For an easy, quick shuttle and scouting opportunities while shuttling, use Forest Service Road 742. If you're coming from Crested Butte, use the Jack's Cabin Road off Highway 135.

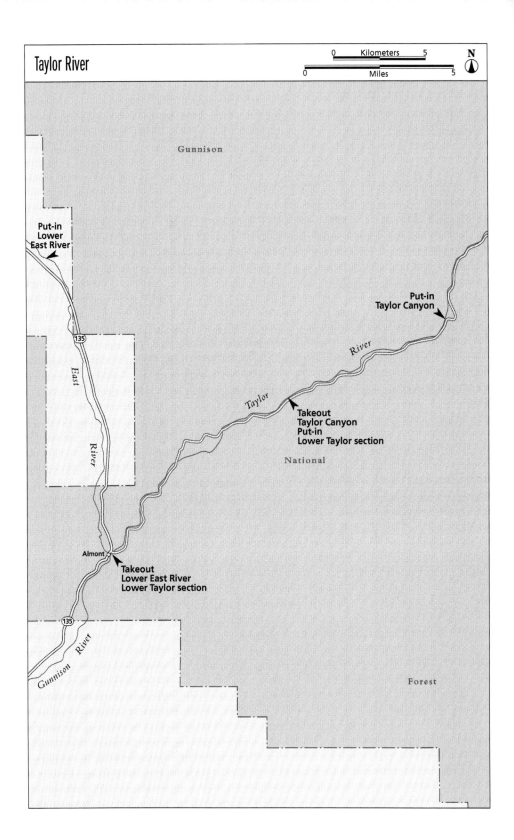

Taylor River

0 Kilometers 5
0 Miles 5
N

Gunnison

Put-in
Lower
East River

Put-in
Taylor Canyon

River

Taylor

Takeout
Taylor Canyon
Put-in
Lower Taylor section

National

East

River

135

Almont

Takeout
Lower East River
Lower Taylor section

135

Gunnison River

Forest

Scenery and wave trains abound on the Lower Taylor. Credit: Kit Davidson

The Paddle

This section of the Taylor is considered to be the uppermost intermediate run below the upstream reservoir. It drops through a narrow and pretty roadside canyon with a storied history of landowners (mostly private fishing lodges) versus boaters. Just below the put-in, the river flows over several ledges that form waves at high water at Initiation rapid (Class III). After that, some surf waves appear at certain levels. Large boulders occasionally choke the granite riverbed, requiring Class III maneuvering. Heads-up for wood, old and new, including the possibility of riverwide fir trees.

The remaining rapids include Toilet Bowl and Tombstone (both Class III). Because of its dam-controlled releases, shady canyon, and slightly higher elevation, water temperatures on this section can be quite chilly, even in summer.

Lower Taylor Section

An advanced beginner paradise of shallow canyon boulder gardens and Class II wave trains.

Nearest city/town: Almont
Start: Five-Mile Bridge (N38 43.53' / W106 46.161')
End: Confluence access point at Almont (N38 39.851' / W106 50.775')
Length: 5.0 miles
Approximate paddling time: 2 to 3 hours

Difficulty rating: Beginner kayaks, canoes, or raft; intermediate river SUP
Rapids: Class II
River type: Continuous, cold high-mountain stream
Current: Swift
Environment: Wide, forested valley

River gradient: 68 fpm
River gauge: 300 to 800 cfs, Taylor at Almont
Elevation Drop: 337 feet
Hazards: Few
Season: May through July, dam controlled
Land status: US Forest Service, Bureau of Land Management, private
Boats used: Kayaks, rafts, canoes, SUPs
Fees or permits: None
Maps: *Gunnison National Forest*
Other users: Kids splashing each other in commercial rafts, anglers
Contacts: US Forest Service, Gunnison National Forest (970-874-6600)

Special considerations: The place for area family floating, advanced beginner/intermediate SUPers, and teaching your significant other to whitewater kayak.

Put-in/takeout information: To reach the takeout, take FSR 742 to the junction with Highway 135 and turn left (south) onto Highway 135. Go a short distance and cross the bridge over the East River. Pull into the parking lot on the east side of the highway at the confluence of the East and Taylor Rivers. To get to the put-in, go upriver on FSR 742 to the well-marked Five-Mile access on river right.

The Paddle

This lower section of Taylor begins settling down as the river exits its upstream canyon. Still cold and swift water flows into mostly Class II wave trains as the granite walls open just below the put-in. Roadside access and easier rapids make this section a great learning section set in a pleasant valley—an intermediate whitewater SUPer's delight!

18 Gunnison River

Formed by the confluence of the Taylor and East Rivers just above the Western-flavored town of Gunnison, the Gunnison River begins a sweeping—and dam-filled—course in a northwesterly direction across the Western Slope before joining the Colorado River in Grand Junction (named because of the confluence of these rivers). The Gunnison springs to life for a few miles of beginner-level paddling before falling into the backwaters of Blue Mesa Reservoir, followed by Morrow Point Reservoir, and finally Crystal Reservoir.

Below here the Gunnison tumbles through the dramatic and expert-only Black Canyon of the Gunnison National Monument. As the Gunny eases out of the "Montrose Box," it courses through the intermediate, often overnighted, section known as Gunnison Gorge and finally tapers down through beginner-friendly open farmlands and low-walled sandstone canyons as it flows north toward the Colorado River.

Confluence-Down

A cruisy, nontechnical open-valley paddle.

Nearest city/town: Gunnison
Start: Three Rivers Confluence at Almont (N38 39.804' / W106 50.821')
End: Shady Island River Park (N38 34.976' / W106 55.227')
Length: 5.0 miles
Approximate paddling time: 2 to 3 hours
Difficulty rating: Beginner
Rapids: Class II
River type: Wide and channelized
Current: Swift
Environment: Rural valley
River gradient: 45 fpm
River gauge: 500 to 3,000 cfs, Gunnison River near Gunnison
Elevation drop: 243 feet
Hazards: Some small whitewater features, mostly formed by man-made materials

Season: April through September
Land status: Gunnison County, Colorado Department of Transportation
Boats used: Kayaks, canoes, rafts, SUPs, drift boats
Fees or permits: None
Maps: Colorado Department of Transportation
Other users: Anglers
Contacts: southwestpaddler.com
Special considerations: Long season
Put-in/takeout information: To reach the takeout, head north out of Gunnison on Highway 135. Shady Island is on river right, just after the highway crosses the river and past Garlic Mike's restaurant. Continue north to the town of Almont to find the put-in on river right just downstream of a highway bridge.

The Paddle

Gentle and steady current pushes paddlers past tall cottonwoods, willows, and open ranchlands. This section is mostly away from roads, and even with numerous homes along the banks, it has a pleasant and lazy rural feel.

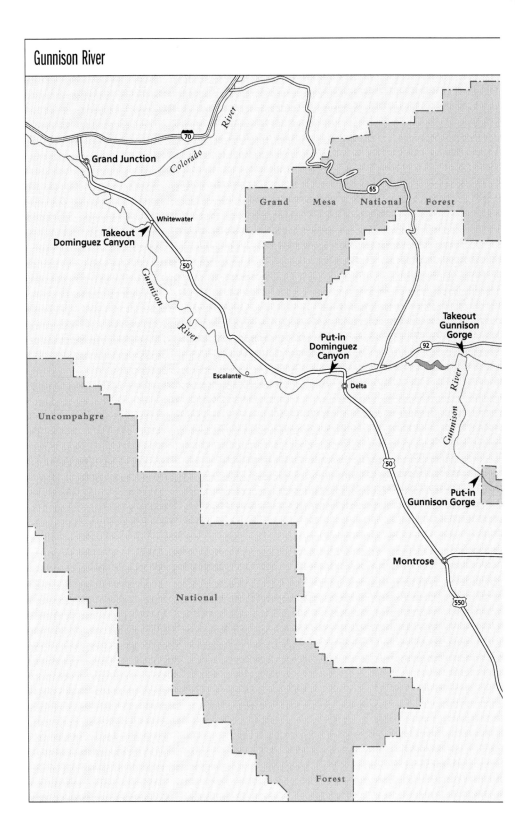

Gunnison River

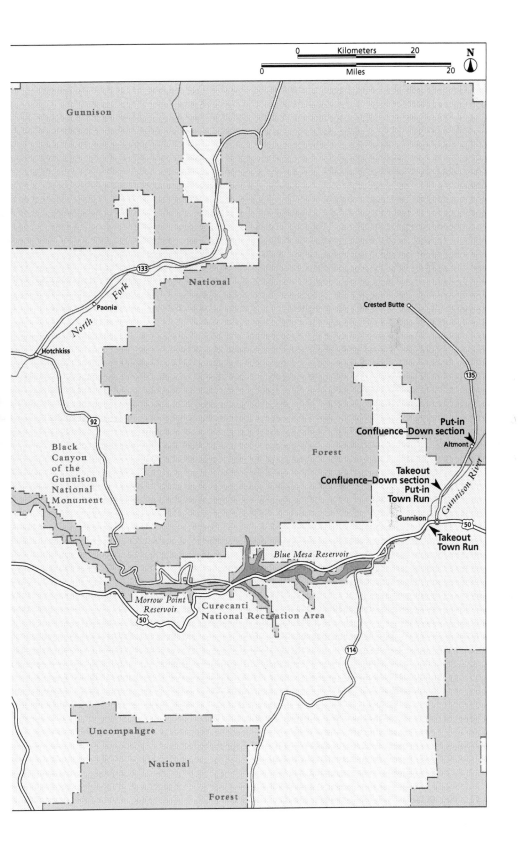

Scenic SUPing on the Gunnison River. Credit: Rob Hurst

Consider extending the run by a few miles of mostly flatwater to take out in Gunnison Whitewater Park, a series of ledgy man-made features for surfing or ferry practice or driving down to find the park-and-play about a mile west of town. Though the Confluence-Down section enjoys a long season, the whitewater park is best enjoyed at flows above 600 cfs. Access the whitewater park by turning south off Highway 50 where it meets County Road 38; it is well-signed.

Gunny Town/Gunnison Whitewater Park

Locals' best after-work run or surf session.

Nearest city/town: Gunnison
Start: Gunnison Whitewater Park (N38 31.954' / W106 56.980')
End: McCabe's Lane (N38 31.056' / W106 59.697')
Length: 4.0 miles

Approximate paddling time: 1 to 2 hours, or one golden hour surf sesh
Difficulty rating: Beginner
Rapids: Class II (3)
River type: Man-made
Current: Swift
Environment: Urban

River gradient: 25 fpm
River gauge: 600 to 5,000 cfs, Gunnison River near Gunnison
Elevation drop: 100 feet
Hazards: Swirly eddylines and monstrous surf holes at high water
Season: April through September
Land status: Gunnison Town
Boats used: Kayaks, canoes, rafts, SUPs
Fees or permits: None
Maps: Gunnison County
Other users: Commercial rafters, anglers, tubers on hot summer days

Contacts: Gunnison Crested Butte Tourism and Prosperity Partnership, gunnisoncrested butte.com
Special considerations: For prime area flows and party vibes, come for the Gunnison River Festival held mid-June each year.
Put-in/takeout information: To reach the take-out, drive west out of Gunnison on US 50. Turn left (south) on McCabe's Lane just past Mesa Campground. Follow this for a quarter mile and park at the picnic area. To get back to the put-in, return to Highway 50 east and go back through the town of Gunnison to the whitewater park.

The Paddle

With the exception of the whitewater park, and its downstream brother Psychedelic Falls, this section is another cruisey beginner run away from the road and passes more ranches and farmlands. Swift current and occasional riffles create a quick get-out-on-the-water experience.

About a quarter mile below the playpark, a poorly built diversion dam forms a three-tiered drop known as Psychedelic Falls—take the right slot, or expect a mind-altering experience on what is otherwise a Class I–II run.

Gunnison Gorge

A fun whitewater float with all the trimmings of a classic Colorado boating and camping adventure.

Nearest city/town: Delta
Start: Chukar Trail (N38 37.318' / W107 49.859')
End: Pleasure Park, near the town of Hotchkiss at the North Fork confluence (N38 47.040' / W107 50.281')
Length: 13.5 miles
Approximate paddling time: 1 to 2 days
Difficulty rating: Intermediate
Rapids: Class III–III+
River type: Walled-in, pool-drop whitewater
Current: Swift
Environment: High desert canyon
River gradient: 21 fpm
River gauge: 300 to 15,000 cfs, Gunnison River below Gunnison Tunnel
Elevation drop: 289 feet

Hazards: approaches Class IV at flows above 3,500 cfs
Season: April through October
Land status: Bureau of Land Management
Boats used: Kayaks, rafts, canoes, packrafts make the hike in easy!
Fees or permits: Pay user fee and self-register for BLM campsites at the put-in
Maps: *Gunnison Gorge, National Conservation Area and Wilderness*
Other users: Anglers, float and wade; a few commercial rafters
Contacts: BLM, Gunnison Gorge National Conservation Area (970-240-5300)
Special considerations: If you use the Pleasure Park outfitter for shuttle, you'll be drinking beer at their bar at the takeout instead of

Wishful thinking? The author after hauling her own stuff to the bottom of Gunnison Gorge for a self-support kayak trip. Credit: Brandon Slate

driving back up. Call them at (970-872-2525) to arrange. While you're at it, call Larry Franks at J and Ray Outfitters in Montrose, (970-323-0115), (jandrayoutfitters.com), to inquire about a horse-pack for the put-in trail.

Put-in/takeout information: The takeout is at Pleasure Park, which is located off Highway 92 approximately 6 miles west of the town of Hotchkiss. Turn south at the sign for Forks of the Gunnison and continue for 1 mile to the

Gunnison River Pleasure Park takeout area. To reach the put-in, drive north on US 50 approximately 9 miles out of the town of Montrose to Falcon Road. Turn right (east) and continue for 4 miles until Falcon Road becomes Peach Valley Road. Follow Peach Valley Road for approximately 10 miles (can be rough dirt/mud when wet) to a BLM picnic/campground at the Chukar trailhead; this is the put-in.

The Paddle

Downstream a ways below the numerous dams and tumultuous Black Canyon, the Gunnison Gorge has it all. A dusty, western-clay-laden access road becomes a slip-n-slide after summer storms. It's a brutal hike in. Manageable canyon whitewater is runnable at surprisingly low flows and reaches broiling, frothy Class IV at high water (3,500 cfs and above). A long day trip, it's best enjoyed as a leisurely overnight.

The biggest challenge may be humping your gear down the 1.5-mile Chukar Trail to the water. Gunny Gorge veterans have breakdown frames and small rafts with backpack straps designed specifically for this purpose. It's also the perfect place to tweak your self-support kayak and carry system before taking on the Class V rapids and portages of the Black Canyon. There is one outfitter permitted to horse-and-mule-pack gear down the steep, rocky trail, for a small fee—totally worth it for large parties or lavish raft expeditions.

Once at the river, steep and arid canyon walls frame pool-drop, technical, intermediate whitewater throughout most of the gorge. Abrupt horizon lines give way to large rocks to maneuver around and good recovery pools at the bottom of most drops. The crux is found between the Squeeze and the Narrows Rapids as the river cuts through a short dark-colored box canyon. This remote and isolated gorge is home to numerous deer, mountain sheep, beavers, golden and bald eagles, red-tailed hawks, and peregrine falcons. River otters have been spotted here, and countless migratory birds briefly land in the gorge in the shoulder seasons. The waters host a healthy population of trout (browns, cutthroats, and rainbows), and many float fishermen make an enjoyable two-day descent of the gorge.

North Fork of the Gunnison (and Anthracite Creek)

For those who have wondered about the industrial-looking mediocre stretch of whitewater below Paonia Reservoir while driving Highway 133.

Nearest city/town: Paonia
Start: Below Paonia Reservoir (N38 56.387' / W107 21.540')
End: Below Somerset (N38 55.638' / W107 28.621')
Length: 7.2 miles
Approximate paddling time: 2 to 3 hours
Difficulty rating: Intermediate/advanced
Rapids: Class III, IV– above 2,000 cfs
River type: Small, boulder-strewn streambed
Current: Swift
Environment: Run-down mine remains
River gradient: 41 fpm
River gauge: 600 to 10,000 cfs, North Fork Gunnison River near Somerset
Elevation drop: 360 feet
Hazards: Weirs and other man-made obstructions
Season: April through June
Land status: Colorado Department of Transportation

Boats used: Kayaks, canoes, small rafts
Fees or permits: None
Maps: *National Geographic: Kebler Pass, Paonia Reservoir*
Other users: Few
Contacts: southwestpaddler.com
Special considerations: Combine this run with Anthracite Creek, putting in below Erickson springs (the traditional takeout for the Class V hair boating stretch above). Check out another beginner-level section of paddling on the Gunnison just downstream of this takeout. There's an intermediate-level put-in in the town of Somerset (an additional 5 miles).
Put-in/takeout information: From Paonia, head north on State Highway 133. The takeout is about 8 miles north of town. To get to the put-in, return to Highway 133 north and drive about 6 more miles. Turn right (east) on County Road 12; the put-in is off this road near the highway.

Floating through the old mining equipment near the town of Somerset on the North Fork Gunnison. Credit: Kit Davidson

The Paddle

The North Fork Gunnison is included more for novelty's sake than for its quality whitewater. Here the river is swift and free flowing through the small mining town of Somerset. It offers fairly continuous shallow current through a small riverbed. If it's high and muddy, while otherwise driving Highway 133 through western Colorado, it may be worth a stop.

Because of its free-flowing nature, it is more challenging with higher early season runoff and tapers down to mellow creeking as the water level drops later in the summer. A small drainage, the North Fork dries up and is too low for paddling by mid- to late summer.

Dominguez Canyon

The Grand Junction–area family desert float. Dogs allowed!

Nearest city/town: Grand Junction
Start: Escalante Boat Launch (N38 45.482' / W108 14.480')

End: Highway 141 bridge in the town of Whitewater (N38 58.287' / W108 27.235')
Length: 29.0 miles (longer or shorter run possible)

Approximate paddling time: 2 to 3 days
Difficulty rating: Beginner
Rapids: Class I–II–
River type: Silty western artery
Current: Moderate
Environment: Desert
River gradient: 6 fpm
River gauge: 800 to 20,000 cfs, Gunnison River near Grand Junction
Elevation drop: 155 feet
Hazards: The no-see-ums can be brutal.
Season: March through October; possibly year-round
Land status: Bureau of Land Management, Mesa County, private
Boats used: Kayaks, rafts, canoes, SUPs
Fees or permits: Free, self-issue BLM permit at the Escalante launch or Bridgeport
Maps: *BLM Dominguez-Escalante National Conservation Area*

Other users: Migrating Canada geese
Contacts: Dominguez-Escalante National Conservation Area (970-244-3300); gjfo_webmail@blm.gov
Special considerations: To lengthen the trip, launch at Confluence Park in the town of Delta (44 total miles; fill out a permit at Escalante while running shuttle). Shorten it to a long single-day float by launching in Bridgeport (14 miles to Whitewater), a narrow boat ramp and access trail best suited for small craft.
Put-in/Takeout information: Find the takeout about 10 miles south of Grand Junction by driving US 50 to the little town of Whitewater. Turn west on Highway 141 and follow it to the bridge over the river; this is the takeout. The put-in is 10 miles north of Delta on US 50. Turn west at the BLM sign for Escalante Area and continue down a dirt road for 3 miles to the bridge across the river; this is the put-in.

The Paddle

This last "wilderness" section of the Gunnison starts with open ranchland before dropping away from most forms of civilization into an 800-foot-deep sandstone-walled canyon with red rock formations. Down here the Gunnison offers up relatively remote (a railroad parallels the river) beginner paddling with swift water, but there're no real rapids above Class II to speak of. It's a great section to SUP or open canoe.

The highlight of this trip is a side hike up Big Dominguez Canyon (located 10 miles below the Escalante Bridge). The journey winds up a creek through its black igneous gorge with a 100-foot waterfall and petroglyphs. The wildlife viewing on this section is on point, including the chance to see desert bighorn sheep, mule deer, golden eagles, turkeys, elk, mountain lions, black bears, and collared lizards. The cottonwood stands provide rookeries for great blue herons.

19 Lake Fork of the Gunnison River

This small, out-of-the-way tributary to the Gunnison is not usually on the radar of quality intermediate paddling in the Gunnison area. Off the "main road" and dumping into Blue Mesa Reservoir, the free-flowing Lake Fork comes off the north side of the San Juan Mountains. Combining good scenery, easy access, and several sections to paddle, the Lake Fork is for those looking for a little-known paddling destination.

Lake Fork Box

Walled-in nature belies its relative ease—mild creeking at best.

Nearest city/town: Gunnison
Start: Ryan Ranch Bridge (N38 07.610' / W107 17.357')
End: Gate Campground (N38 14.770' / W107 15.640')
Length: 11.0 miles
Approximate paddling time: 3 to 5 hours
Difficulty rating: Intermediate
Rapids: Class II-III− (continuous)
River type: Walled-in serpentine gorge
Current: Swift
Environment: Road runs along canyon rim out of sight for most of the run.
River gradient: 31 fpm
River gauge: 400 to 1,000 cfs, Lake Fork at Gateview Campground
Elevation drop: 340 feet
Hazards: Strainers, sometimes riverwide
Season: May through mid-July

Land status: Mostly private
Boats used: Kayaks, canoes, small rafts
Fees or permits: None
Maps: Bureau of Land Management Recreation Web Map
Other users: Anglers
Contacts: BLM Gunnison Field Office (970-642-4940)
Special considerations: The run downstream from Gate Campground to Red Bridge contains particularly sensitive access through private land; thus, no beta is provided. There is also an easy Class II+ run with easy access through Lake City town.
Put-in/takeout information: Highway 149 is used for the easy shuttle on the section. A sign marks the takeout, located near mile marker 89. Look for the put-in near mile marker 79, 10 miles south of the takeout.

The Paddle

This section of the Lake Fork is located 5 miles north of the quaint, scenic town of Lake City. This piece of river drops down into a 100-foot-deep steep-walled canyon below the road, which lends a committed backcountry feel. Don't be alarmed by walls closing in; the Lake Fork Box merely makes sweeping turns on continuous current, with smaller wave trains throughout. The occasional log may require heads-up maneuvering.

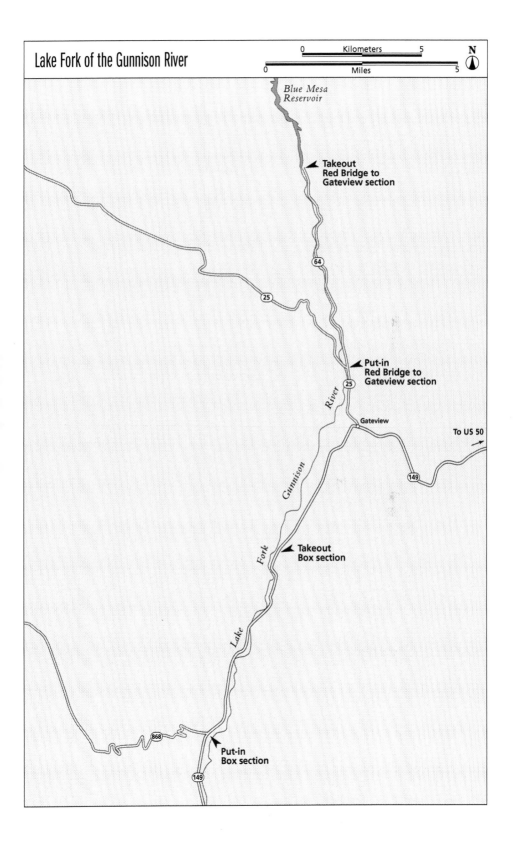

Lake Fork of the Gunnison River

Blue Mesa
Reservoir

Takeout
Red Bridge to
Gateview section

64

25

Put-in
Red Bridge to
Gateview section

25

River

Gateview

To US 50

149

Gunnison

Takeout
Box section

Fork

Lake

868

Put-in
Box section

149

Kilometers 0 5

Miles 0 5

N

Red Bridge to Gateview

"A short run with small waves, except in a very good snow year, when it's a short run with big waves."—*Colorado Rivers and Creeks*, Second Edition

Nearest city/town: Lake City
Start: Red Bridge Campground (N38 19.441' / W107 13.619')
End: Gateview Campground (N38 23.092' / W107 14.644')
Length: 4.5 miles
Approximate paddling time: 1 to 3 hours
Difficulty rating: Intermediate/advanced
Rapids: Class III, IV at flows above 1,000 cfs
River type: Big-water-style play set in a small drainage
Current: Swift
Environment: High desert canyon
River gradient: 53 fpm
River gauge: 400 to 2,500 cfs, Lake Fork Gunnison at Gateview
Elevation drop: 240 feet
Hazards: Strainers, sometimes riverwide, and logjams
Season: Late April through mid-July

Land status: Bureau of Land Management, contentiously private
Boats used: Kayaks, rafts
Fees or permits: None
Maps: Bureau of Land Management Recreation Web Map
Other users: Anglers
Contacts: BLM Gunnison Field Office (970-642-4940)
Special considerations: Bring a playboat.
Put-in/takeout information: To get to the takeout at Gateview Campground, take 25 Road north off Highway 149 at the well-marked turn in mile 92 and follow it for about 2.5 miles. Then bear right to follow 64 Road (dirt) to its end; this is the takeout. Drive back upstream to the intersection of 25 Road and 64 Road; the put-in is at Red Bridge Campground where 25 Road crosses the river.

The Paddle

The lowest section of the Lake Fork is a playful intermediate creek run that cuts through a craggy canyon before becoming a long arm of Blue Mesa Reservoir just below the takeout. The crux is Rattlesnake Rapid, located in the middle of the run. With plenty of holes and the potential for getting stuffed into a logjam, this rapid can be easily scouted/portaged from the road along river right.

20 San Miguel River

The San Miguel tumbles out of the stunning San Juan Mountains directly through the historic mining town of Telluride, now better known for its skiing and celebrity sightings than as a paddling destination. Still, where there's snow there's water, and here it's coupled with views of high cliffs veiled in streaming waterfalls. The river provides the local creek-boaters with their Class V fix through Keystone Canyon before offering up a few beginner/intermediate options. The largest tributary to the Dolores River, the San Miguel is a cold and free-flowing river due to snowmelt with a short window of runnable flows.

Throughout its length before joining the Dolores, the San Miguel makes a transition from alpine/mountain-flavored scenery in a river canyon lined with fir and aspen trees to a desert-flavored, sandstone-walled canyon lined with scrub oak and sagebrush. In recent years commercial raft and fishing outfitters have claimed their market share of summer tourism, and their spot on the San Miguel. Combining these runs with a camping trip in the semi-wilderness of Norwood Canyon can make for a pleasant moving-water overnighter.

Sawpit

Standard ski-town summer fare: fast, cold, shallow whitewater that swells in excitement with spring snowmelt.

Nearest city/town: Telluride
Start: Silverpick Road (N37 58.016' / W107 58.228')
End: Fall Creek Road (N37 59.619' / W108 01.333')
Length: 7.3 miles
Approximate paddling time: 2 to 3 hours
Difficulty rating: Intermediate
Rapids: Class III (1)
River type: Colorado snowmelt special
Current: Swift
Environment: Forested alpine canyon
River gradient: 69 fpm
River gauge: 500 to 5,000 cfs, San Miguel River near Placerville
Elevation drop: 545 feet
Hazards: Fast cold water, shallow obstacles, spring wood
Season: April through June
Land status: Bureau of Land Management, private

Boats used: Kayaks, canoes, rafts
Fees or permits: None
Maps: BLM San Miguel River Recreation Area
Other users: Anglers
Contacts: BLM Uncompaghre Field Office (970-240-5300)
Special considerations: The area true beginner run is just downstream, from Fall Creek to Specie Creek, and no less scenic. The next section down to Norwood Bridge is the popular commercial rafting stretch. There is also a pretty and innocuous Class II–III run through town. Put in near the confluence with Bear Creek and take out at the bridge on Mahoney Drive.
Put-in/takeout information: The takeout is on Fall Creek Road, which turns south off Highway 145 about a mile west of Sawpit. To get back to the put-in, return to Highway 145 and travel east (south) toward Telluride. Turn south on Silver Pick Road and follow to the river by bearing west.

San Miguel River

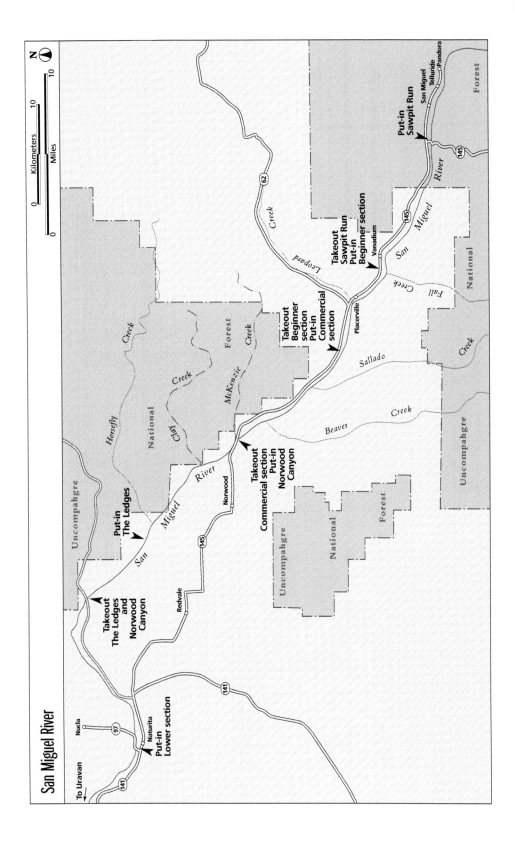

N

Kilometers
0   10

Miles
0   10

To Uravan

Nucla

141

97

Naturita
Put-in
Lower section

141

Uncompahgre

National

Forest

Redvale

145

Norwood

Takeout
The Ledges
and
Norwood Canyon

San   Miguel   River

Put-in
The Ledges

Horsefly   Creek

Clay   Creek

McKenzie   Creek

Takeout
Commercial section
Put-in
Norwood Canyon

Beaver   Creek

Sallado   Creek

Takeout
Beginner section
Put-in
Commercial section

Placerville

Leopard   Creek

62

Uncompahgre

National

Forest

Takeout
Sawpit Run
Put-in
Beginner section

Vanadium

Fall   Creek

San   Miguel   River

145

Put-in
Sawpit Run

San Miguel
Telluride
Pandora

Uncompahgre

National

Forest

The Paddle

Starting out just below Telluride and its veil of waterfalls streaming off the valley's high cliffs, the Upper San Miguel is a swift-moving section with steady gradient and cold water.

Smaller waves and rapids dot the earlier portion of this otherwise fast-but-featureless run. The largest rapid—Sawpit (Class III)—is after its namesake mining hamlet just above the takeout. It requires dodging a few long holes above Navajo Rock, which creates a slot move amid other midstream boulders. This move gets exciting at levels above 1,300 cfs.

Be careful of this run at its highest flows. It can be a continuous, eddyless flush should the need for rescue occur.

Norwood Canyon/Ledges

The San Miguel's only semi-wilderness stretch, coupled with friendly surf waves at high water.

Nearest city/town: Norwood
Start: Highway 145 bridge between Norwood and Placerville (N38 07.543' / W108 12.482')
End: Green Truss Bridge (N38 15.504' / W108 23.699')
Length: 16.3 miles (shorter run possible)
Approximate paddling time: One long day or two short ones
Difficulty rating: Intermediate
Rapids: Class II-III
River type: Granite boulder garden giving way to smooth bedrock
Current: Swift
Environment: Alpine to high desert canyon
River gradient: 50 fpm
River gauge: 600 to 5,000 cfs, San Miguel near Placerville
Elevation drop: 745 feet
Hazards: Downed trees
Season: May, June, sometimes July
Land status: Bureau of Land Management, private
Boats used: Kayaks, rafts, canoes

Fees or permits: None
Maps: *TOPO–Gurley Canyon; Sanborn Park; Big Bucktail Creek*
Other users: Anglers
Contacts: BLM Uncompahgre Field Office (970-240-5300)
Special considerations: Some paddlers come to this section solely for the soul surfing at Ledges when the tide is up. Here, the craggy canyon gives way to smooth, diagonally ledged bedrock for which the spot is named. Look for flows above 1,300 cfs and put in with the locals about 3 miles up the dirt river road (BB36 Road) from the takeout.
Put-in/takeout information: To reach the takeout, look for EE30 Road, just after the junction of Highways 145 and 141 near Naturita. Turn right and follow this road uphill, staying to the right until eventually reaching the Green Truss Bridge; this is the takeout. The put-in is located just east of the town of Norwood, down the hill on Highway 145 where it crosses the river.

The Paddle

This section of the San Miguel features the only semi-wilderness run, with little traffic on the dirt roads along its bank. At the put-in, the river immediately drops into a wooded canyon flanked by sandstone cliffs. The first 6.0 miles offer easy paddling as you approach Horsefly Creek, entering on river right. This is a good side hike and an excellent fishing spot.

Below here be wary of a runnable low-head dam—run far left. This lower portion of the run features more numerous waves that are great for surfing or charging straight through, depending on your style and skill. All the rapids can be easily negotiated without scouting—a good read and run.

Then, there's the bottom 5 miles. Known as the Ledges, it's a high-water play run in and of itself for Telluride kayakers. Sandstone shelves create uniformly wide surf waves that are very user friendly, even for rafts. The majority of these can be scouted while bouncing along the dirt road heading to the put-in, about 5 miles up BB36 Road from the Green Truss Bridge.

Halfway decent camping options exist; watch for private property and, of course, gold medal trout fishing.

21 Uncompahgre River

The Uncompahgre River starts high in the south San Juan Mountains and flows north into the scenic climbing-and-fly-fishing-oriented town of Ouray—whose visitor's bureau coined the name Little Switzerland. As the Uncompahgre flows out of town, it tumbles swiftly and continuously through a very narrow riverbed and then eases a bit as it passes continuous ranchland with barbed wire lacing the river. At the small town of Ridgway, the Uncompahgre is evidence of the whitewater park building era, with its associated river festival and "Junk of the Unc" anything-but-boats race during runoff each June. There is one more runnable section, and new whitewater park, around Montrose, the next borough considered a city by mountain standards (no beta box).

Rollans Park to Ridgway Reservoir

A fun, quick run to prove the Uncompahgre is good for something besides fly-fishing in Ridgway.

Inflatable kayak paddlers ply the muddy waters of the Uncompahgre near Montrose.
Credit: Kit Davidson

Uncompahgre River

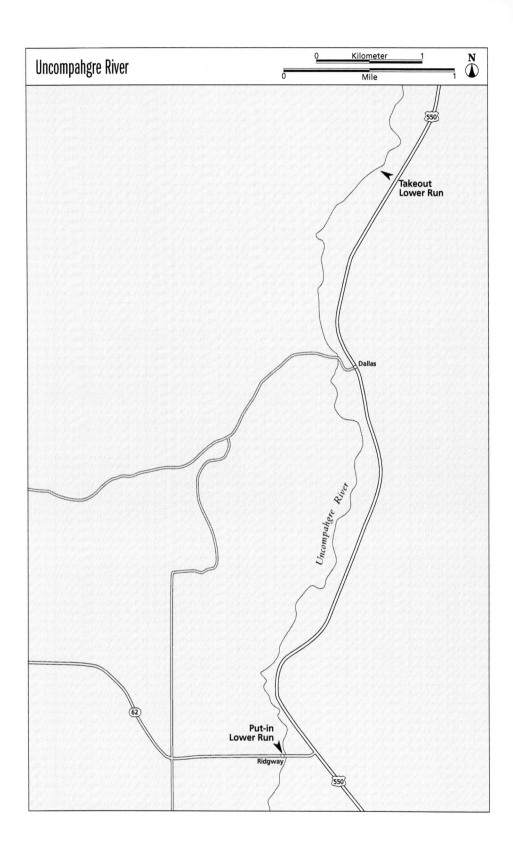

0 Kilometer 1

0 Mile 1

N

550

Takeout
Lower Run

Dallas

Uncompahgre River

62

Put-in
Lower Run

Ridgway

550

SUPing between the walls of Slickrock Canyon. Credit: Rob Hurst

Nearest city/town: Ridgway
Start: Rollans Park (N38 09.120' / W107 45.120')
End: Dallas Creek access in Ridgway State Park (N38 11.460' / W107 44.880')
Length: 3.2 miles
Approximate paddling time: 1 to 2 hours
Difficulty rating: Intermediate
Rapids: Class II+
River type: High-mountain fly-fishing stream

Current: Swift
Environment: Ranchland
River gradient: 35 fpm
River gauge: 500 to 2,500 cfs, Uncompahgre near Ridgway
Elevation drop: 112 feet
Hazards: Wade fishermen
Season: April through late June
Land status: Private, Colorado Parks and Wildlife

Boats used: Rafts, kayaks, canoes, SUPs, drift boats
Fees or permits: Pay CPW parking fee at takeout; free with state parks pass.
Maps: San Juan County
Other users: Anglers
Contacts: Ridgway State Park (970-626-5822)
Special considerations: A river trail parallels the entire section for hiking/jogging shuttle options.

Put-in/takeout information: To reach the takeout, head north out of Ridgway on US Highway 550. After 5 miles look for a sign for Ridgway State Park. Turn left (west) into the park and pay the entrance fee. Turn left at the first junction and follow signs to the takeout at the Dallas Creek access. The put-in is located just below the Highway 62 bridge in Ridgway, at the whitewater park.

The Paddle

This section of the Uncompahgre starts right in the middle of Ridgway with a few nice man-made ledges for a warm-up or surf session. Below here the river meanders a few miles through a relatively open valley lined with cottonwood trees before dropping into a shallow, steep-sided section with more technical rapids. This fun, quick run provides some on-the-fly play opportunities before dropping into the backwaters of Ridgway Reservoir.

22 Dolores River

Talk about a river that goes through a transition. The Dolores River covers some distance and varied terrain as it makes its way out of the aspen forests off the west side of the San Juan Mountains, then flows northwest into Utah and joins the Colorado River just above the sandstone-covered town of Moab.

Free flowing in its upper reaches, the Dolores follows a short but steady course until it flows into the backwaters of McPhee Reservoir. Unfortunately, this reservoir has been disastrous in terms of offering adequate and consistent boatable flows downstream of the dam. When, in big snowmelt/runoff years, the dam releases sufficient water to provide the recommended level for paddling, the Lower Dolores offers numerous remote, multi-day sections for beginning/intermediate desert-loving paddlers looking to get away from it all for a while.

Upper River to Stoner Section

A steady stream of waves and holes among dense forest and few crowds. Flows subject to spring snowmelt.

Nearest city/town: Dolores
Start: Bear Creek trailhead (N37 535' / W108 10.884')
End: Stoner Bridge (N37 35.338' / W108 19.207')
Length: 14.0 miles
Approximate paddling time: 3 to 5 hours of soul-surfing with no wait
Difficulty rating: Intermediate
Rapids: Class III (multiple)
Current: Swift
Environment: Forested, high-mountain valley
River gradient: 50 fpm
River gauge: 500 to 2,000 cfs, Dolores near Rico
Elevation drop: 680 feet
Hazards: Large, powerful whitewater features at flows above 1,000 cfs
Season: May, June
Land status: US Forest Service San Juan National Forest

Boats used: Playboats, rafts, canoes, SUPs
Fees or permits: None
Maps: *RiverMaps, Guide to the Dolores River of Colorado and Utah*
Other users: Anglers
Contacts: Dolores Water Conservancy District (970-565-7562)
Special considerations: The best intermediate surf waves/play spots on this section are found between mile markers 29 and 26 for a short, wham-bam, 3.0-mile-long, Class III play run known as the Stampede. Beginning paddlers can put in at Stoner and continue downstream to the town of Dolores for an additional 15 miles of Class II water. Numerous roadside pullouts provide easy access.
Put-in/takeout information: Use Highway 145 for both the put-in (near mile marker 34) and takeout (near mile marker 21).

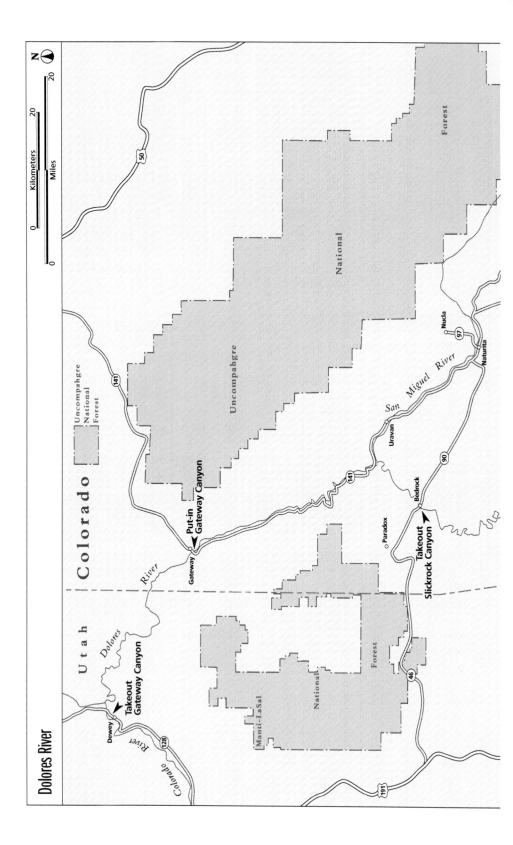

Dolores River

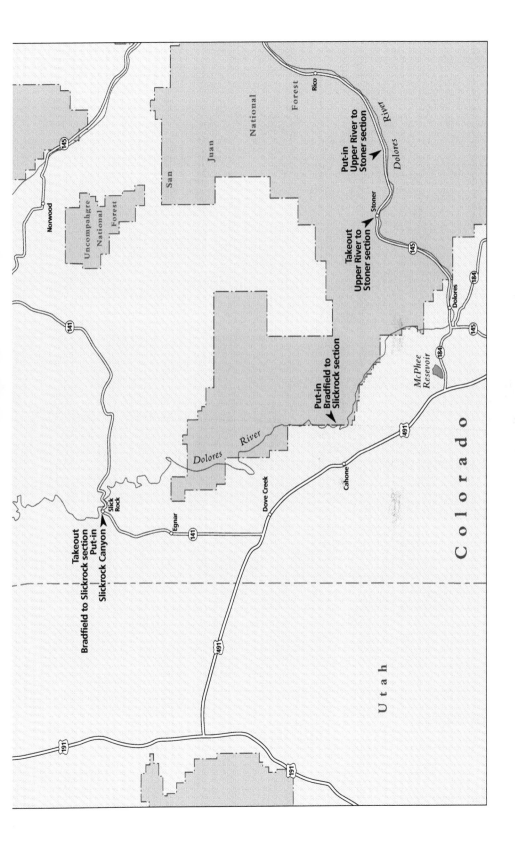

The Paddle

Here the Upper Dolores River flows through a beautiful high-mountain, aspen-filled valley. It is free flowing at this point and so flows strong, fast, and cold when in early summer. Most of this section offers up straightforward continuous waves and steady current but little technical difficulty. Be careful in higher water—the same steady, continuous current can make swimming and rescuing boats a long and unpleasant experience.

In the heart of the run, a section of great surf waves offers the most technical features. You can charge through them if surfing is not your thing. Sloping sandstone bedrock shelves form an even river bottom that creates shallow surf waves. After this section, the Dolores settles back down and finishes off in the scenic little hamlet of Stoner.

Bradfield to Slickrock

Catch it if you can!

Nearest city/town: Dolores
Start: Bradfield Launch Site (N37 39.387' / W108 44.157')
End: Slickrock access (N38 01.790' / W108 53.109')
Length: 47.0 miles
Approximate paddling time: 3 to 4 days
Difficulty rating: Intermediate/advanced
Rapids: Class III (multiple), Class IV (1)
River type: Rarely running, dam-controlled desert artery
Current: Swift
Environment: Forested canyon transitioning to high-mountain desert
River gradient: 23 fpm
River gauge: 500 to 4,000 cfs, Dolores below McPhee Reservoir
Elevation drop: 1,080 feet
Hazards: Fast current and jagged rock obstacles
Season: Four to six weeks in April through mid-June, if at all
Land Staus: Bureau of Land Management

Boats used: Kayaks, rafts, canoes, SUPs (with a portage)
Fees or permits: None
Maps: *RiverMaps, Guide to the Dolores River of Colorado and Utah*
Other users: Ranchers, for irrigation water
Contacts: BLM Tres Rios Field Office (970-882-7296)
Special considerations: Though no permit is as yet needed for this run, which rarely has runnable dam-release flows, campers are required to register at the put-in and carry the requisite desert Leave No Trace gear—groover, firepan, dishwater strainer, and kitchen floor.
Put-in/takeout information: To reach the put-in, travel west on US Highway 491 out of Cortez. In the small town of Cahone, turn right (east), following signs to Bradfield launch site onto County Road R. Follow CR R approximately 3 miles and then turn right onto County Road 16. Go approximately 1.5 miles, turn left onto County Road S, and continue into the access area to put in.

The Paddle

Because of the unfortunate operations of McPhee Dam just upstream of the put-in, this section of the Dolores River is perhaps one of the best but least paddled

The walls close in from all sides on the Dolores. Credit: Rob Hurst

intermediate multi-day river trips in the West. Catching this section with ample flow is the challenge, but once the water is flowing, paddlers will thoroughly enjoy a Douglas fir–, ponderosa pine–, and juniper-lined canyon in the upper parts of this run. Up here the canyon reaches almost 2,500 feet in depth. It is easy to find pleasant campsites beneath the towering sandstone walls and ample trees.

The river cruises along with steady current and fairly straightforward rapids that fall in the Class II–II+ range, mostly found on corners and at the mouth of side canyons. The canyon was once home to Ancestral Puebloans, and cliffside remnants can be seen just below Glade Canyon on river right. After the river makes a sweeping turn to the north around Mountain Sheep Point, the whitewater picks up. Lunchbox and Molar Rapids provide a warm-up before the big one—Snaggletooth Rapid (Class IV). This chunky rapid can easily be scouted and portaged on a dirt track on river left. With high pin potential, Snaggletooth's namesake craggy, fingerlike obstacle can pose a challenge for gear raft rowers.

Below this drop the Dolores keeps charging northward through Wall and Mile Long Rapids (both Class III). After these rapids the canyon makes a noticeable transition to a more open feel. Scrub oak, sagebrush, and cacti are the primary vegetation. The river then settles down as it drifts placidly for the last 8.0 miles or so to the takeout.

Slickrock Canyon

A mellower multi-day desert-flavored trip through an intimate canyon, a great open-canoe trip.

Nearest city/town: Monticello, Utah
Start: Highway 141 bridge, Slickrock (N38 01.798' / W108 53.109')
End: Highway 90 bridge, Bedrock (N38 18.277' / W108 53.665')
Length: 50.0 miles
Approximate paddling time: 2 to 3 days
Difficulty rating: Beginner/intermediate
Rapids: Class II (multiple), Class III (1)
River type: Serpentine desert canyon
Current: Moderate
Environment: Colorful sandstone walls
River gradient: 10 fpm
River gauge: 800 to 5,000 cfs, Dolores near Bedrock
Elevation drop: 440 feet
Hazards: A few rapids that approach Class III in difficulty
Season: May, June
Land status: Bureau of Land Management
Boats used: Rafts, canoes, kayaks, SUPs
Fees or permits: None
Maps: *RiverMaps, Guide to the Dolores River of Colorado and Utah*
Other users: Ancestral Puebloans, whose rock art is visible at river level and in side canyons

Contacts: BLM Tres Rios Field Office (970-882-7296)
Special considerations: A lower put-in near the entrance to Slick Rock Canyon is often used at Gypsum launch site. This avoids 15 miles of flatwater that passes relatively uninteresting ranchland. Though no permit is as yet needed for this run, which rarely has runnable dam-release flows, campers are required to register at the put-in and carry the requisite desert Leave No Trace gear—groover, firepan, dishwater strainer, and kitchen floor.
Put-in/takeout information: To reach the takeout, head north on Highway 141 from the town of Naturita. Just west of town look for signs for Highway 90; turn left (west) and follow Highway 90 through Paradox Valley to the river bridge and takeout in Bedrock. The actual takeout is located upstream on river left. The put-in is located at the river access area at the Highway 141 bridge in the town of Slick Rock. Highway 141 is off Highway 491 just west of the town of Dove Creek.

The Paddle

If you put in at Slick Rock, the river starts slowly and wanders through ranchland. (A lower put-in is available at the entrance to the canyon; see Special Considerations for details.) Once entering the canyon, the river sweeps and meanders around tight corners flanked by sheer-walled sandstone cliffs. This means that campsites are sparse and among the piñon, juniper, and prickly pear—don't expect wide expanses of sandy beach.

Swift current carries paddlers easily downstream at good water levels, and smaller rapids (nothing more than Class II) are found at the mouth of side canyons that enter the river. There's a good campsite and a side hike opportunity at Spring Canyon, which enters on river right in the middle of the run. Three miles downstream is Coyote Wash, which enters on river left and affords the best campsite in the canyon, as well as a short side hike that leads to Ancestral Puebloan rock art. If the campsite is already taken, at least stop and go for a side hike to check out the petroglyphs. Below here is a nice day's paddle to the takeout at the classically western Bedrock Store.

Gateway Canyon

The last canyon section of the Dolores River before it dumps into the Colorado River just across the Utah border.

Nearest city/town: Moab
Start: Gateway launch site (N38 40.841' / W108 58.862')
End: Dewey Bridge, Utah (N38 48.685' / W109 18.477')
Length: 32.0 miles
Approximate paddling time: 2 to 3 days
Difficulty rating: Intermediate
Rapids: Class II-III (multiple), Class III+ (1)
River type: High-volume desert artery
Current: Moderate
Environment: Sandstone canyon
River gradient: 14 fpm
River gauge: 250 to 5,000 cfs, Dolores near Cisco, UT
Elevation drop: 450 feet
Hazards: Large boulder sieves and island strainers
Season: May, June
Land status: Bureau of Land Management
Boats used: Kayaks, rafts, canoes, SUPs

Fees or permits: Yes, unlike the upstream sections. Get it and the rest of your western permits at recreation.gov.
Maps: *RiverMaps, Guide to the Dolores River of Colorado and Utah*
Other users: Few
Contacts: BLM Moab Field Office (435-259-2100)
Special considerations: None
Put-in/takeout information: This is a long but reliable shuttle if using Highway 141 east from the put-in through Grand Junction, then Interstate 70 west, and then Highway 128 south to Dewey Bridge takeout.

A more rugged (and possibly closed due to spring snow) option is to take County Road 44 from the put-in heading west to the junction with Forest Service Road 207. Turn right (west) onto the Castleton Valley Road, then right (north) at the Highway 128 (Utah) junction to Dewey Bridge.

The Paddle

The river cruises downstream of the put-in in a wide valley with a dirt road following the first 8 miles down to the biggest rapid of this section—Stateline Rapid (Class III at lower water levels, up to Class III+–IV at higher water levels).

The canyon walls begin to squeeze in here, and the river tumbles through a long island rapid that requires a scout on river right. Below here the river officially enters into Gateway Canyon and the whitewater picks up in frequency. Be aware of Beaver Falls—another technical, boulder-filled Class III rapid—at the mouth of Beaver Creek outwash, which enters from river left. The river then bends back to the north, and the canyon is at its narrowest and most dramatic point down here in the heart of Gateway Canyon far away from it all.

Multiple side canyons offer pleasant off-river hiking options through this section of the canyon. Eventually the Dolores comes out of the intimate canyon and slowly flows across broad, open land until it joins the mighty Colorado. Only 1 mile downstream of this confluence is the historic Dewey suspension bridge. The takeout is upstream of the bridge on river right.

23 San Juan River

The San Juan River falls off the south side of Wolf Creek Pass in the southwest corner of the state, just above the eclectic crossroads town of Pagosa Springs. Wolf Creek Pass often reports the highest recorded snowfall in the state each winter, averaging over 400 inches per year. The free-flowing Upper San Juan bursts to life with cold, fast, high water every snowmelt season. Paddlers can find the highest boatable sections on the West Fork, as well as a brief section on the East Fork.

The Upper San Juan officially starts at the East Fork and West Fork confluence 10 miles above Pagosa Springs, which recently joined the ranks as a true Colorado mountain town with the addition of a whitewater park and several breweries. Below this confluence the river eases through a broad valley as it approaches town, where there is a mediocre whitewater park. Below town the San Juan drops into a more remote section known as Mesa Canyon, with intermediate whitewater.

Below this section the San Juan eases slowly for miles before it drops into the backwaters of Navajo Reservoir, where it is dammed. These sections of the Upper San Juan, while still in Colorado, offer beginner/intermediate paddling in more of a forested landscape. The Lower San Juan is more of the same style of paddling, but in a sandstone-desert environment, as the river dips into Utah.

Mesa Canyon

The Pagosa area's favorite Class III cruise.

Nearest city/town: Pagosa Springs
Start: Pagosa Whitewater Park (N37 15.263' / W107 00.652')
End: Trujillo Road (N37 01.370' / W107 12.708')
Length: 13.4 miles
Approximate paddling time: 3 to 6 hours
Difficulty rating: Intermediate
Rapids: Class III– (1)
River type: Man-made whitewater features and one side-canyon rock garden
Current: Moderate
Environment: High-alpine canyon
River gradient: 32 fpm
River gauge: 400 to 2,500 cfs, San Juan River at Pagosa Springs
Elevation drop: 32 fpm
Hazards: Cantankerous landowners—stay in your boat if it's safe to do so

Season: May through July
Land status: US Forest Service, Pagosa Springs town, private
Boats used: Kayaks, canoes, rafts
Fees or permits: None
Maps: Pagosa Springs town/highway
Other users: Anglers, tubers in the playpark at low water
Contacts: Pagosa Springs visitor's bureau, visitpagosasprings.com
Special considerations: Consider adding the few miles upstream of Pagosa Springs, or all the way up to the confluence of the East Fork and West Fork San Juan, for more beginner paddling. Plan a pre- or post-paddle soak at the hot springs resort along the river in town.
Put-in/takeout information: From the visitor center located in downtown Pagosa Springs, head west on US 160 through town. Drive

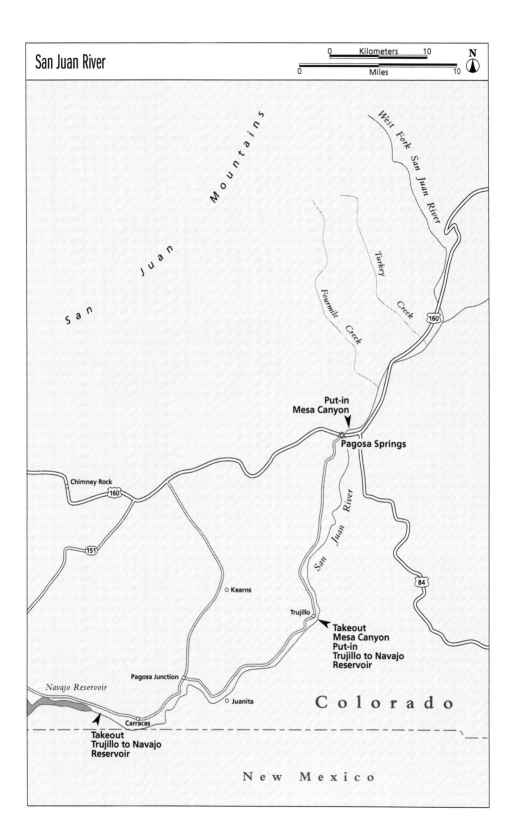

San Juan River

Kilometers 0 — 10
Miles 0 — 10

N

West Fork San Juan River

San Juan Mountains

Turkey Creek

Fourmile Creek

160

**Put-in
Mesa Canyon**

Pagosa Springs

Chimney Rock

160

151

San Juan River

84

○ Kearns

Trujillo ○ ◄ **Takeout
Mesa Canyon
Put-in
Trujillo to Navajo
Reservoir**

Pagosa Junction ○

○ Juanita

C o l o r a d o

Navajo Reservoir

Carracas

◄ **Takeout
Trujillo to Navajo
Reservoir**

N e w   M e x i c o

south on 8th and turn right onto Apache Way, which turns into CR 500 out of town as it becomes dirt and eventually parallels the river near the end of this run. Approaching the hamlet of Trujillo, CR 500 crosses the river; this is the takeout.

The Paddle

Dodge the tubers and sunbathers around the hot springs in town before dropping away from it all into a scenic canyon. Ponderosa pines, piñons, and junipers line the banks, home to abundant raptor life, including red-tailed hawks and golden eagles. The riverbanks are shared between Forest Service land in the top portion of the run and Southern Ute Indian Tribe land in the lower part.

Several half-moon-shaped ledges within the boundaries of a well-marked private ranch can disturb the peace for newer paddlers. More advanced boaters will welcome the excitement of a few steep horizon lines and benign holes. Don't be fooled—the fourth and largest in the series of ledges is natural, not man-made, and can be snuck on the left. The crux of the run is Rock Garden Rapid (Class III−) near the mouth of Squaw Canyon about halfway through the run. Eventually the canyon opens up near mile 10, and the river eases its way down to the takeout. About 30 miles of flatwater lie between here and the river's next stop at Navajo Reservoir.

24 Piedra River

Piedra River literally means "river of rocks," as early Spanish explorers aptly named it. Flowing southward out of the Weminuche Wilderness Area (the largest wilderness area in Colorado) and off the Continental Divide, the Piedra is a free-flowing torrent that's fast and cold with early-season snowmelt.

The Piedra is a technical little gem of a river that offers remote intermediate paddling in its upper reaches, a challenging lower gorge for advanced paddlers, and a mellow rural section before dumping into the backwaters of Navajo Reservoir, which dams the San Juan River. It's two significant gorges are uniquely named backward as Second Box and First Box.

Second Box

A beautiful remote run with technical intermediate to advanced whitewater.

Nearest city/town: Pagosa Springs
Start: Upper Piedra Campground (N37 25.609' / W107 11.580')
End: First Fork Bridge (N37 21.184' / W107 19.475')
Length: 10.0 miles
Approximate paddling time: 2 to 4 hours
Difficulty rating: Intermediate
Rapids: Class III (2)
River type: Boulder garden
Current: Swift
Environment: Forested high-alpine canyon
River gradient: 50 fpm
River gauge: 800 to 4,000 cfs, Piedra near Arboles
Elevation drop: 561 feet
Hazards: Shifting geology and other debris
Season: May, June (early peak)
Land status: US Forest Service
Boats used: Kayaks, rafts, decked canoes
Fees or permits: None
Maps: *Coyote River Gear, Mania's Lost Souls River Guide: Animas and Piedra*
Other users: Few

Contacts: 4Corners Riversports (970-259-3893), riversports.com
Special considerations: Just downstream of the takeout for this section, the Piedra drops into First Gorge—a committing and technical Class IV section for advanced/expert paddlers. Boaters may be committed to both sections during early season if the road to First Fork Bridge is closed due to snow.
Put-in/takeout information: From Pagosa Springs head west on US Highway 160. Continue for 19 miles to First Fork Road, just before the US 160 bridge over the river. Turn right (north) onto First Fork Road and continue upstream for 10 miles to the takeout at the First Fork Bridge/Campground. To reach the put-in, drive back east toward Pagosa Springs on Highway 160. Turn left (north) onto Piedra River Road (Forest Service Road 631) about two miles west of town, and follow it for 16 miles until it crosses the river; this bridge is the put-in.

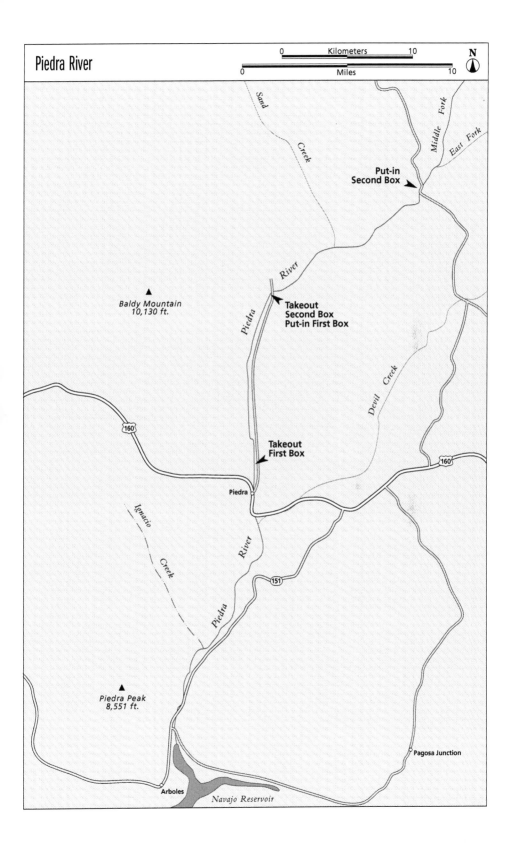

Piedra River

0 Kilometers 10
0 Miles 10

N

Sand Creek

Middle Fork

East Fork

**Put-in
Second Box**

River

Baldy Mountain
10,130 ft.

**Takeout
Second Box
Put-in First Box**

Piedra

Devil Creek

**Takeout
First Box**

160

160

Piedra

Ignacio

Creek

Piedra River

151

Piedra

Piedra Peak
8,551 ft.

Pagosa Junction

Arboles

Navajo Reservoir

The Paddle

With snow-covered peaks as a put-in backdrop, the Piedra drops into a tight canyon where wilderness abounds. Paddlers have seen deer, elk, bear, and wild turkey through this section.

Numerous side creeks enter into the river and boost its flow as it heads downstream. The bigger rapids of this section (Lone Pine and Limestone, both Class III) are found in a lower, 2-mile-long box canyon. This practically roadless section of river is not to be missed if it's flowing when you're in the area.

First Box

The Piedra's harder, more committing lower gorge—with a hot spring!

Nearest city/town: Pagosa Springs
Start: First Fork Bridge (N37 21.184' / W107 19.475')
End: Lower Piedra Campground (N37 14.541' / W107 20.559')
Length: 9.2 miles
Approximate paddling time: 3 to 5 hours, with scouting
Difficulty rating: Advanced
Rapids: Class IV (3)
River type: Pool-drop rock piles
Current: Swift
Environment: Forested high-alpine canyon
River gradient: 55 fpm
River gauge: 800 to 1,000 cfs, Piedra River near Arboles
Elevation drop: 495 feet
Hazards: Sieves in shifting geology
Season: May, June
Land status: US Forest Service
Boats used: Kayaks, small rafts

Fees or permits: None
Maps: *Coyote River Gear, Mania's Lost Souls River Guide: Animas and Piedra*
Other users: Few
Contacts: 4Corners Riversports (970-259-3893), riversports.com
Special considerations: Boaters may be committed running the Second Box section above this during early season if the road to First Fork Bridge is closed due to snow. This makes for a long, 20-mile day and is possible to do as a wilderness overnighter.
Put-in/takeout information: From Pagosa Springs head west on US Highway 160. The takeout is the campground a mile upstream and north of where the highway crosses the river. To get to the put-in, go back east on US Highway 160 almost to Pagosa Springs, and turn right (north) onto First Fork Road. Continue upstream for 10 miles to the put-in at the First Fork Bridge/Campground.

The Paddle

The First Box Piedra is its upstream counterpart's wilder, woolier cousin. The rapids here are decidedly steeper, cutting through the same eroding canyon walls and their piles of discarded boulders. Below First Fork bridge, this section splashes through some manageable Class III wave trains before Piedra Falls (Class IV). The next two drops, at the crux of the run, form from active mudslides on river right. The first one is aptly named Mudslide (Class IV), with several lines, where most boaters choose to run far left. There is pin potential for rafts here above 1,000 cfs. Scout from the right

A paddle team faces the runout to Eye of the Needle Rapid in the First Box Piedra.
Credit: Rob Hurst

taking care to avoid poison ivy. Consider setting safety because Eye of the Needle (Class IV) lies just downstream and is considered the biggest drop on the run. At Eye of the Needle, most of the current piles into an ugly boulder river center—scout, portage, or line boats from river right. Be sure to scout the runout, with a feature affectionately known as Lucifers, where wood collects in the left channel. The recommended line is to run the left side of the right channel, hugging a midstream island with a sieve at the top. The rapids mellow out to Class III for the remaining three quarters of the run. There is a lukewarm hot spring on river left at low flows a few miles above the takeout.

25 Animas River

The free-flowing Animas River tumbles downhill in a cold, swift torrent off the south side of the San Juan Mountains in the remote southwest corner of Colorado. The Animas begins its navigability in the town of Silverton as it drops through the expert-only Upper Animas Gorge—a cold, continuous 25 miles of thrilling whitewater set beneath snow-covered peaks. The upper reach of the Animas may be best enjoyed, or shuttled, via its scenic tourist train ride.

The Animas is choked between sheer walls as it exits out of the mountains just above Durango. It settles down through peaceful meanderings in a wide valley offering miles of great flatwater river touring. As the Animas flows into town, it picks up some speed and offers a good short commercial rafting run through town, as well as a great after-work rinse-off section for playboaters.

Below Durango the Animas settles into a friendly but busy pace as it flows out of the state and joins the San Juan River just across the New Mexico border. While the Animas and its surrounding drainages are usually considered Class V creek-boater territory, there are a few sections available for mere mortal paddlers. There is also a world-class kayak school in Durango at 4Corners Riversports.

Animas Valley

The first piece of the Animas accessible for beginning paddlers near Durango.

Nearest city/town: Durango
Start: Baker's Bridge (N37 27.546' / W107 47.953')
End: Trimble Lane (N37 23.100' / W107 50.219')
Length: 6.6 miles
Approximate paddling time: 2 to 4 hours
Difficulty rating: Beginner
Rapids: Class I–II
River type: Wide and mostly unobstructed
Current: Moderate
Environment: Western-flavored ranchlands
River gradient: 15 fpm
River gauge: 500 to 4,000 cfs, Animas at Durango
Elevation drop: 180 feet
Hazards: None or easy to avoid
Season: April through September
Land status: Contentiously private; please abide

Boats used: Kayaks, canoes, rafts, SUPs
Fees or permits: None
Maps: *Coyote River Gear, Mania's Lost Souls River Guide: Animas and Piedra*
Other users: Anglers
Contacts: 4Corners Riversports (970-259-3893), riversports.com
Special considerations: Use one of the only other legal access points at Oxbow River Park or 33rd Street in Durango to add about 13 miles of flatwater to this stretch. Be sure to allow enough time to float this section—landowners do not take kindly to trespassing boaters.
Put-in/takeout information: Use US Highway 550 as the main road for the shuttle. To reach the takeout, head north out of Durango to the small borough of Trimble. Look for Trimble Lane just to the south. Turn right (east) and follow this road to the takeout at the bridge over

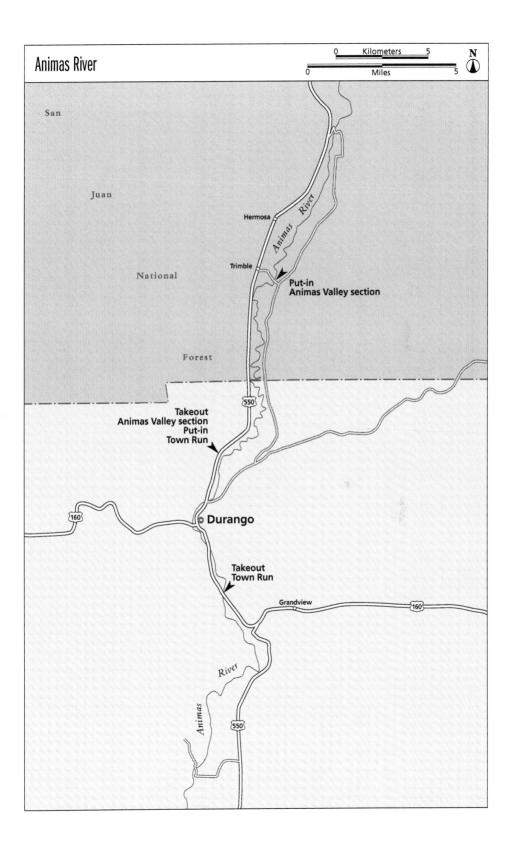

the river. To get back to the put-in, head north through Hermosa and look for signs for CR 250. Turn right (east) onto CR 250 and follow it down to the put-in at the bridge over the river.

The Paddle

If you're looking for a longer section of river for a family float or a great river touring section, then here you go. Meandering miles of flatwater offer paddlers a scenic cruise in the wide-open Animas Valley as the river floats beneath sandstone cliffs in the distance while passing by open ranchland and horse properties.

Higher water will help push paddlers downstream; lower water tends to be a bit more of a slog and a long flatwater paddle. Wave to tourists—the historic and famous Durango-Silverton Narrow Gauge Railroad parallels part of this section of river.

Durango Town Run

A watery route from the north end to the south end of Durango; one of the rowdiest "town runs" of the west.

Nearest city/town: Durango
Start: 32nd Street boat ramp (N37 18.180' / W107 51.839')
End: Dallabetta Park (N37 13.287' / W107 51.655')
Length: 5.8 miles
Approximate paddling time: 2 to 4 hours
Difficulty rating: Beginner/intermediate
Rapids: Class III (multiple)
River type: Urban whitewater with man-made features
Current: Swift
Environment: Bustling mountain college town
River gradient: 27 fpm
River gauge: 500 to 6,000 cfs, Animas at Durango
Elevation drop: 131 feet
Hazards: Multiple bridge abutments, diversions, and other man-made debris
Season: Year-round
Land status: City of Durango
Boats used: Kayaks, rafts, canoes, SUPs
Fees or permits: None
Maps: *Coyote River Gear, Mania's Lost Souls River Guide: Animas and Piedra*

Other users: Homeless encampments
Contacts: 4Corners Riversports (970-259-3893), riversports.com
Special considerations: Beginning paddlers can shorten this section by taking out at the fish hatchery. To access the best play, use Santa Rita Park as a put-in and take out behind 4Corners Riversports.
Put-in/takeout information: To reach the takeout, head south on Main Street and veer to the right, following signs for US 550 just past a Burger King. Stay on US 550/160 east as the road heads past a Wal-Mart on the right. Shortly thereafter turn right (south) onto River Road next to a Home Depot. Head down to the river, cross over it, and then turn right into the newly constructed Dallabetta River Park.

Use U.S. 550/Main Street as the main route for the shuttle to the put-in. Head north through downtown to 32nd Street. Turn right (east) onto 32nd Street and cross the river. Make an immediate left (north) and go one block to the put-in at the boat ramp.

The Paddle

The first few miles from the put-in offer a good flatwater warm-up or instruction. Just below a fish hatchery on river right, the whitewater picks up a bit and continues swiftly downstream, with a rapid just under the railroad bridge as well as the Main Street bridge.

The real crux of the section is found below the US Highway 160 bridge as paddlers approach Little Smelter Rapid. Big Smelter Rapid (Class III) is found downstream in Santa Rita Park. This is the site of many a swim for budding paddlers, as well as a test of skills for numerous playboaters and slalom racers.

Just below Smelter Rapid, the Animas tumbles around the corner, heading through Corner Pocket Rapid. Farther downstream the river flows over Santa Rita Hole just underneath the US 160 and River Trail bridges. This rapid marks the last of the big ones. The river settles down a bit through Sawmill and High Bridge Rapids farther downstream.

Various put-ins and takeouts can be used to shorten this section or lessen the difficulty based on paddlers' skill levels.

Flatwater Tours—Lakes and Reservoirs (North-South)

In addition to its rivers and creeks, Colorado also hosts numerous reservoirs and lakes that offer abundant opportunities for flatwater tours. Many of these paddles feature majestic mountain backdrops, as well as relative seclusion away from most traffic.

Access is great throughout most of the state's reservoirs, as many of them feature state parks and designated launch areas. This section highlights a few of the more popular lakes and reservoirs for flatwater touring plus some other noteworthy locations. Look here for a flatwater workout, kayak roll practice, or SUP tour, keeping an eye out for the occasional outrigger canoe club or dragon boat race.

26 Horsetooth Reservoir

A 1,900+-acre reservoir within striking distance of downtown Fort Collins.

Distance: 1.0 to 5.0 miles (as long as desired)
Launch site: Satanka Bay boat ramp (N40 36.010' / W105 10.580')
Craft: Rec boats, canoes, kayaks, SUPs
Approximate paddling time: 1 to 3 hours
Season: April through October; year-round possible
Access: From downtown Fort Collins, head south on US Highway 287 to Drake Road. Turn right (west) onto Drake Road and continue until a T-intersection with South Overland Trail. Turn right (north) onto South Overland Trail, and then very shortly turn left (west) onto County Road 38E. Take this uphill to the edge of the reservoir and another T-intersection. Turn right onto County Road 23, which parallels the eastern edge of the reservoir. Follow CR 23 all the way around the northern edge of the reservoir to Lory State Park. Pay the entrance fee and follow signs for the Satanka Bay boat ramp; this is the launch site.

Additional information: For more information on Lory State Park, visit http://parks.state.co.us/Parks/lory. For information on Horse-tooth Reservoir, call (970-679-4554).
Honorable mentions: Boyd Lake State Park, south of Fort Collins; the western edge of Carter Lake, southwest of Loveland

The Paddle

Lying just on the west side of Fort Collins, Horsetooth Reservoir is set beneath the aptly named Horsetooth Rock. A busy, motor-laden boat ramp is located on the south side of the reservoir, but the more isolated north end is more appealing to recreational paddlers. Using the easy access and amenities within Lory State Park on the northwest side of the reservoir, paddlers will find a good boat launch for an afternoon tour.

Head south along the western side of the lake to get away from all the roads. Explore the numerous small coves (Soldier, North Eltuck, South Eltuck, and Orchard) along this steep, hilly side of the reservoir and enter Horsetooth Mountain Park just to the south. Numerous nearby trails are also available for stretching out your legs after a paddle.

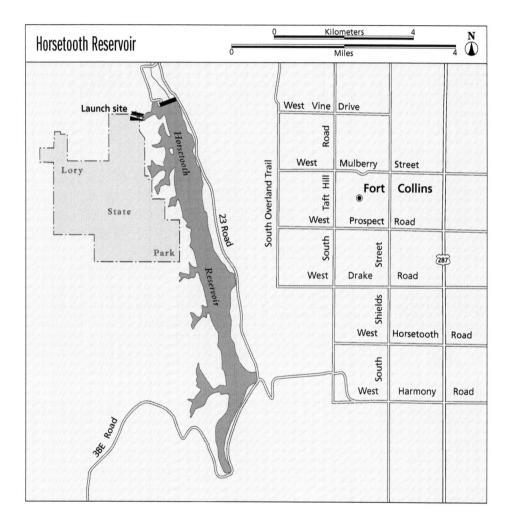

Horsetooth Reservoir

Kilometers
0   4

Miles
0   4

N

Launch site

Lory

State

Park

Horsetooth

Reservoir

23 Road

38E Road

South Overland Trail

West Vine Drive

Taft Hill Road

West Mulberry Street

Fort Collins

West Prospect Road

South Shields Street

West Drake Road

287

West Horsetooth Road

South Shields

West Harmony Road

27　Boulder Reservoir

The only real beach and lake for recreating near the active small city of Boulder.

Distance: 1.0 to 5.0 miles (as long as desired)
Launch site: South Beach (N40 04.281' / W105 13.556')
Craft: Rec boats, canoes, kayaks, SUPs, outrigger canoes
Approximate paddling time: 1 to 3 hours
Season: April through October; year-round possible
Access: From downtown Boulder, head east on Pearl Street out to the Foothills Parkway past 30th Street. Head north on the Foothills Parkway then the Diagonal Highway toward Longmont and look for Jay Road at a traffic light. Turn left (west) onto Jay Road. Shortly thereafter, take your first right (north) onto 51st Street and follow signs for the reservoir. Turn right into the park. Pay the entrance fee and park near the boat ramp on the south side of the reservoir; this is the launch site.
Additional information: For more information on Boulder Reservoir, call (303-441-3468) or visit www.bouldercolorado.gov.
Honorable mention: Gross Reservoir, west of and above Boulder

The Paddle

Set on the eastern edge of town, Boulder Reservoir is surrounded by small rolling hills set out on the Front Range plains rather than within the mountains. This can be a busy place in the warm summer months, but because no motors are allowed on the lake, it can still feel peaceful.

For the best paddling—and to escape the crowds on the south-side beach—head to the western edge of the reservoir and paddle the coastline around to the northern edge of the reservoir. The crowds are left behind, the roads are a bit in the distance, and abundant waterfowl can be encountered in the marsh grasses.

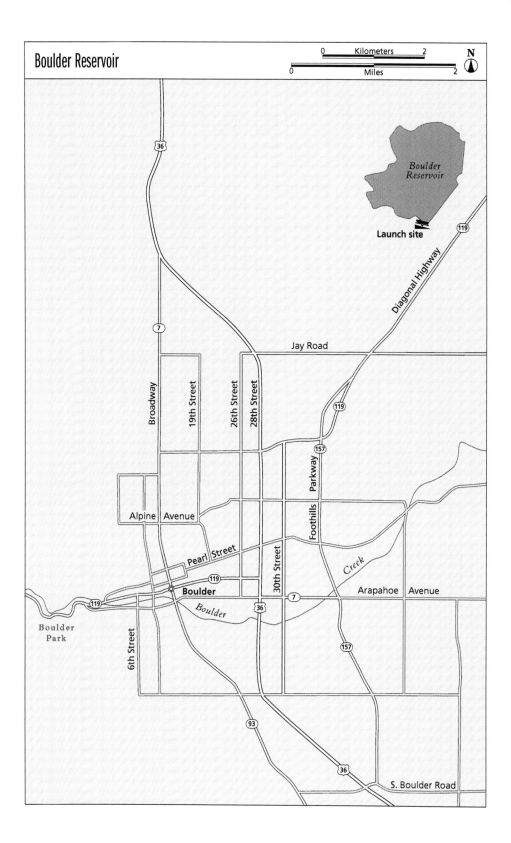

Boulder Reservoir

Kilometers
Miles

N

Boulder Reservoir

Launch site

Diagonal Highway

Jay Road

Broadway

19th Street

26th Street

28th Street

Parkway

Foothills

Creek

Alpine Avenue

Pearl Street

30th Street

Arapahoe Avenue

Boulder

Boulder

Boulder Park

6th Street

28 Chatfield Reservoir

A 5,300+–acre flatwater oasis in a sea of urban-ness.

Distance: 1.0 to 3.0 miles
Launch site: South Ramp (N39 32.614' / W105 03.587')
Craft: Rec boats, canoes, kayaks, SUPs
Approximate paddling time: 1 to 3 hours
Season: May through September
Access: From downtown Denver, head south on Interstate 25 to exit 207B. Veer right (west) onto US Highway 85 (Santa Fe Drive). Continue heading south approximately 7 miles to Highway C-470; enter C-470 turning right and heading west. Get off at the next exit, which is Wadsworth Boulevard. Head south on Wadsworth, eventually crossing over the southern arm of the lake. At a T-intersection turn left (north) onto County Road 5 and follow signs to Chatfield State Park. Pay the entrance fee and follow signs for the South Ramp; this is the launch site.

Additional information: For more information on Chatfield State Park go to http://parks.state.co.us/Parks/Chatfield/.

Honorable mentions: Bear Creek Lake Park, east of Morrison; Cherry Lake, Cherry Creek State Park in Aurora

The Paddle

Because of its proximity to the Denver metro area, Chatfield is a busy, busy place. Avoiding the crowds and motors, flatwater paddlers will find a worthy afternoon tour that will feature a less populated area of the reservoir that is home to more waterfowl and wildlife.

From the launch site, paddle toward the western edge of the reservoir and head up the southern arm. This is the outflow of the now-dammed South Platte River and is also home to a heron rookery. Farther upstream at the mouth of the river, the marshlands also offer a protected cove away from it all.

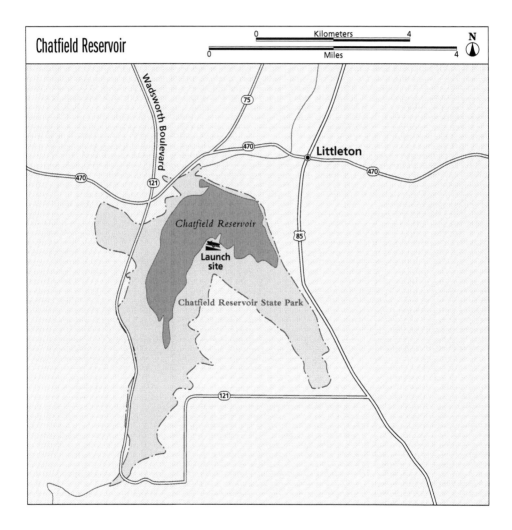

29 Cottonwood Lake

A hidden, high-alpine gem.

Distance: Less than 1.0 mile
Launch site: Cottonwood boat ramp (N38 47.033' / W106 17.032')
Craft: Rec boats, canoes, kayaks, SUPs
Approximate paddling time: 1 to 3 hours
Season: May through September
Access: From Buena Vista, take Main Street (County Road 306) west as it starts to head up Cottonwood Pass. Turn left on County Road

344 and follow it for 4 dusty, bumpy miles until you reach the campground near the south shore of Cottonwood Lake. Follow the road around the lake to the north side to access the main boat ramp, with ample parking nearby.
Additional information: No motorized craft allowed
Honorable mention: Turquoise Lake and Twin Lakes farther north near Leadville

The Paddle

At 40 acres, what Cottonwood Lake lacks in size it makes up in stunning views of towering granite cliffs, and the chance to see wildlife including moose or mountain goats. This high-mountain lake is actually a tiny reservoir on Cottonwood Creek, an Arkansas River tributary. The water is notoriously cold; tourists and locals alike flock here on hot summer days. It's also a great locale for aspen leaf peeping in fall. Perfect for rec boats or an SUP tour—be sure to check forecasts and plan accordingly for late afternoon winds.

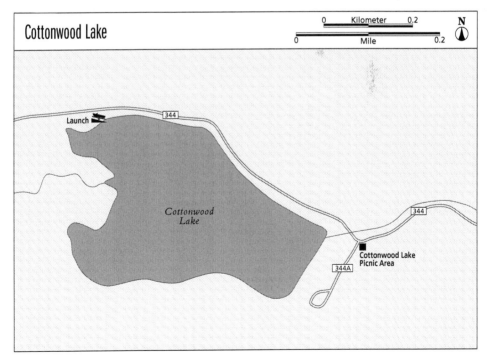

30 Lake Pueblo

A nice state park for a flatwater tour on the western edge of 4,600+-acre Lake Pueblo.

Distance: 1.0 to 6.0 miles
Launch site: Northshore Marina (N38 16.324' / W104 46.105')
Craft: Rec boats, canoes, kayaks, SUPs
Approximate paddling time: 1 to 3 hours
Season: April through October; year-round possible
Access: From downtown Pueblo, head east to Interstate 25; enter the interstate heading north. Get off at exit 101 for US Highway 50 and head west on US 50 toward Pueblo West.

Pass Purcell Boulevard. Turn left (south) onto McCulloch Boulevard and follow this down around toward the entrance station at Lake Pueblo State Park. Pay the entrance fee and follow signs for Northshore Marina; this is the launch site.
Additional information: For additional information on Lake Pueblo State Park, visit cpw .state.co.us/placestogo/parks/LakePueblo.
Honorable mention: The small St. Charles Reservoir, south of Pueblo

The Paddle

The northwestern end of Lake Pueblo is more suitable to flatwater paddling, as there are fewer larger craft in the area. From the launch site, head across the reservoir to the southern edge and then head west along the coastline, heading upstream. Paddling farther to the west will have you encountering the outflow of the now-dammed Arkansas River. Part of the northern end of the lake is called Swallows. Once a small community that was flooded when the lake was formed, Swallows is home to a large number of birds and is a layover spot for migrating pelicans twice a year. Enjoy this area set beneath the Wet Mountains just to the west.

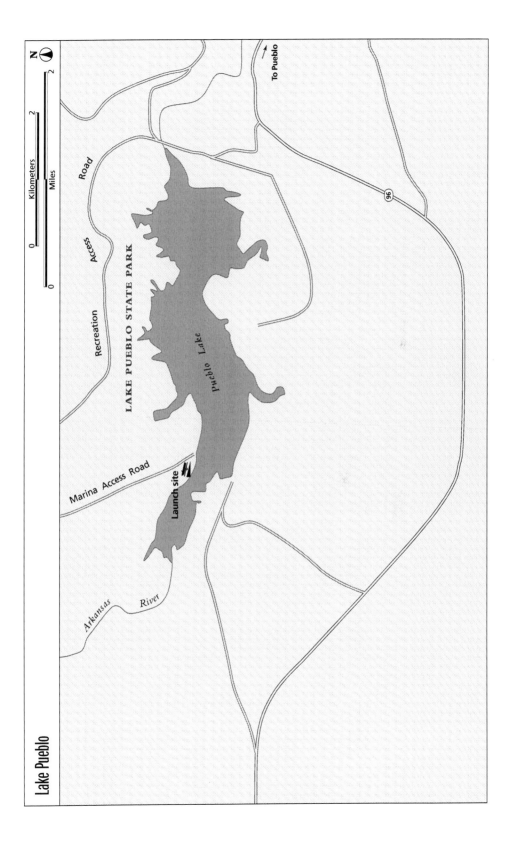

Lake Pueblo

31 Lake Granby

Endless miles of flatwater touring with a majestic mountain backdrop.

Distance: 1.0 to 10.0 miles (or as long as desired)
Launch site: Sunset Point, Arapaho National Recreation Area (N40 09.276' / W105 52.416')
Craft: Rec boats, canoes, kayaks, SUPs
Approximate paddling time: 1 to 4 hours
Season: May through October
Access: From Interstate 70 head north on US Highway 40 toward Winter Park. Head up and over Berthoud Pass, drop down into the Fraser River Valley, and continue heading north through Fraser and Granby. Just west of Granby turn right (east) onto US Highway 34 and head

east into Arapaho National Recreation Area. Look for signs for Sunset Point; this is the launch site.
Additional information: For additional information on Lake Granby, go to www.grand -county.com/Granby.aspx. For additional information on Arapaho National Recreation Area (Sunset Point), visit www.fs.fed.us/r2/arnf/ recreation/anra/index.shtml.
Honorable mentions: The eastern edge of Shadow Mountain Lake, just to the north of Lake Granby; Williams Fork Reservoir, to the west of Lake Granby

The Paddle

With 7,250 acres and more than 40 miles of shoreline, Lake Granby is the second-largest body of water in Colorado. Set at the foot of the Continental Divide just outside the western boundary to Rocky Mountain National Park, Lake Granby impedes the Colorado River just downstream of its headwaters. Crowds and motors can be an issue here, but there is room for everyone, and there is a nice, more-isolated tour along the northern edge of the reservoir.

From the launch site, paddle across the reservoir, island hopping along the way. Or take a detour and paddle up the Grand Bay arm of the lake. Stay along the northern edge of Lake Granby for a more-isolated hillside paddle. Trails closely parallel this side of the reservoir.

Return back across the reservoir or continue all the way down to the eastern arm of the lake to Arapaho Bay and paddle back along the southern shore.

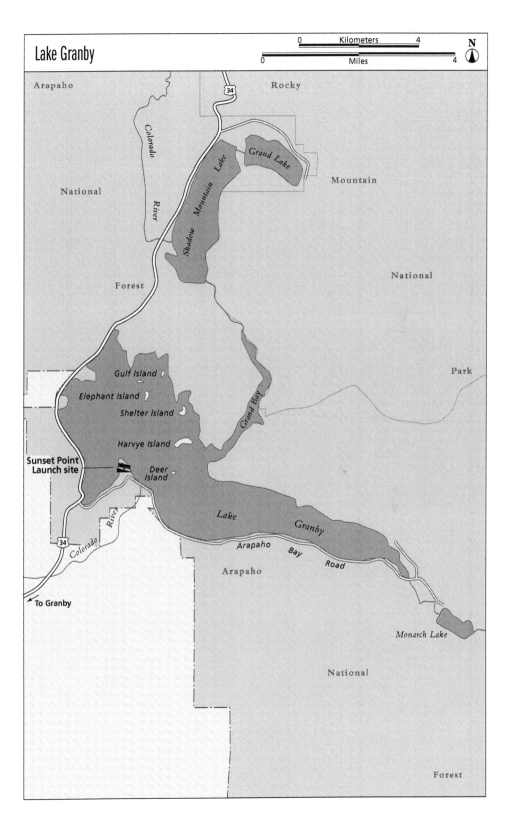

Lake Granby

Kilometers
0   4
0   4
Miles

N

Arapaho   Rocky

Colorado

River

National

Shadow Mountain Lake

Grand Lake

Mountain

National

Forest

Park

Gulf Island

Elephant Island

Shelter Island

Grand Bay

Harvye Island

Sunset Point
Launch site

Deer
Island

Lake   Granby

Arapaho   Bay   Road

Colorado   River

Arapaho

To Granby

Monarch Lake

National

Forest

32 Lake Dillon

The off-duty ski area employee sailboat special, also suitable for flatwater paddlecraft.

Distance: 1.0 to 8.0 miles
Launch site: Dillon Marina (N39 37.526' / W106 02.629')
Craft: Rec boats, canoes, kayaks, SUPs
Approximate paddling time: 1 to 5 hours
Season: May through September
Access: From downtown Denver, head west on Interstate 70, head through Eisenhower Tunnel (underneath the Continental Divide), and drop down toward Dillon. Take exit 205 (Silverthorne), and then head east for 2 miles on US Highway 6, going underneath the interstate, toward Dillon. Follow signs for the Dillon Marina; this is the launch site. Another launch site is available at the Frisco Bay Marina, which is accessed off I-70 exit 203.

Additional information: For additional information on Lake Dillon, visit www.townofdillon.com. For information on the launch site, visit www.dillonmarina.com.
Honorable mention: The western edge of Green Mountain Reservoir to the north

The Paddle

Lake Dillon, the largest lake in the area, is set at 9,000+ feet beneath the dramatic Continental Divide, which towers above the eastern edge of the reservoir. The lake was originally created to divert water out of the Blue River Basin into the South Platte River Basin to quench Denver's thirst. Sprawling out at 3,200+ acres with approximately 27 miles of shoreline, Lake Dillon offers flatwater recreation for all types of users—motorboats and sailboats as well as canoes and kayaks.

The most frequently used access is from Dillon Marina on the north side of the lake. For a nice paddle, go along the east edge of the reservoir, heading up the quiet and fish-friendly area within the Snake River Arm. A longer add-on option is to come out of the Snake River Arm and keep heading to the south, checking out the eastern edge of the Blue River Arm. Fir trees line the banks, and trails closely parallel this entire side of the reservoir.

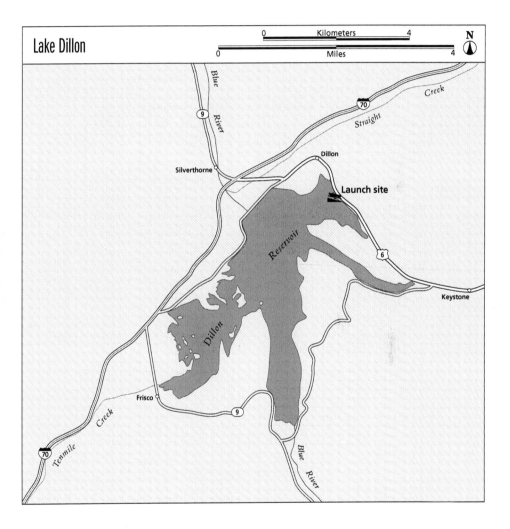

Lake Dillon

33 Blue Mesa Reservoir

The largest body of water in the state.

Distance: 1.0 to 20.0 miles (as long as desired)
Launch site: Dillon Pinnacles trailhead (N38 28.174' / W107 15.243')
Craft: Rec boats, canoes, kayaks, SUPs
Approximate paddling time: 1 to 6 hours
Season: May through October
Access: From downtown Gunnison, head west on US 50, paralleling the Gunnison River. The river drops into the backwaters of Blue Mesa Reservoir. Continue on US 50 west. Just before US 50 crosses the reservoir, there is a sign for Dillon Pinnacles Access. Turn right and wind down toward the reservoir; this is the launch site. Another launch site is available at Sapinero, farther west on US 50, for exploration up the Lake Fork Arm.

Additional information: For additional information on Blue Mesa Reservoir and Curecanti National Recreation Area, visit www.nps.gov/cure. Park headquarters can be reached by calling (970-641-2337).
Honorable mention: Ridgway Reservoir, within Ridgway State Park, southwest of Blue Mesa

The Paddle

At 20 miles long with over 95 miles of shoreline, Blue Mesa Reservoir is the largest body of water in the state. Blue Mesa is set within the Curecanti National Recreation Area and offers numerous designated campsites, picnic areas, launch sites, and trails. Once on the water, countless inlets and coves offer ample paddling exploration options, but along with the miles of exploration come hordes of crowds—mostly with motors.

The reservoir is also well known for its fishing, having broken the state record with a 50-plus-pound trout pulled out of its waters. Fear not—there are a few quieter coves worthy of exploring that also offer fine kayak fishing.

The picturesque Dillon Pinnacles trailhead on the west side of the US Highway 50 bridge is a good launch site that offers a variety of flatwater options. Putting in here, it is possible to stay along the north edge of the reservoir, heading up into the quiet West Elk Arm.

If you're looking for a longer edition on this northern side of the reservoir, paddle back down the West Elk Arm. Instead of returning to the launch site, continue heading west up Soap Creek Arm. This is a busier arm of the reservoir, as there is a boat launch area at the northern end.

For a longer day tour from the same launch site, explore the Lake Fork Arm on the south side of the reservoir. With all this water, there are plenty of options for paddling.

Blue Mesa Reservoir

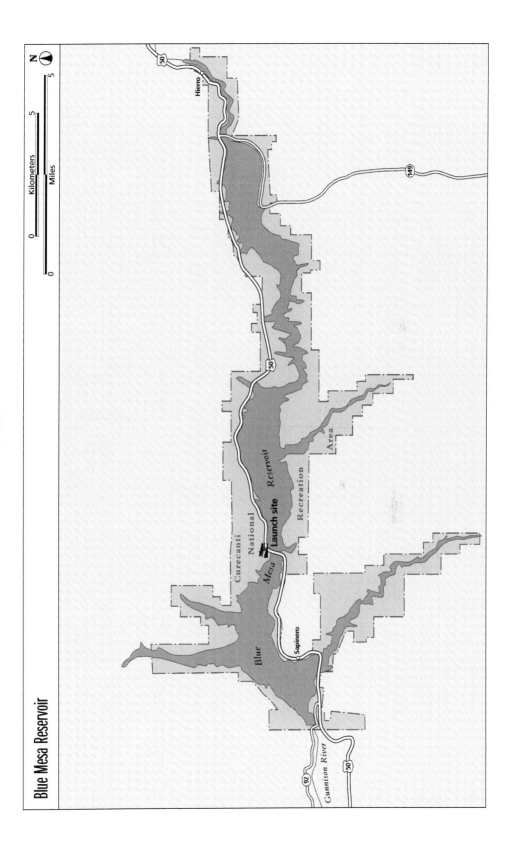

34 Vallecito Reservoir

A beautiful flatwater getaway less than an hour's drive from the Western-flavored town of Durango.

Distance: 1.0 to 6.0 miles
Launch site: North end of lake (N37 25.553' / W107 33.220')
Craft: Rec boats, canoes, kayaks, SUPs
Approximate paddling time: 1 to 4 hours
Season: May through October
Access: From downtown Durango, head east on US Highway 160 to the traffic light in Bayfield; turn left (north) onto County Road 501 (Vallecito Road). Head up the Pine River Valley, eventually passing Vallecito Dam and driving around the western edge of the lake. Stay on CR 501; on the northern side of the lake, the road turns to dirt. Within 0.5 mile after CR 501 becomes dirt, look for dirt pullouts along the right-hand side of the road next to the lake. These pullouts are launch sites.

Additional information: For additional information on Vallecito Lake, call (970-247-1573) or visit www.vallecitolakechamber.com.

Honorable mentions: The nice mountain lakes of Haviland and Electra, to the north of Durango; the northern arm of McPhee Reservoir, just north of Cortez

The Paddle

Tucked away in the southwest corner of the state, Vallecito Reservoir gathers several small streams that drain the Weminuche Wilderness Area (the largest wilderness area in Colorado). Set beneath towering mountains Vallecito provides 2,700+ acres of flatwater.

The most common access is to launch on the northern end of the reservoir next to the inflow from Vallecito Creek (this is also a great fishing area). You will find a bit quieter paddle along the northeastern edge of the lake by heading south. Pine and fir trees fall into the steep-sided reservoir as paddlers pass Forest Service picnic/camping areas on their way to the mouth of the Los Pinos River inflow into the reservoir (another good fishing spot).

It is possible to continue paddling down the eastern edge of the reservoir all the way to the dam. Simply reverse course and get a great view of the mountains while returning to the launch site on this fine half-day paddle.

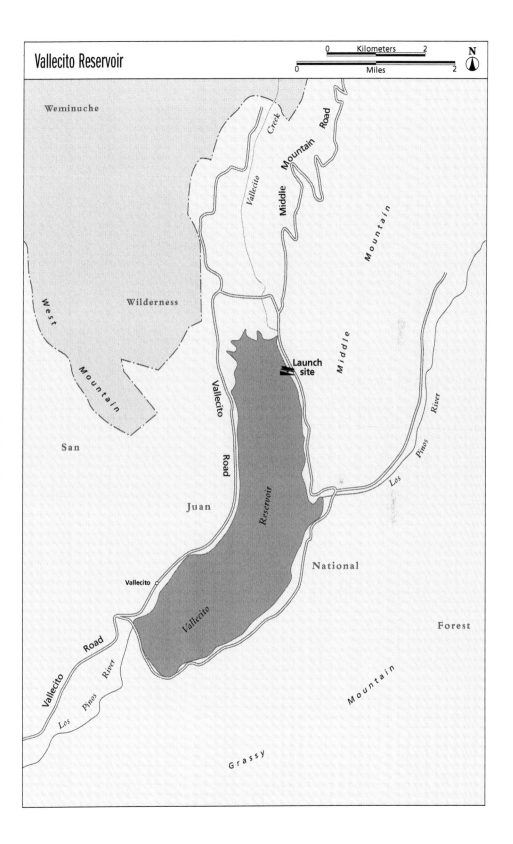

Vallecito Reservoir

Kilometers 0 — 2
Miles 0 — 2

N

Weminuche

West

Mountain

San

Juan

Wilderness

Vallecito Creek

Middle Mountain Road

Mountain

Middle Mountain

Launch site

Vallecito Road

Los Pinos River

Reservoir

Vallecito

National

Forest

Vallecito

Vallecito Road

Los Pinos River

Mountain

Grassy

Appendix: Paddling Resources

Books

Banks, Gordon, and Eckhardt, Dave. *Colorado Rivers and Creeks*, Second Edition (Boulder, Colorado: 1999).

DeLorme Maps. *Colorado Atlas and Gazetteer* (Yarmouth, Maine: 2007).

Stafford, Evan, and McCuthchen, Kyle. *Whitewater of the Southern Rockies* (Wolverine Publishing: 2007).

Wheat, Doug. *The Floater's Guide to Colorado* (Falcon Press Publishing, Inc.: 1983).

Websites

American Whitewater—National paddling resource website
www.americanwhitewater.org

Mountainbuzz—Colorado's boating forum website
www.mountainbuzz.com

Paddling Life—National online paddling magazine
www.paddlinglife.com

Facebook Paddling Groups

Arkansas River People
BV Paddlers
Colorado Creeking Beta
Colorado Kayakers
Crested Butte Watersheds
Eagle River Valley Boaters
Front Range Kayakers
Glenwood Area Boaters
Glenwood Canyon Live Boating Conditions
Kayaking, Canoeing, Paddle Boarding in Colorado (mostly flatwater)
Poudre Paddlers Canoe and Kayak Club of Northern Colorado
Roaring Fork Paddlers
Roaring Fork Valley Whitewater Paddlers
Rubber Pushers of Colorado—Rafting Group
Summit County Paddle
Western Colorado Rafting

Paddlers scout Snaggletooth Rapid on the Dolores. Credit: Rob Hurst

River Flow Information

US Geological Survey (USGS)—National Water Information System
http://waterdata.usgs.gov/co/nwis/rt

Flows can also be checked at www.americanwhitewater.com

Paddle Shops/Schools/Clubs

Alpine Quest Sports
Edwards, CO and Glenwood Springs, CO
www.alpinequestsports.com

Aspen Kayak and SUP
Aspen, CO
www.aspenkayakacademy.com

Backdoor Sports
Steamboat Springs, CO
www.backdoorsports.com

Boulder Outdoor Center
Boulder, CO
www.boc123.com

Canoe Colorado
Denver, CO
www.canoecolorado.net

Centennial Canoes
Palisade, CO
www.centennialcanoe.com

CKS Main Street
Buena Vista, CO
www.cksmainstreet.com

Colorado River School
www.coriverschool.com

Colorado Whitewater Association
Englewood, CO
www.coloradowhitewater.org

Confluence Kayak and Ski
Denver, CO
www.confluencekayaks.com

The Edge Ski and Paddle
Pueblo, CO
www.edgeskiandpaddle.com

4Corners Riversports
Durango, CO
www.riversports.com

Golden River Sports
Golden, CO
www.goldenriversports.net

Gunnison Kayak Program
Gunnison, CO

Pikes Peak Whitewater Club
Colorado Springs, CO
www.pikespeakwhitewaterclub.com

Poudre Paddlers
Fort Collins, CO
www.poudrepaddlers.org

Pueblo Paddlers
Pueblo, CO
http://pueblopaddlers.blogspot.com/

Rocky Mountain Adventures
Fort Collins, CO
www.shoprma.com

Rocky Mountain Canoe Club
Englewood, CO
www.rockymountaincanoeclub.net

Rocky Mountain Outdoor Center
Buena Vista, CO
www.rmoc.com

Rocky Mountain Sea Kayak Club
Lakewood, CO
www.rmskc.org

Three Rivers Resort
Almont, CO
www.3riversresort.com

Whitewater Workshop
Golden, CO
www.whitewaterworkshop.com

Colorado River Conservation Organizations

American Whitewater
P.O. Box 1540
Cullowhee, NC 28723
(828) 293-9791
www.americanwhitewater.org

Colorado Environmental Coalition
1536 Wynkoop Street, #5C
Denver, CO 80202
(303) 534-7066
www.ourcolorado.org

Friends of the Yampa
PO Box 771654
743 Oak Street
Steamboat Springs, CO 80487
www.friendsoftheyampa.com

San Juan Citizens Alliance
PO Box 2461
1309 E 3rd Avenue
Durango, CO 81302
www.sanjuancitizens.org

Colorado River Events

Animas River Days (early June)
Animas River, Durango, CO
www.animasriverdays.com

Bailey Fest (Labor Day weekend)
North Fork of the South Platte River, Bailey, CO
www.coloradowhitewater.org

Dolores River Festival (early June)
Dolores River, Dolores, CO
www.doloresriverfest.org

Fibark (mid-June)
Arkansas River, Salida, CO
www.fibark.net

GoPro Mountain Games (mid-June)
Eagle River, Vail, CO
www.summer.mountaingames.com

Gore Canyon Race (late August)
Colorado River, Kremmling, CO
www.americanwhitewater.org

Gunnison River Festival (June)
Gunnison River, Gunnison, CO
www.gunnisonriverfestival.com

Flying high at FIBArk. Credit: Kevin Hoffman

Lyons Outdoor Games (late May/early June)
St. Vrain River, Lyons, CO
www.burningcancolorado.com

Oh Be Joyful Race (early June)
Oh Be Joyful Creek, Crested Butte, CO
Oh Be Joyful Race Facebook group

PaddleFest (mid-May)
Arkansas River, Buena Vista, CO
www.ckspaddlefest.com

PouFest (early June)
Cache la Poudre River, Bellvue, CO
www.poufest.com

Ridgway River Fest (last weekend in June)
Uncompahgre River, Ridgway, CO
www.ridgwayriverfest.org

Royal Gorge Whitewater Festival (late July)
Arkansas River, Canon City, CO
www.royalgorgewhitewaterfestival.com

Yampa River Festival (mid-June)
Yampa River, Steamboat Springs, CO
www.friendsoftheyampa.com

About the Reviser

Kate Stepan grew up on a farm in Pennsylvania. Her life changed forever when, at five years old, Kate's dad signed her up for flag football instead of cheerleading. In high school, barely knowing how to ski, Kate became a ski instructor at Blue Mountain in the Poconos. Ski instructing led to raft guiding, which led to kayak instruction, which led her to Buena Vista, Colorado, and the Rocky Mountain Outdoor Center in 2009. With a degree in journalism from George Washington University in Washington, D.C., Kate also did a two-year stint in southern California as an editor at *Canoe and Kayak* magazine.

She started guiding in 2003 on the Lehigh River, then worked as a raft guide and video boater on West Virginia's infamous New and Gauley Rivers. Kate has paddled in Pennsylvania, New York, West Virginia, Maryland, North Carolina, South Carolina, Georgia, Tennessee, California, Arizona, New Mexico, Utah, Wyoming, Idaho, Oregon, Washington, and Colorado. She has surf kayaked off the northern California coast, and sea kayaked in Alaska and Florida.

Kate learned to canoe when she took a NOLS River Instructor Course in 2014. She has taught expedition-based leadership, whitewater raft/kayak and canoe courses for NOLS on the Green River in Utah, the Main Salmon in Idaho, and the Kali River in India. She's boated in Chile, Mexico, Ecuador, New Zealand, Fiji, India, and Nepal. Kate now teaches whitewater kayaking, rafting, swiftwater rescue, and wilderness first aid/CPR at Rocky Mountain Outdoor Center, where she also trains younger guides as staff manager. She lives in Buena Vista, where she is still learning to ski while teaching lessons at Copper Mountain.

Road tripping around Colorado's rivers circa 2010. Credit: Kevin Hoffman

About the Author

Freelance photographer and writer Dunbar Hardy has been focusing on the paddle-sports industry for more than 15 years, with articles and photos published in national and international publications. He has also held the position of senior editor for *Kayak Session* and *Paddle World* magazines.

Dunbar is recognized as one of the most experienced and accomplished expedition paddlers/leaders in the world. He has successfully completed first descents and paddling expeditions throughout Colorado and the United States, as well as in such exotic places as Bhutan, Russia, Morocco, China, Mexico, Honduras, Guatemala, Costa Rica, Panama, Venezuela, Ecuador, Peru, Chile, Argentina, New Zealand, Italy, France, Switzerland, and Canada. He is also a co-owner/lead instructor of Tarkio Kayak Adventures (www.teamtarkio.com), based in Missoula, Montana, which offers domestic and international multi-day instructional kayaking clinics.

After literally traveling the world paddling, Dunbar is proud to call Colorado his home.

Credit: Rob Hurst